PRACTICAL WORK IN
SCHOOL SCIENCE

Practical work has been part of science education for just over 100 years and is accepted as an essential and exciting part of understanding this discipline. Although it can be costly and sometimes messy, it simply has to be done if students and teachers are to progress in their understanding.

Schools and universities invest millions of pounds in it and the National Curriculum reveres it – but what exactly is going on in classrooms around the country and how are the leading practioners moving with the times?

This book attempts to reflect on the value and the purpose of practical work as part of the scientific curriculum. Why are practical exercises so necessary and what do they contribute to the learning process? The chapters examine many issues, such as:

- how practical work is perceived by students and teachers;
- whether we will, or should, move on to the 'virtual lab';
- the limitations of current 'hands-on' work and valuable alternatives to it;
- the connections between practical work in science education and 'authentic' science;
- what role experimentation plays in current educational practice.

Jerry Wellington is Reader in Education at Sheffield University, and has taught science at all academic levels.

PRACTICAL WORK IN SCHOOL SCIENCE

Which way now?

Edited by Jerry Wellington

London and New York

First published 1998
by Routledge
11 New Fetter Lane, London EC4P 4EE

Simultaneously published in the USA and Canada
by Routledge
29 West 35th Street, New York, NY 10001

© 1998 selection and editorial material Jerry Wellington, individual
chapters the contributors

Typeset in Garamond by
J&L Composition Ltd, Filey, North Yorkshire
Printed and bound in Great Britain by
T.J. International, Padstow, Cornwall

British Library Cataloguing in Publication Data
A catalogue record for this book is available from the British Library

Library of Congress Cataloguing in Publication Data
Practical work in school science: which way now? / edited by Jerry
Wellington
p. cm.
Includes bibliographical references and index.
(pbk. : alk. paper)
1. Science–Study and teaching–Great Britain. 2. Science–Study
and teaching–Laboratory manuals. I. Wellington, J. J. (Jerry J.)
Q183.4.G7P7 1998
507.8–dc21 98-3969
CIP

ISBN 0–415–17492–9 (hbk)
ISBN 0–415–17493–7 (pbk)

CONTENTS

CONTENTS

LIST OF ILLUSTRATIONS

Figures

Tables

CONTRIBUTORS

Jerry Wellington taught science in Tower Hamlets, East London, before joining the University of Sheffield where he is now Reader in Education. He has written or edited a number of books and journal articles on education. His main interests are in the nature of science and scientific method, and the role of language in science education.

Linda Baggott is a lecturer in biology and education at the University of Exeter, where she also runs teacher training courses. Her academic background is in physiology, and she worked as a secondary science teacher in London. She first became interested in using computers in teaching science in the mid 1970s and has been involved in this area of curriculum development and action research ever since, recently becoming particulary interested in simulation.

Roy Barton is a senior lecturer in Education in the School of Education and Professional Development at the University of East Anglia. Previously he has taught science in a number of secondary schools over a period of eighteen years. Currently his research interests are centered on the use of ICT for teaching and learning, particularly in science education and in teacher education.

Noel Gough is Associate Professor and Deputy Director, Deakin Centre for Education and Change, Deakin University, Victoria, Australia. His current research focuses on narrative theory and popular media culture in education, with particular reference to poststructuralist research methodologies, curriculum change, environmental education and science education. He is the Australian Editor of the *Journal of Curriculum Studies*, an Executive Editor of *The Australian Educational Researcher*, and has published extensively in his areas of research interest.

Jenifer V. Helms is an assistant professor in science education at the University of Colorado in Boulder, Colorado. Her teaching and research interests centre on students' and teachers' interpretations of the nature of science; inclusive, project-based science teaching; and feminism and science.

Derek Hodson, whose major interests concern the relationships among history, philosophy and sociology of science and science education, has thirty years experience in schools and universities in the UK, New Zealand and Canada. He is currently Professor of Science Education at the Ontario Institute for Studies in Education, Toronto.

Christine Howe is Head of Psychology at Strathclyde University. In addition to science education and computer-assisted learning, she has research interests in language acquisition, children's conceptual development, gender and dialogue, and collaborative problem solving. She has published numerous books, chapters, articles and reports, including *Gender and Classroom Interaction: a Research Review* (1997) and *Conceptual Structure in Childhood and Adolescence: the Case of Everyday Physics* (1998).

Edgar Jenkins is Professor of Science Education Policy at the University of Leeds where is also the Director of the Centre for Studies in Science and Mathematics Education. He has taught chemistry in a variety of secondary schools and, in addition to books for schools, has published widely on a range of policy issues in both the historical and contemporary contexts. His most recent book (1998) is *Junior School Science Education in England and Wales since 1900: From Steps to Stages.*

John Leach lectures in science education at the University of Leeds, where he is co-ordinator of the Learning in Science Research Group. His research interests include the role of understanding about the nature of science in science learning. He formerly taught chemistry and science in British secondary schools.

Richard Masters holds a Master's degree from the University of Otago in New Zealand and a DPhil from the University of York in England. At present he is a lecturer in applied psychology in the School of Sport & Exercise Sciences at the University of Birmingham. His main research interests are in the function of implicit knowledge in learning and skill acquisition and the relationship between anxiety and performance.

Robin Millar taught physics and science in schools in the Edinburgh area for eight years before moving to the University of York, where he is now Professor of Science Education. He is involved in initial and in-service teacher education, and in science curriculum development. His main research interests are in students' learning in science, the role of practical work and investigations, and the public understanding of science.

Mick Nott taught science and managed science departments in comprehensive schools in the 1970s and 1980s. He is now based at Sheffield Hallam University, and lectures on and researches into science education.

His current research interests are the nature of science in science education and the history and sociology of science education.

Jonathan Osborne is a senior lecturer in science education at King's College London. Prior to that he was an advisory teacher and taught physics and science in Inner London schools for twelve years. He has a wide range of research interests, from primary science through to alternatives in practical work, informal science education and the impact of contemporary science on the curriculum.

Pamela Smith is a lecturer at the Anna Freud Centre, London. Apart from science education, her research interests lie in early mathematics and in psychological perspectives on medicine and health.

Joan Solomon is Professor of Science Education at the Centre for Science Education at the Open University and Visiting Professor at Kings College London. After about thirty years of teaching physics, science and STS in secondary classrooms she retains an active research interest in aspects of formal and informal science education which relate to the professional status of science teachers, to practical work in classrooms and interactive science centres, and also in active exploration of the public awareness of Science and Technology. Her interests extend beyond the UK, to other countries in the European Union and further afield.

Clive Sutton has published widely about language and learning in science. His books include *Communicating in the Classroom* (ed.) Hodder and Stoughton (1981) and *Words, Science and Learning*, Open University Press (1992). His current interest centres on pupils' awareness of the historical and cultural processes that have led to the scientific knowledge they encounter.

John Wardle has wide experience in the field of information technology and science education, developed through a career involving work as a secondary school science teacher, head of physics, advisory teacher and science project officer for the National Council for Educational Technology (NCET, now BECTA). John's current role of senior lecturer at the Centre for Science Education, Sheffield Hallam University, involves working with initial teacher training students, INSET provision for teachers and curriculum development work. He directed the DTI funded **Schools OnLine Science** project which developed science education resources, strategies, support and training for schools using the Internet.

Brian E. Woolnough is Lecturer in Science Education at Oxford University Department of Educational Studies. Having previously taught in secondary schools he is now responsible for the science curriculum work on the PGCE course at Oxford UDE. His research and writing lie in the areas of practical work, especially project work, in school science and technology; of developments in the school curriculum for science and technology; of the relationship between authentic science, tacit learning, and pupils' motivational differences; and of the effectiveness of engineering education schemes.

PREFACE

The aim of this book is not to bury or condemn practical work in science, but to reappraise it. The approach of the end of the millennium seems a good time to take stock of where practical work in science has come from, to appraise its position now and to begin to formulate new principles for its future position in science education. We have experienced over 100 years of school science practical work and witnessed the coming (and sometimes going) of the heuristic approach, discovery methods, the 'Nuffield philosophy', investigational work, the process movement and the 'problem-solving' approach, to mention but a few.

Practical work has been applauded for its ability to enthuse, to illustrate phenomena and to enhance understanding. It has also been criticised and even condemned for its huge expense, its potential for conceptual confusion, its gender bias, and its power to encourage both teachers and pupils to behave badly (unethically) in the classroom.

Now is an opportune time to put together a book on the role and purpose of practical work for the future, with a critical but positive message. With the potential of new information technology beginning to emerge in education, the book has an underlying theme of analysing what is best in past and present practice whilst offering practical ideas for practitioners in the future.

The focus of the book will be on the actual practice of practical work, what has and has not worked in practical science, and what practice in the future might look like. Each chapter contains a critical element but will also include a section on practical implications for teachers. Not all chapters sing the same song. Just as many of the authors dismiss the idea of one unified scientific method, none is advocating one single approach to practical work. Nor do the chapters form a cohesive whole with a coherent message – there is a lot more work to be done before that will be achieved. The chapters have been grouped into themes or sections but the decision on how that was done was an arbitrary one. Our intention is that the chapters should provide a platform and a catalyst for practitioners, researchers, curriculum developers and policy makers to re-examine practical work with the grand aim of improving it in the next century. This book should be seen as another contribution to the debate on practical work, not as a vehicle for concluding it. Views on practical work (like science and scientific method itself) will constantly change depending on their historical, social and political context.

In summary, the intention of the book is to bring together a number of authors with a wide range of experience in science education to look at the past, the present and the future, and to examine the following overarching questions:

- What are the aims and purposes of practical work? That is, why do we, and should we, invest so much time and money in it?
- How have we arrived at our present practices in and philosophies of practical work?
- What views and images do teachers and students have of school practical work, and how does this relate to their images of science itself? What are their expectations of it, and attitudes towards it?
- What light can research into science education shed on these questions? What are the implications for classroom practice?
- What 'types' of practical work are there and what are their alleged purposes?
- How does the use of computers impinge on traditional practical work? What 'added value' will be provided by IT? Will important skills be replaced?
- Can multimedia act as a surrogate for practical work? Which 'practical activities' will move out of the lab and into the multimedia system?
- What is 'authentic' practical work? What practical activities can be done outside the lab to make them more 'authentic'?
- How does the use of talk, discussion, writing and language in general relate to practical work?
- Can or should practical work attempt to mirror or 'mimic' the nature of science?
- What directions should practical work in the future take?

J.J. Wellington

ACKNOWLEDGEMENTS

I would like to thank all the authors who have contributed to this book, first for agreeing to write a chapter and second for being so efficient and co-operative. Tina Cartwright's help in organising and preparing chapters, compiling the index and contacting authors by post and by e-mail has been invaluable. Her work, and the support of the University of Sheffield Research Fund, have enabled the book to proceed smoothly from the initial research stage to final publication. The encouragement of my family (Wendy, Dan, Rebecca and Hannah) has been an enormous help, as always.

Finally, I would like to acknowledge the publishers who have given permission to reproduce illustrations and excerpts from other work. The extract on pp. 169–70 is taken from Primo Levi, *The Periodic Table*, translated by Raymond Rosenthal (Michael Joseph 1985) copyright © 1975 Giulio Einaudi editore. s.p.a., English translation copyright © 1984 by Schoken Books Inc., and is reproduced by permission of Penguin Books Ltd and A.M. Heath & Company Limited.

Part I

INTRODUCTION

1

PRACTICAL WORK IN SCIENCE
Time for a re-appraisal

Jerry Wellington

School science is now firmly embedded in the laboratory. The TIMMS (Third International Mathematics and Science Study, 1997) report compared the curricula of 13-year-old pupils in a range of countries – practical laboratory activities in science were more frequent in England than in any other country. This may be a cause for celebration – but is the practical, hands-on approach to science working? The aim of this book is to begin to look behind the TIMMS data and to ask what is going on in practical laboratory activities, and why. The purpose of this chapter is to set the scene and introduce, as briefly as possible, the main issues which will be explored later in the book.

The laboratorising of school science

As Jenkins points out in the third chapter of this book, the process of locating school science education in the lab has taken place over a period of at least a century. In tracing the history of practical science education, Nott (1997: 49) argues that by 1897 the laboratory had already 'been identified as an essential item for school science education'. In the century which has followed, the school lab has become a symbol of the status of science in the curriculum, 'rather than a space appropriate for teaching and learning science' (Nott 1997: 54).

In 1988, an article written by three sociologists (Delamont *et al.* 1988) described a view of secondary school science from an outsider's perspective. The title of their article ('In the beginning was the Bunsen') was used to signal what they call the 'ritualistic or fetishistic' way in which the Bunsen burner has become the icon of school science. They describe how pupils' first few lessons in secondary science are an initiation into a new domain. The subject becomes consecrated and demarcated, away from other curriculum areas because of features like its danger and its precision:

The laboratory is introduced to pupils as an esoteric locale, with its own special objects, ceremonial observances, demands and dangers. Entry into the world of school science is managed as a *rite de passage:* the initiates embark on a perilous and closely supervised adventure. In the course of their initiation they are introduced to artefacts which are endowed with special status.

(Delamont *et al.* 1988: 316)

This is the way science lessons are seen by outsiders, albeit sociologists. Surely there must be some justification for these rites, icons and artefacts? There must be more to lab life than Nott's cynical end remark: 'Why do we do so much practical work in science in English schools? Perhaps because there are so many laboratories' (1997: 60).

Recent phases and fads in practical work

It is inevitable that science education and its practical work will and should change over time. It is as much a function of its social, historical and technological context as science and scientific method itself. Jenkins' chapter and valuable articles such as Nott (1997) and Gee and Clackson (1992) give an account of its history over a long period, in the latter case going back to the days of John Locke in the late seventeenth century. More recently, Hodson (1996) has talked of 'three decades of confusion and distortion', starting from the 1960s. In my view, from a UK perspective, there have been three important movements in that period which could (rather cruelly and with hindsight) be called phases or fads. I will term them the discovery approach, the process approach, and (after Jenkins) 'practical work by order'.

The discovery phase involved pupils in 'being scientists for the day' and invoked slogans such as 'I do and I understand'. Hodson (1996: 116–19) gives a full account of this phase and its origins in the United States in the writing of Schwab and Bruner. Courses, curricula and publications were born and were most evident in the Nuffield programmes developed in the late 1960s. Those who taught with the Nuffield materials (myself included in the 1970s) will have fond memories of the creativity embedded in the approaches, the ideas and the practical work of the Nuffield movement. Many of the 'experiments' and the newly designed items of apparatus live on and have become institutionalised – more icons of school science. It is easy to be critical of that era and so I will be brief. The approach has been criticised largely for its distorted view of scientific inquiry; that is, it presented scientists rather like 'Sherlock Holmes in a white coat' (Wellington 1981). Observation was presented as theory-free, the jump from experimental data to laws and theory was presented as an inductive process. Hodson (1996:

118) summed up the discovery movement up as 'philosophically unsound and pedagogically unworkable'.

The second recent phase, in my view, deserves less attention than the discovery era, which, although based on a shaky image of science, did at least produce a number of valuable teaching ideas and materials. The so-called 'process approach' was based not only on a totally distorted view of science but also led to a range of published teaching materials in the 1980s which promoted a completely one-sided and potentially harmful approach to science education. The distorted view of science was based on the myth that the skills and processes of science (observing, inferring, predicting and so on) could be divorced from the knowledge base; namely the laws and theories of science. Processes were to be disembedded from their context and content, learned and taught separately, in the hope that they could become transferable to other contexts. The so-called 'less able' learners, it was felt, could cope with these transferable processes even if they could not grasp the difficult concepts of science 'content' – thus science would be accessible to all. Again, we will not devote space here to a critique of the process movement (Hodson 1996: 119–22). With hindsight it seems remarkable that in 1989 a whole book (Wellington 1989) was considered necessary as one effort to counter this flawed approach to science and science education.

The third phase, from an English and Welsh perspective, although similar orders have been laid down elsewhere, came with National Curriculum legislation which decreed not only the content to be covered in science education but also the approach which should be taken to practical and investigative work. Indeed 'approach' is too weak a term for, since 1988, different templates have been made law which dictate how investigative work should be done and which model of science and scientific method it should follow. The first template relied heavily on a control-of-variables model of science which bore no resemblance to the history of science or to its current practice. The model was ridiculed by some (discussed in Wellington, 1994), since its application to the work of scientists such as Mendel, Hawking, Newton or Einstein (who probably never controlled a variable in his life) condemned them to reaching barely level one on the statutory ten-point scale. More seriously, its imposition in schools led to the hostility, resentment and 'bitterness' (Donnelly 1995: 99) of teachers who were forced to implement and assess this rigid model of scientific inquiry. The model was later revised and re-christened 'Experimental and Investigative Science'. There is less emphasis on variables and their control and quite rightly the importance of evidence and its evaluation are stressed – but it still promotes *one* model or template for science and scientific enquiry. The idea of having one format or one algorithm for science is, as I and other authors here argue, flawed.

5

Reasons for doing practical work now –
and their limitations

I find that teachers are always surprised, even shocked, when asked to consider what practical work in science education is for. Donnelly (1995: 97) reports the same reaction in asking teachers in a research project to suggest the purposes of pupil laboratory work:

> 'I haven't even thought about it. . . . I mean, that's what science is.'

> '. . . it's what science is all about really, is getting on with some experiments. Science is a practical subject . . . you know, end of story I think.'

I recently asked a sample of forty-eight science graduates embarking on a teaching career to write down on a small, blank piece of paper why we do practical work in school science. Inevitably, I received a wide range of answers to such an open question, for example: 'to back up the theory'; 'to give pupils something to remember the theory by'; 'to make theory more visual and accessible to kids'; 'makes things easier to remember'; 'to give experience – seeing is believing'; 'to bring science to life'; 'develop manipulative skills'; 'to develop skills useful to life and to home'; 'to develop practical skills'; 'to develop an inquiring mind'; 'to learn transferable skills like a fair test, or planning and observation'. On a more practical level some wrote: 'to make a change from theory work'; 'something else to do apart from lessons'; 'keep kids quiet'; 'make lessons more interesting'; 'they break up lessons to keep the kids entertained'; 'fun – sometimes!'; 'nice change'; 'to make boring, dry topics more fun'; 'give interest and variety'.

This wide range of responses is interesting to consider in the light of research over the last thirty years into teachers' reasons and rationales for doing practical work. The research and critical analysis of Kerr (1963), Buckley and Kempa (1971), Thompson (1975), Beatty and Woolnough (1982) and others have indicated a range of important reasons for doing practical work in science. These were summarised and critically discussed nowhere more clearly than in Hodson (1990), and are also discussed in the next chapter, by Millar. My own reading of the literature is that the reasons and rationales put forward can be grouped into three main areas: one relating to knowledge and understanding (the cognitive domain); one relating to skills and processes, often deemed to be transferable; and a third relating to attitudes, enjoyment and motivation (the affective domain). I found it interesting that all the free-range responses given by learner teachers above fall into these three groups.

Below, for the sake of brevity, I give a crude summary of arguments in each area and counter arguments to them:

1 *Cognitive arguments* It is argued that practical work can improve pupils' understanding of science and promote their conceptual development by allowing them to 'visualise' the laws and theories of science. It can illustrate, verify or affirm 'theory work'.

The counter argument to this, of course, is that practical work can confuse as easily as it can clarify or aid understanding (especially if it 'goes wrong' – see later section). Hence the counter-slogan which came from an unknown source in the 1980s: 'I do and I become confused.' It can be argued that theory comes first and is needed in order to visualise – not the other way round: 'Experience does not give concepts meaning, if anything concepts give experience meaning' (Theobald 1968).

This may be a good argument for doing practical work after teaching and discussing theory. But practical work is still not a good tool for teaching theory – theories are about ideas, not things. Theories involve abstract ideas which cannot be *physically* illustrated: 'In the context of the school laboratory it is clear that students cannot develop an understanding through their own observations, as the theoretical entities of science are not there to be seen' (Leach and Scott 1995: 48).

2 *Affective arguments* Practical work, it has been argued, is motivating and exciting – it generates interest and enthusiasm. It helps learners to remember things; it helps to 'make it stick'.

Few who have taught science would deny this. But this is not the case for all pupils – some are 'turned off' by it, especially when it goes wrong or they cannot see the point of doing it. All teachers can relate to the lovely quote from the pupil in Qualter *et al.* (1990: 5), 'Oh no, Sir! Not another one of your problems', as she responds to her teacher's attempt to turn a piece of practical work into a 'problem-solving' investigation. Evidence from Murphy (in Woolnough 1991) indicates that more girls than boys react negatively to practical work in science.

3 *Skills arguments* It is argued that practical work develops not only manipulative or manual dexterity skills, but also promotes higher-level, transferable skills such as observation, measurement, prediction and inference. These transferable skills are said not only to be valuable to future scientists but also to possess general utility and vocational value.

There may be some truth in the claim for manipulative skills and possibly measurement, but there is little evidence that skills learnt in science are indeed general and transferable or that they are of vocational value. As one of the leading writers in the field of situated cognition puts it:

The results of learning transfer experiments range from positive to negative . . . as a whole perhaps equivocal and unstable describes them best. But when we investigate learning transfer directly across situations, the results are constantly negative, whether analysing performance levels, procedures or errors.

(Lave 1988: 68)

In a slightly different area of skill (personal skills and teamwork) it has been claimed that the small group work which inevitably goes on in practical science can develop such skills as communication, interaction and co-operation. Again, this may be partially true, but when group work is closely observed and analysed it often reveals domination by forceful members, competition, lack of engagement for some, and a division of tasks which may leave one pupil simply recording results or drawing out a neat table without even seeing, let alone touching, any apparatus (discussed in Wellington 1994, ch. 8).

Finally in this domain, it has been argued that practical science develops the general skill of 'scientific inquiry' or scientific method. This training or inculcation into the method of science is said to be transferable and again of vocational value to all students even if they choose other career paths (as the vast majority do). Counter-arguments to this claim have been put forward in many publications (for instance, several chapters in Wellington (1989); and Chapman (1993), who talks of the 'overselling' of science education). But perhaps the most telling quote comes from Ausubel (1964), whose work, ironically, has been used to support certain phases in practical work in the recent past:

Grand strategies of discovery do not seem to be transferable across disciplines . . . it hardly seems plausible that a strategy of inquiry, which must necessarily be broad enough to be applicable to a wide range of disciplines and problems, can ever have sufficient particular relevance to be helpful in the solution of the specific problem at hand.

(Ausubel 1964: 298)

This section has introduced and summarised some of the arguments and counter arguments for and against practical work. Many of the points will be followed up and expanded upon in later chapters. In Chapter 2 Millar goes on to show how the stated purposes of practical work relate to five specific examples of activities in typical teaching labs. Our aim here has been to introduce a tone of healthy scepticism for the potential and outcomes of practical work.

'Real' science, teachers' science, pupils' science and school science

One of the accusations levelled against practical work in school science is that it has failed to reflect 'real' science. This, in my view, begs two questions: first, how could it and anyway, why should it? And second, what is 'real' science? Both questions are addressed by various authors in this book but again I introduce them and briefly discuss them here.

Take the second question first. The world of science covers a huge range of diverse activities. If we consider all the activities or disciplines that we would probably list as 'sciences' it is likely to include: astrophysics, biochemistry, biotechnology, botany, cosmology, ecology, and zoology. From this list, it is almost impossible to define or distil out the essential, defining features of being a science or of 'scientific method'. Each will have certain features in common but these are more like 'family resemblances' (Wittgenstein 1953) than a single unifying feature or an essential core. The methods they use are different; the culture and the history varies from one science to another. In some ways, considering sciences as a family is like considering the range of games that exist. Different games have different rules, different numbers of players and different times of duration. Some games use a board, some have teams, while others need individuals; some involve physical contact, some do not. We all know a game when we see one, but we would all be hard pushed to state the defining features of games as a family.

So it is hardly surprising that the various 'phases and fads' over the decades in practical work in science education have failed to mimic or to capture 'scientific method'. It is not just a difficult task for school science – it is an impossible one. This is the reason why a single, prescriptive framework for experimental and investigative work in practical science will never succeed. It is also the reason why, as Jenkins points out in this book, any attempt to impose a single format or prescription for practical work receives resentment, cynicism and scepticism from the science teaching profession.

However, this does not imply that science education can convey nothing about the nature of science. Indeed, this is still one of its most important roles, especially if it is to improve the public understanding of science – (Millar 1996) gives a full discussion of a science curriculum aimed at fostering public understanding. There are certain messages about science as an activity which can be conveyed (either implicitly or explicitly – 'caught *and* taught'). These are discussed fully in later chapters (Hodson, Leach, Woolnough and others). For this introductory chapter, I condense them as follows:

1   In science, experiments are not conducted which are independent of theory; that is, experiments are not done in a theoretical vacuum.

2 As a result, predictions, observations and inferences are theory-laden.
3 Scientists normally work as members of communities, often in institutions – science is a social activity which involves people. These people have personal attitudes, views, opinions and prejudices.
4 Scientists work in a social, cultural, historical and political context. This context determines: what methods they are able to use; what questions get asked; how far they are funded and pursued. Research pursued and methods used in Victorian England or Nazi Germany have not been, and will not be, acceptable in other eras.
5 Scientific theories do not follow logically from experimental data (the fallacy of induction). Experiments may be derived from or suggested by theories – but theories are not fully determined by or derived from experiments (things like human beings and 'leaps of the imagination' are needed in the middle).
6 Unlike Premier League football managers, established theories are not dismissed just because of a few bad results. Similarly, the choice between competing theories is not made purely on empirical/experimental grounds. Theories are not confirmed or proven, but can be supported, by experimental results. Theories can be shown to be false (falsified) by experimental data.
7 Science has methods but does not have *one method*. No scientific method follows a set, algorithmic procedure or a set of rules. Science also involves tacit, implicit, personal knowledge (see Nott and Masters, and Woolnough in this book).

It is a tall order to expect science teachers, most of whom will have spent little or no time during their science degrees in considering the nature of science, to convey all these messages about science in busy laboratories – or to find the time and the strategies to teach these ideas explicitly. This is made especially difficult for teachers by the fact that pupils' perceptions of science, and indeed those of the public generally (Wellington 1991 on media science), are totally at odds with the seven statements above. As Leach points out in his chapter, young people's views and beliefs about science pose a challenge for the science teacher in the laboratory – the place where a number of cultures meet. Leach and other authors discuss strategies and approaches to address this problem. Again, here my aim is simply to condense a few of the teaching points that can be conveyed to pupils which later chapters take much further. First, learners need to be shown or taught how to observe things. They will not see a field around a magnet, or reflection/refraction in a ripple tank or a cell under a microscope unless they know what they are looking for. As Hodson has argued in this book and in other papers, children need to learn the observational language of science – they need to 'see things as . . .'. This is why science processes cannot be separated from science content; all the processes of science –

inferring, classifying, predicting, hypothesising, seeing, observing, are embedded in science knowledge and theory (Wellington 1989). Science processes are situated in science; they are not context-free and transferable.

For similar reasons, science teachers cannot teach theory through practical work. Pupils cannot just be exposed to phenomena or events or observations in the hope that they will somehow induce or discover 'the theory'. Discovery learning may work for teaching knowledge *that* – for example, a metal bar expands when you heat it – but cannot be expected to teach *knowledge why* (for instance, theories such as the particle model of matter which can help to explain expansion). Practical work can illustrate phenomena but it cannot explain why they happen. Pupils need to be taught that not everything in science can be related to lab experience and doing things. This is why conversation, discussion and imagination are so important (see the chapters by Osborne, Solomon and Sutton); namely, working with the ideas, concepts and principles of science.

A third point which pupils need to be told when doing practical work is that a few 'dodgy' (that is, anomalous) results do not lead to the abandonment of a theory – it takes a lot more than that. However, a lot of judgement (prior theoretical knowledge) is required to decide which results are 'dodgy' or anomalous. Teachers do this all the time when they collect results in at the end of an 'experiment' and decide which ones to write on the blackboard and which ones 'don't fit' and can be ignored (especially when looking for lines of best fit). This leads to the next point – very few 'experiments' in school science are really experiments. It's just that we have all (teachers and pupils) got into the habit of calling them that.

'Experiment' – the all-purpose word

One of the issues which teachers *and* pupils need to become clearer about is the range of different types of practical work and the purposes they serve. There is a tendency for both teachers and pupils to call every type of practical activity they do in a school lab. an 'experiment'. In fact, many of the practical activities done in school science are plainly not experiments – they may be illustrations of a phenomenon (either done in small groups or on the front bench); they may simply be providing experiences or getting a feel for a phenomenon for pupils; they may simply be exercises or routines for pupils to follow, aimed perhaps at developing a particular skill or becoming used to a piece of equipment or an instrument (categories such as these were discussed helpfully by Woolnough and Allsop in 1985).

Equally, there are all sorts of 'experiments'. Some may (quite rightly, since this goes on in 'real science' all the time) simply involve replicating a piece of practical work which has already been done, either recently or in many cases a few hundred years ago. Replication is an important part of

11

scientific activity. Others may be genuine investigations although these are probably far less common. Some, incidentally, do not involve any apparatus (like thought experiments).

Whatever practical work is done in school labs, teachers should be wary of using the blanket term 'experiment'. This is more than a semantic point; pretending that all activity is experiment has generated much of the cynicism amongst pupils towards lab work, which is summed up so well in this quotation from a children's story:

> We were supposed to be reading the instructions for an experiment we were going to perform in class that day. Now there's another stupid thing. Year after year, this same teacher makes his students perform the same experiments. Well, if the experiments have been done so many times before, how can they still be experiments? The teacher knows what is going to happen. I thought experimenting meant trying new things to see what would happen. We weren't experimenting at all. We were playacting.
>
> (From Martin 1990: 2)

These points are followed up in later chapters, not least by Gough. The point argued later is that types of practical work are all horses for courses. If we observe typical science teaching labs we see at least six types of activity going on that we would probably all class as practical work: teacher demonstrations; class practicals, with all learners on similar tasks, working in small groups; a circus of 'experiments', with small groups engaged in different activities, rotating in a 'carousel'; investigations, organised in one of the above two ways; and problem-solving activities. (More discussion on the meaning of these types and their purposes is given in Wellington 1994: 132–7). Another way of classifying practical work was suggested by Woolnough and Allsop (1985: 47–59). They gave a useful breakdown using three categories: exercises, experiences and investigations.

Each type of practical work serves a different purpose: different type, different aim (Gott and Duggan 1995: 21). We need to convey this to pupils; for instance, if they are going to replicate what someone already knows, tell them: don't kid them that they are discovering something.

Institutionalised practicals – icons, rituals and malpractice

One of the legacies of the past in practical work has been the growth in or evolution of 'standard' practicals which are passed on from one generation of teachers to the next, and by teacher training institutions. They become embedded in published schemes and programmes, and are even transferred without checking from one textbook to another. In his chapter, Jenkins talks about this process in the late nineteenth and mid-twentieth centuries and the role which laboratory manuals have played in the handing down and evolution of a set of practical activities which work in class. There are many good reasons for this of course, and part of it involves the inheritance of the considerable 'craft knowledge' required to carry out an effective piece of practical work.

However, there is also a slightly more sinister side to this generation game. As Kirschner puts it: 'Years of effort have produced "foolproof" experiments when the right answer is certain to emerge for everyone in the class if the laboratory instructions are followed' (1992: 278). More recent research by Nott and Smith (1995) has highlighted the interesting behaviour of science teachers in 'rigging' and 'conjuring' of so-called experiments in order that things do not go wrong. The ability to rig, of course, could be put down to craft knowledge, but the tendency to conjure – such as to inject oxygen from a tank in order to 'prove' that photosynthesis of pondweed has occurred – is a rather more dubious practice. Further work by Nott and Wellington (1996) has shown that the practice of conjuring may well be widespread and is often passed on by mentors in schools (or just as often by lab technicians) during teacher training.

The imposition of what Jenkins and colleagues (see his chapter) have called 'Investigations by order' has led to the development of similarly institutionalised practicals, but in this case masquerading as investigations, all designed and tailored to fit the national template and its assessment framework. An alien observer travelling around the schools of England and Wales would soon begin to wonder why so many pupils were dissolving jellies, bouncing ping-pong balls and watching coffee cool in the labs of the nation.

Time for a reappraisal

We cannot dwell on this here and it is easy to be sarcastic and cynical, so we stop now. No one doubts that the experiences of practical work and getting a feel for materials, apparatus, events and phenomena are a vital part of science education. The aim of this book is to see where we have come from with practical work, to assess its value, to search for more 'authentic' practical work and to suggest ways of improving it for the future.

In the second chapter of this introductory section, Millar examines different types of practical work in science by looking closely at five concrete examples of the type of practical work currently done in school labs. By examining each example in detail he is able to show what practical work can, and cannot, achieve. Millar relates these specific examples to statements from the past about the purposes of practical work and shows the large gap between the rhetoric of past statements or claims for practical work, and the reality of real teaching labs. Millar's five cases or examples are invaluable in portraying five real teaching situations to which later discussions can be pinned and connected.

Later, we hope to show the importance of practical work in real settings and of genuine project work; we try to show the value and importance of conversation, discussion and imagination when linked with practical activity; other chapters discuss the key role of personal and implicit knowledge in practical science. One major change since the eras which Jenkins summarises has been the growth of information and communication technology (ICT). The implications of ICT for doing science and for learning it are enormous and in many ways require a whole book to explore them fully. Here we illustrate a few examples of the potential of ICT in three short chapters which indicate how practical work will be fundamentally changed by new technology.

At the end of the book we take stock of key points in the chapters and offer specific suggestions for future curriculum development and teaching practices.

References

Ausubel, D.P. (1964) 'Some psychological and educational limitations of learning by discovery', *The Arithmetic Teacher,* 11(5): 290–302.

Beatty, J. and Woolnough, B. (1982) 'Practical work in 11–13 science: context, type and aims of current practice', *British Educational Research Journal* 8(1): 23–30.

Buckley, J.G. and Kempa, R.F. (1971) 'Practical work in sixth form chemistry', *School Science Review* 53: 24–36.

Chapman, B. (1993) 'The overselling of science education in the eighties', in E. Whitelegg, J. Thomas, and S. Tresman, (eds) *Challenges and Opportunities for Science Education,* London: Paul Chapman.

Delamont, S., Beynon, J. and Atkinson, P. (1988) 'In the beginning was the Bunsen: the foundations of secondary school science', *Qualitative Studies in Education* 1(4): 315–28.

DES (1985) *Science 5-16: A Statement of Policy,* London: HMSO.

Donnelly, J. (1995) 'Curriculum development in science: the lessons of Sc1', *School Science Review,* 76(277): 95–103.

Gee, B. and Clackson, S. (1992) 'The origin of practical work in the English school science curriculum', *School Science Review* 73(265): 79–83.

Gott, R. and Duggan, S. (1995) *Investigative Work in the Science Curriculum,* Buckingham: Open University Press.

Hodson, D. (1990) 'A critical look at practical work in school science', *School Science Review* 70(256): 33–40.

—— (1993) 'Rethinking old ways: towards a more critical approach to practical work in school science', *Studies in Science Education* 22: 85–142.

—— (1996) 'Laboratory work as scientific method: three decades of confusion and distortion', *Journal of Curriculum Studies* 28(2): 115–35.

Kerr, J.F. (1963) *Practical Work in School Science,* Leicester: Leicester University Press.

Kirschner, P. (1992) 'Epistemology, practical work and academic skills in science education', *Science Education* 1: 273–99.

Lave, J. (1988) *Cognition in Practice,* New York: Cambridge University Press.

Leach, J. and Scott, P. (1995) 'The demands of learning science concepts – issues of theory and practice', *School Science Review* 76(277): 47–51.

Martin, A.M. (1990) *Claudia and the Great Search,* New York: Apple Paperbacks, Scholastic.

Millar, R. (1996) 'A science curriculum for public understanding', *School Science Review* 77(280): 7–18.

Murphy, P. (1991) 'Gender differences in pupils' reaction to practical work', in B.E. Woolnough (ed.) *Practical Science,* Milton Keynes: Open University Press.

Nott, M. (1997) 'Keeping scientists in their place', *School Science Review* 78(285): 49–61.

Nott, M. and Smith, R. (1995) '"Talking your way out of it", "rigging" and "conjuring": what science teachers do when practicals go wrong', *International Journal of Science Education* 17(3): 399–410.

Nott, M. and Wellington, J. (1996) 'When the black box springs open: practical work in school science and the nature of science', *International Journal of Science Education* 18(7): 807–18.

Qualter, A., Strang, J. and Swatton, P. (1990) *Explanation – a Way of Learning Science,* Oxford: Blackwell.

Theobald, D.W. (1968) *An Introduction to the Philosophy of Science,* London: Methuen.

Thompson, J.J. (1975) *Practical Work in Sixth Form Science,* Oxford: Oxford University Press.

TIMMS (1997) *Third International Mathematics and Science Study,* Slough: NFER.

Wellington, J.J. (1981) '"What's supposed to happen, Sir?": some problems with discovery learning', *School Science Review* 63(222): 167–73.

—— (ed.) (1989) *Skills and Processes in Science Education*, London: Routledge.

—— (1991) 'Newspaper science, school science: friends or enemies?' *International Journal of Science Education* 13(4): 363–72.

—— (ed.) (1994) *Secondary Science: Contemporary Issues and Practical Approaches,* London: Routledge.

Wittgenstein, L. (1953) *Philosophical Investigations,* Oxford: Oxford University Press.

Woolnough, B.E. (ed.) (1991) *Practical Science,* Milton Keynes: Open University Press.

Woolnough, B.E. and Allsop, T. (1985) *Practical Work in Science,* Cambridge: Cambridge University Press.

2

RHETORIC AND REALITY

What practical work in science
education is *really* for

Robin Millar

The subject matter of science is the material universe. The aim of the scientific enterprise is to obtain the sort of knowledge and understanding of the material universe which can be relied upon for action (Ogborn 1997). We value science because of the extent to which it has been successful in achieving this aim. The aim of science education is to pass on to young people some elements of this knowledge and understanding which we (as a society) feel are of value to them.

Given its subject matter, it is natural that communicating scientific knowledge will involve acts of 'showing' as well as of 'telling'. The subject matter is all around us; it is obvious that we will want to use it in the task of communicating information and ideas about it. For that reason, asking the question 'why do we do practical work in science education?' seems almost irrelevant, beside the point, a mere academic exercise. As many science teachers would answer, we do practical work 'because science is a practical subject'. There are, however, good reasons for asking the question. Perhaps the principal one is that much of what is said about practical work and the reasons for it simply do not hold up to close examination. The rhetoric of science education contains a number of popular myths about practical work and its educational purpose, and these can significantly distort practice. By becoming clearer about the *real* purposes of practical work, we may be better able to plan appropriate practical activities which are more effective and efficient uses of learning time.

In two major research exercises in the 1960s and 1970s, Kerr (1963) and Thompson (1975) asked teachers to rank in order of importance lists of possible aims of practical work. More recently, Hodson (1990) has tried to identify the different justifications offered for practical work in school science. In all these studies, two of the main groups of aims (or justifications) identified are those which concern the role of practical work in supporting the teaching of scientific knowledge, and in teaching about the processes of scientific enquiry. In this chapter, I will, for reasons of space, discuss only the first of these. This should not be taken to imply that the second is of less importance, or that similar points about the relationship between rhetoric and reality could not also be made in that context. Indeed, the recent work of Donnelly *et al.* (1996) on Science Attainment Target 1 indicates very clearly some of the features of the rhetoric–reality gap in this area.

In the next section I will consider some of the things which are said about practical work and will try to indicate why I think they provide a false rationale for practical work. Then, in the following section, I will go on to consider some specific examples of practical work, of the sort which pupils might be asked to do at some point during their secondary school science course. For each of these, I will try to indicate what seem to me the real reasons for undertaking these tasks in a teaching and learning context. From this, I will try to develop a rationale for practical work within a perspective which sees science education as the passing on of well-attested knowledge rather than as personal enquiry leading to the 'construction' of knowledge.

Practical work: what we say

Much of what is said and written about practical work in science education stems from the widely held image of 'the pupil as scientist'. This viewpoint was articulated particularly clearly in the Nuffield Science Teaching projects of the 1960s with their aim of making the pupil 'a scientist for the day'. It is explicit in many of the things school textbooks say about science in their introductory chapters, and implicit in much of what science teachers say and do.

It is not difficult to see where the idea comes from. Children are curious about the world around them; they learn much of what they know about the world by observing it, and by manipulating and acting on it in various ways. In educational contexts, encouraging children to pursue their own enquiries is attractive because it taps into this natural curiosity, and allows children to extend their knowledge in a way which seems natural and developmental, rather than coercive. It sits more comfortably, therefore, with contemporary views on the appropriate allocation of power in social institutions, by appearing to offer a means of handing on a body of well-attested knowledge without undue emphasis on the authority of the 'expert'. An 'investigative' or 'enquiry' approach also encourages children to be more independent and self-reliant, to think of themselves as able to pose their own questions about the physical world and to find answers to them through their own efforts. In this way it contributes to general educational goals concerning the development of individuals and their capacity for purposeful, autonomous action in the world.

The problem is not with these entirely appropriate social and general educational aims. It is that on to them has been grafted an epistemological justification of an enquiry approach in science education which is open to serious objection. This finds its purest expression in the idea of 'discovery' or 'enquiry' learning, the idea that learners can, by exploring a phenomenon carefully for themselves, assemble the 'facts of the matter' and then come to the accepted scientific understanding. The role of the teacher is to guide the learner, by proposing activities, providing well-chosen materials and instances, drawing attention to salient features (and perhaps away from irrelevant or erroneous ones) and generally 'shaping' the learner's experience – without the need to 'tell' them what 'should happen' or how it 'should be' explained. The problems which this approach generates in practice – essentially of pupils recognising that the 'answer', although unknown to them, is well known to others, and acting accordingly – are well documented (Driver 1975; Atkinson and Delamont 1976; Wellington 1981). Learners clearly find the role of 'scientist' a difficult one to sustain in the teaching laboratory – and for good reason.

More fundamental, however, than these practical difficulties are the epistemological difficulties of the 'enquiry learning' view. These are of two kinds. The first is the assumption that the collection of data, through observation and measurement, is a straightforward common-sense activity. In practice, however, any natural object, material or event has so many features and aspects that any observation of it must begin with a selection process, deciding what to observe and what to ignore. This selection is based on a view about what is salient to observe; in other words, it embodies a particular stance, or perspective, on the thing being observed. Also the quantities (or variables) we use in making and recording our observations are not 'given' by the phenomenon; they are part of the framework of ideas that we bring to the act of observation. So we cannot approach anything and 'just observe it'; we always bring our own particular set of 'spectacles' to the act of observing. This influences *what we choose* to observe, and our prior ideas also influence *what* we observe.

To say that is not, however, to go so far as to claim (as some have done) that all observations are 'theory-laden', and that no clear distinction can therefore be drawn between 'data' and 'explanations' (or, to use other terms, between 'evidence' and 'theory'). There is, I think, a continuum ranging from observations which are readily agreeable by everyone, and based largely on categories and quantities which are part of everyday non-technical discourse, to observations which more obviously carry a theoretical 'load' (such as the 'observation' of an electric current by noting the position of a pointer on an ammeter). The essential point is rather that the framework of ideas, both those learned from previous experience and those designed into the learning situation by the teacher, are a crucial component of any observation event.

The second problem with the epistemology of enquiry learning is about how we get from observations to explanations. 'Enquiry learning' in science is based on the idea that explanations will 'emerge' from observations, if these are carefully structured and sequenced by the teacher and the teaching scheme. This, in philosophical terms, is naïve empiricism – the view that our knowledge begins from unbiased observations, in which we can then discern patterns and regularities, and hence arrive at an explanation. Even a brief excursion into the history of science will tell us, however, that patterns which are clear with hindsight were often not apparent to those exploring a field and that explanatory ideas do not simply 'emerge' from collected data. The development of new fields often begins with the collection, by many people, of data which are believed to be relevant and reliable, and to stand in need of explanation. At some point, one of the individual scientists proposes an explanation which accounts for most of the data (the rest either being set aside for the moment as 'unexplained', or, in some cases, deemed now to be erroneous or irrelevant). After a period of time, the community of scientists is persuaded of the value of this explanation, and it leads (usually) to productive new lines of work. So whilst explanations almost always come from someone who is very familiar with all the available data, the step of generating an explanation is essentially a creative and imaginative one. The explanation (or theory) is an intellectual creation, entirely separate from the data it tries to account for in the sense that the data still stand whatever the fate of the proposed explanation. There is no 'automatic mechanism' by which an explanation 'must emerge' if enough valid data are assembled.

The same is also true at school level. We can, for instance, make many observations about the behaviour of rubbed plastic rods and other objects, noting how they attract and repel, and stick to other objects. These do not inevitably lead to the conclusion that some invisibly small particles are transferred between objects in the process of rubbing, and that these carry an electrical charge – a fundamental property of matter that is not normally observed because it exists in positive and negative forms which are usually present in equal amounts. It is implausible that most learners would ever come to an idea such as this without being told it by someone else. The reason why we celebrate the genius of the great scientists is precisely because the generation of explanatory ideas such as these is not an automatic, routine process of taking care in observation and measurement and following 'a method'. It requires lengthy periods of immersion in and struggle with the phenomena involved, and peculiar insight. Learning situations cannot provide the former, and it would be wholly unrealistic to expect the latter of all learners.

It is therefore a mistake to equate 'learning' with 'rational conviction' (Ogborn 1997). The evidence we can collect and present in the teaching laboratory is never sufficient to establish an idea. It is not reasonable to hope that students will be able to give rational grounds for their acceptance of all the scientific knowledge we would want them to learn. More realistically, we might aim to ensure that they have sufficient understanding of where these ideas came from to explain the 'general shape' (Norris 1992: 217) of the justification for accepting the idea.

I have referred, throughout the discussion above, to 'enquiry learning'. Matthews (1994) has argued that similar points can be made about the epistemology underlying constructivist teaching approaches. In such approaches, the learner is first encouraged to articulate clearly their current understanding. Practical tasks are then used to enable the learner to make observations which challenge this (cognitive conflict) or which extend positive aspects of it (bridging). From these the learner is intended to 'construct' an improved understanding. Matthews' central point is that this, too, rests on an empiricist view of knowledge, that a particular set of experiences can lead the learner into making the intended 'construction' for themselves. In fact, abstract ideas are not constructed anew by learners, but have to be passed on by the teacher 'telling' the learner. To believe that learners should rediscover (or construct for themselves) all their knowledge of the material universe is to deny the key advantage which language gives humans over other species in the transmission of knowledge across the generations.[1]

Practical work: what we do

Let us turn then from the rhetoric of practical work in science education – the things which are said about it – to some examples of practical tasks of the sort which are actually used in school science teaching.

Example 1: Visking tubing

A class of 15-year-old students is working in small groups of two or three, carrying out a practical task which they themselves would almost certainly call 'an experiment'. It involves taking a short length of thin plastic tubing, which they have been told is called Visking tubing. This has been soaked in water beforehand to make it pliable. The students have to tie a knot in one end of their piece of tubing and then, using a dropper pipette, put some glucose solution and some starch suspension into it. Then they have to tie the other end of the tubing, making sure both ends are securely tied, so that none of the glucose or starch can leak out of the resulting 'sausage' through the ends. Then they have to put the sealed length of tubing into a boiling tube of water and leave it for a time (Figure 2.1). Then they take samples of liquid from the boiling tube and test these for the presence of glucose and starch, using standard tests with which they are already familiar from previous science lessons, involving Benedict's reagent and iodine, respectively.

Procedure

1 Set up the apparatus as shown in the diagram.

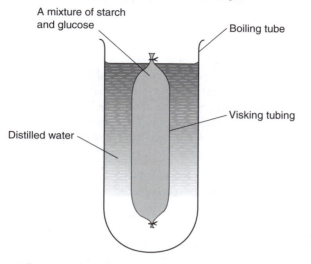

2 Test the distilled water with Benedict's solution and with iodine solution as soon as you have set up the apparatus.
3 Repeat the tests at two minute intervals by taking further samples from the boiling tube.
4 Record your observations in the form of a table.

Figure 2.1 The Visking tubing practical task
Source: M. Jenkins (1987) *Examining GCSE Human Biology*, London: Hutchinson, p. 135
© Stanley Thornes (Publishers) Limited, Cheltenham, UK

If all goes according to plan, they should obtain a positive test for glucose but a negative one for starch. From this, they will be helped, through class discussion, to deduce that glucose has been able to pass through the Visking tubing into the water outside, but starch has not. This, in turn, will be explained in terms of the smaller size of the molecules of glucose, which enables them to pass through 'gaps' in the Visking tubing which the starch molecules are too large to pass through. The final step in the chain of argument is to suggest that this arrangement is a model of digestion in the human gut: during digestion, other chemicals (enzymes) react with starch to produce glucose which, unlike the starch, can pass through the walls of the intestine into the bloodstream and so be transported to all parts of the body.

So what is this piece of practical work actually for? Why do this practically, rather than just talking about the ideas involved? Clearly, the task is intended to help the students perceive the structure of the digestive system and the process of digestion in a certain way. The physical model which they construct is intended to help them picture the intestine as a tubular structure, through which certain things can pass. And the use of chemical tests for the two types of foodstuff carries the implicit message that digestion is essentially a chemical process. Strikingly, however (and my reason for choosing to begin with this particular example of practical work), this practical task provides no warrant whatsoever for accepting this account of digestion. The practical work is not carried out on the real system we want the students to understand, but on a model of it. There is no way in which we can logically infer anything about the behaviour of the human gut from that of a piece of plastic tubing. That does not, of course, mean that the practical task is of no value – just that it would be wrong to see it as providing supporting evidence for an explanation.

Example 2: cooling and insulation

Most practical work is, unlike the first example above, carried out on the 'real system' we want to understand. For example, consider another class, again of 14- or 15-year-olds, investigating the rate at which hot water in a beaker cools, when different materials are wrapped around it. They take several beakers, and wrap each in a different material (such as felt, cotton wool, plastic foam or bubble-wrap); they may also have one beaker which is left unwrapped for comparison purposes (Figure 2.2). Then they pour hot water into each beaker and measure the water temperature at 1-minute intervals for about 15–20 minutes. They make measurements of this sort on several beakers, either simultaneously or in sequence, and draw graphs to show how the temperature of the water in each varies with time.

What are the students supposed to learn from this practical activity? They are very unlikely to be expected to recall the detailed outcomes of their work – to remember, for instance, which material is better than another for keeping the water hot. Usually, in this activity, no effort is made to ensure that the thickness, even less the mass per unit area, of the materials is kept the same, so any comparison can only be of the available specimens of the various materials used. The students will, however, be expected to recall that all of the materials result in the water staying hot for longer than it does with no wrapping around the beaker, and to be able to explain this in terms of a model of energy (heat) moving spontaneously from the hot water in the beaker to the cooler surroundings and of the different materials slowing down this process to differing degrees. The practical activity as a whole is a kind of enactment of the scientific model of the thermal process involved: the actions undertaken, and the interpretation of the results obtained, make sense when viewed from within this particular mental model of thermal processes. The practical activity provides an opportunity for the students to think, and to talk and write, about this phenomenon from within the 'mental landscape', and using the terminology, of an

Keeping warm

Help
Sheet

Think about

- You can use different materials to insulate some beakers.

- You can leave one beaker with no insulation, as a 'control'.

- You will need to put a lid on each beaker (to reduce evaporation and make it a fair test). You can make a hole in each lid for a thermometer:

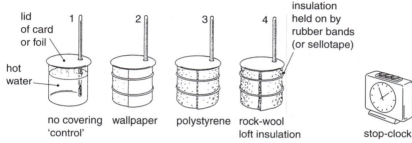

- You can half-fill each beaker with the **same** amount of very hot water. Can you think of a way of doing this accurately and quickly, so that all 4 beakers start off (almost) together?

⚠ hot water

- What else must you do, to make it a **fair test**?

- You can take the temperature of each beaker, every 2 minutes, for 20–30 minutes. You can use a table like this:

Time (mins):	0	2	4	6	8	10	12	14	16	18	20	22	24	26	28	30
no insulation																
wallpaper																
polystyrene																
loft insulation																

(left axis label: Temperature (°C))

Figure 2.2 The cooling and insulation task
Source: K. Johnson, S. Adamson and G. Williams (1995) *Spotlight Science, Teachers' Guide 9*, Cheltenham: Stanley Thornes, p. 81 © Stanley Thornes (Publishers) Limited, Cheltenham, UK

imagined model. What they do makes sense within this model. The model also determines how they interpret their observations. The primary purpose of the task is to encourage students to view thermal processes in this way, by working 'within a model' and by 'talking the language of the model'. This is a powerful means of consolidating ideas, because it involves *acting* and not merely thinking (see Solomon's chapter).

Example 3: green leaves

The first two examples above illustrate the role of some practical tasks in helping learners to understand a model, by having them act in ways which only make sense from within the perspective of the model. The actual results are less important than the overall framework – in the first case because the system used is not the 'real thing', in the second because the detailed results are not worth committing to memory. Some practical tasks seem, at first sight, however, to depend more strongly on getting the 'right result'. Consider, for example, another class of 15-year-olds, carrying out some investigations on the green leaves of plants. A few days previously the students have carefully wrapped some of the leaves of a growing geranium in aluminium foil, to exclude light from them. For the practical task, each group uses one wrapped leaf and one unwrapped leaf from the same plant. They cut discs from each leaf and, taking care to keep the discs from the two leaves separate, they extract the green colour from them by immersing them in boiling ethanol for several minutes. They then wash the leaf discs and place them on a spotting tile, where they can add a few drops of iodine solution to each (Figure 2.3). They should find that the discs from leaves which have been covered in foil are unaffected by the iodine, but those from leaves which were not wrapped turn dark blue – indicating that starch is present in these leaves.

What is this practical task for? Clearly it is intended to help the students to grasp the idea that green plants produce starch and that light is essential to this process. In other lessons in the same topic, they may carry out other practical tasks, involving plants which have been kept for some time in an atmosphere from which carbon dioxide has been removed, or using variegated leaves, to help them build up a model of a process (photosynthesis) going on in the leaves of green plants, in which carbon dioxide is converted into starch, when light shines on them.

But does that mean that this practical task provides a warrant (or one part of the warrant) for accepting the scientific account of photosynthesis? To answer that, we need to ask: what would be the consequence of failing to obtain the expected outcome – of getting positive starch tests from leaves kept in the dark, or negative ones from leaves kept in the light? However this is handled in the classroom, we *know* that it does not really pose a challenge to the accepted scientific account of events. Nor should it. Accepted scientific knowledge is supported by much more extensive evidence than this, and has gone through a lengthy period of scrutiny before being generally accepted. Further work based upon it has demonstrated the usefulness of the knowledge in other contexts. Results obtained in a short time by novices, and using rudimentary equipment, cannot threaten this. The sensible response is to look for other ways to account for the deviation from the expected – in the quality of the apparatus, and the level of expertise of the investigators.

Testing a leaf for starch

Most of the sugar made in the leaves of a plant is changed to starch.
You can test for this starch with iodine.
If the leaf turns blue-black with iodine then starch has been made.

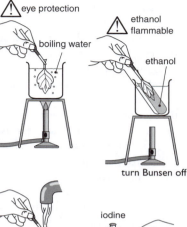

- Dip a leaf into boiling water for about 1 minute to soften it.

- Turn off the Bunsen burner.

- Put the leaf into a test-tube of ethanol. Stand the test-tube in the hot water for about 10 minutes.

- Wash the leaf in cold water.

- Spread the leaf out flat on a petri dish and cover it with iodine, What colour does the leaf go?

h Why was it important that you turn off the Bunsen burner when you were heating the ethanol?
i What was the leaf like after you heated it in the ethanol?
j Was there any starch in the leaf that you tested?

Into the light

If starch is present we can say that the leaf has been making food.
Plan an investigation to see if a plant can make food without any light.

Figure 2.3 Testing leaves for starch
Source: Johnson *et al.* (1995), p. 147 © Stanley Thornes (Publishers) Limited, Cheltenham, UK

Tasks like the three discussed above have to be understood as *pedagogic* and not as *epistemic* events. Their function is not to discover something new about the world, but to help learners to perceive the world in certain ways – ways which are known in advance to the teacher and to the expert community of which he or she is a representative. Newman makes the point succinctly:

> The young child is often thought of as a little scientist exploring the world and discovering the principles of its operation. We often forget that while the scientist is working on the border of human knowledge and is finding out things that nobody yet knows, the child is finding out precisely what everybody already knows.
>
> (1982: 26)

If an unexpected outcome to this practical task does not challenge the accepted account, does obtaining the expected outcome provide support for the accepted account? Logically, if I argue that the failure of a teaching laboratory practical task to display the expected outcome does not undermine the accepted account, it would appear to follow that its success does not add any support to, or grounds for accepting, that account. This is not, however, quite so. For obtaining the expected outcome, particularly after a long and complex series of operations, *does* lead us to place more confidence in the chain of reasoning which led to the prediction of the expected outcome. In short, failure to get the result we predict is endemic; success is noteworthy. The reason is that there are always many possible explanations for something not going according to expectations, but it is unlikely to agree with a precise prediction if that is based on erroneous reasoning.

This brings us closer, I think, to seeing the real reason for carrying out practical tasks like the leaf-testing task. The aim is simply to *produce the phenomenon*. The purpose of the task is to get things to work as expected. This, as Hacking has also noted, is also the aim of much practical activity in the science research laboratory:

> To experiment is to create, produce, refine and stabilise phenomena. If phenomena were plentiful in nature, summer blackberries there just for the picking, it would be remarkable if experiments didn't work. But phenomena are hard to produce in any stable way. That is why I spoke of creating and not merely discovering phenomena. That is a long hard task. . . . The pre-apprentice in the school laboratory is mostly acquiring or failing to acquire the ability to know when the experiment is working.
>
> (1983: 230)

As Hacking goes on to note, this is the reason why experiments in science are rarely replicated; if a phenomenon has been produced convincingly by one scientist, there is no need to do it again. If the production of a phenomenon is unconvincing, however, attempts may be made to devise other, and better, ways to produce the phenomenon reliably, but these will usually involve new approaches rather than direct replications of an earlier experiment.

In a teaching context, producing the phenomenon is also a kind of ritualised display of the power of the scientific knowledge involved. The event implicitly proclaims: 'see, we (that is, the scientific community as embodied in the teacher) know so much about this that we can get this event to happen, reliably and regularly, before your very eyes!' The less likely the event, the more powerful this is. Practical tasks carried out by the students are really 'auto-demonstrations', so they carry the even stronger implicit message that 'our understanding, and consequent control of materials and events, is so good that I (the teacher) don't even have to do it for you but you can do it for yourself'.

The other implicit message in all of this is the one that Hacking has drawn attention to: that phenomena are not easy to produce. It requires skill to devise a situation which allows a phenomenon to be seen clearly, instead of being masked by other phenomena and processes, as it usually is in a complex situation. It is therefore not unreasonable to treat a successful (that is, expected) outcome of a practical task as our best evidence that a learner has carried out the task correctly and with sufficient care and skill.

Example 4: circuit predictions

The lengthy discussion of the previous example included the point that unexpected outcomes in teaching laboratory practical tasks can always be explained away, without challenging the accepted account. How, if this is so, can practical work be used to challenge students' ideas, where these differ from the scientific account? Cannot the students, with justification, explain their observations away in a similar manner?[2] To explore this a little, consider a class of 14-year-olds who have been learning about electric circuits. The teacher proposes the predict-observe-explain task shown in Figure 2.4.

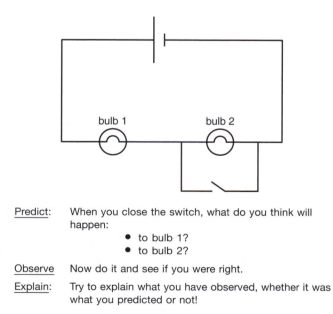

Predict: When you close the switch, what do you think will happen:
                   • to bulb 1?
                   • to bulb 2?

Observe   Now do it and see if you were right.

Explain: Try to explain what you have observed, whether it was what you predicted or not!

Figure 2.4 A predict–observe–explain task on electric circuits

Pupils with a sequential model of circuit behaviour may predict that bulb 2 will go out when the switch is closed, but that bulb 1 will stay the same brightness as before, as current gets to it 'before' it encounters the switch. The teacher's plan is that such pupils will observe that bulb 1 becomes brighter and be obliged to review their thinking to take account of this new information.

The issue which concerns us here is not whether such a review does indeed lead to better understanding, but whether we can legitimately claim that this task provides evidence which conflicts with such pupils' expectations. The answer to this is implicit in the previous discussion. What we are really doing here is producing a phenomenon which is predicted by our (that is, the accepted scientific) account of electric circuit behaviour. It may be possible for someone to defend a different explanatory account by appealing to other explanations of the discrepancy – thus 'saving the appearances'. But the facts of the matter are likely to be more readily agreed than in the green leaf task – partly because the effect (brightness of a bulb) is more directly observable than the presence/absence of, say, starch in a leaf; and partly because the observation is more quickly made, and so can be repeated several times with different bulbs and switches to check an initial observation.

Example 5: metals and acid

As a final example, consider a group of pupils carrying out a series of observations on the reactions of metals with dilute acids. They have been given samples of magnesium, zinc, iron and copper, and a supply of dilute hydrochloric acid. They are to add samples of each metal in turn to a small sample of acid in a test tube, to observe what happens and to put the metals into order according to the vigour of the reaction.

What is the point in doing this practically, as opposed, for example, to telling pupils the outcome? Clearly there is a phenomenon (indeed phenomena) to produce, but its production requires little expertise. Also the outcome, especially of the reaction with magnesium, is a memorable event which pupils may remember and recall as an event. This function of practical tasks, of providing a memorable episode, applies equally to the Visking tubing, the cooling water, and the green leaf tasks discussed above. It is an important element of the justification of such tasks, as there is some evidence that our memories store whole episodes rather than separate ideas or principles – see White 1988, ch. 3. This can, however, be a mixed blessing, as often the important learning point is associated with the *interpretation* of the event and not with its surface features as a whole event, yet these are what may be retained in memory.

As with other practical tasks discussed, we could question the extent to which the task provides a warrant for accepting the order of reactivity the pupils will eventually be expected to recall. In my description, I carefully omitted aluminium from the list of metals provided, as many teachers would in practice. Their reason is that they know its behaviour in this reaction is not consistent with its place in the reactivity series – for other reasons which would be a distraction if mentioned at this point in the learning process. So the task is simplified, to ensure the desired outcome. What if aluminium were provided? Then the observations would not be allowed to dictate the conclusion about order of reactivity, but a form of special pleading would take place. But surely that also, implicitly, under-mines the significance, as evidence, of all the observations actually made. How, logically, could we rule out any other piece of special pleading that would alter the observed order of reactivity? The case of aluminium then serves to indicate that the observations, in fact, provide no conclusive evidence about the order of reactivity of these metals.

Surely the real purpose of this practical is to teach learners something about what a metal–acid reaction is like, and to provide some concrete referents for ideas like 'gas evolved', 'vigorous reaction', 'less vigorous reaction' and so on. Imagine trying to explain any of these ideas using words alone to a person who had never seen an actual example. Of course it will be easier to communicate the idea by showing the real thing. What is going on here is teaching by ostension – what Wittgenstein (1953) calls 'ostensive definition'. Pupils are learning new ideas by being shown exam-ples of them, rather than by being given formal definitions, or other verbal accounts, of them. Much of our learning follows this route, as Kuhn (1977) has pointed out (with useful examples). When we get pupils to investigate the relationship between force and acceleration for a trolley, for instance, we are showing what the scientific ideas of 'force' and of 'acceleration' mean, by giving concrete examples of them. If the pupils can produce the phenom-enon of a linear graph of acceleration against force, so much the better. The rationality of accepting Newton's Second Law of Motion is neither enhanced nor undermined by the outcome, whatever it happens to be!

A general observation

To conclude this discussion it may be worth drawing out one point which is implicit in all the above discussion. It is that the purpose of much practical work in science is to build a bridge – between the realm of objects and observable properties on the one hand, and the realm of ideas on the other. If we do practical work 'because science is a practical subject', then it is almost equally true that we do it 'because science is a theoretical subject'. All the five tasks I have discussed try, in different ways, to encourage students to make links between things they can see and handle, and ideas they may entertain which might account for their observations. The links may be built by asking students to 'see it this way' (Ogborn *et al.* 1996, ch.7; and Sutton and Solomon in this book), using a particular model to view phenomena. They may also be asked to produce phenomena which a particular model predicts, or which will be used as the raw material for speculating about possible explanations. Finally, they may be shown examples of categories or classes of materials or events, so that they can attach meaning to these concept labels.

Supporting the learning of scientific knowledge: how practical work works

To summarise the discussion above, I have argued that the outcomes of practical tasks in the teaching laboratory can provide *some* support for the accepted scientific account of phenomena – but only because phenomena are difficult to produce reliably and so their successful production makes us more inclined to accept as valid the knowledge which predicted them. The less likely the phenomenon is, the stronger the impression it makes. Producing a phenomenon does not, of course, 'prove' that the knowledge which predicted it is 'true'. In the teaching laboratory, however, failure to produce a phenomenon does not threaten an accepted piece of knowledge. Popper's notion of falsification (or the naïve version of it) certainly does not apply in the teaching laboratory (even if it applies in 'real science').[3]

Practical work of this sort – intended to support the teaching and learning of scientific knowledge – has to be understood, and judged, as a communication strategy, as a means of augmenting what can be achieved by word, picture and gesture. Parallels with the activity of 'real scientists' in research laboratories are unhelpful and may be misleading. There are no necessary parallels between the way in which a piece of knowledge was first established and the way it is best communicated to someone who doesn't yet know it. In the discussion above, I have tried to show, using examples, the significant difference between the things which are said about the role of practical work in science education and the purposes which are implicit in the things which are actually done. There is more need, I think, to change what we say than what we do – though a clearer understanding of what practical work can and cannot do might also lead to better designed and more effectively targeted practical work.

Notes

1 Of course learners may well have to 'reconstruct' their own personal views, convictions and beliefs in the light of such learning. But that is very different from claiming that they are constructing 'knowledge'.
2 The key phrase here is 'with justification'. We know that students *do* do this; the question is, is it rationally justified?
3 Though this, too, has been seriously challenged; see, for example, Newton-Smith (1981 ch. 3), Chalmers (1982 ch. 5).

References

Atkinson, P. and Delamont, S. (1976) 'Mock-ups and cock-ups – the stage management of guided discovery instruction', in M. Hammersley and P. Woods (eds) *The Process of Schooling*, London: Routledge and Kegan Paul, pp. 133–42.

Chalmers, A. (1982) *What is this Thing called Science?*, Milton Keynes: Open University Press.

Donnelly, J., Buchan, A., Jenkins, E., Laws, P. and Welford, G. (1996) *Investigations by Order*, Nafferton: Studies in Education Ltd.

Driver, R. (1975) 'The name of the game', *School Science Review*, 56(197): 800–4.

Hacking, I. (1983) *Representing and Intervening*, Cambridge: Cambridge University Press.

Hodson, D. (1990) 'A critical look at practical work in school science', *School Science Review* 71(256): 33–40.

Kerr, J. (1963) *Practical Work in School Science*, Leicester: Leicester University Press.

Kuhn, T.S. (1977) 'Second thoughts on paradigms', in T.S. Kuhn, *The Essential Tension*, Chicago: University of Chicago Press, pp. 293–319.

Matthews, M. (1994) *Science Teaching: the Role of History and Philosophy of Science*, London: Routledge.

Newman, D. (1982) 'Perspective-taking versus content in understanding lies', *Quarterly Newsletter of the Laboratory of Comparative Human Cognition*, 4: 26–9: cited in B. Rogoff, (1991), 'The joint socialisation of development by young children and adults', in P. Light, S. Sheldon and M. Woodhead (eds) *Learning to Think*, London: Routledge, pp. 67–96.

Newton-Smith, W. (1981) *The Rationality of Science*, London: Routledge and Kegan Paul.

Norris, S.P. (1992) 'Practical reasoning in the production of scientific knowledge', in R.A. Duschl and R.J. Hamilton (eds) *Philosophy of Science, Cognitive Psychology and Educational Theory and Practice*, Albany, NY: State University of New York Press, pp. 195–225.

Nott, M. and Wellington, J. (1996) 'When the black box springs open: practical work and the nature of science', *International Journal of Science Education*, 18(7): 807–18.

Ogborn, J. (1997) 'Science and the made world', in M. Ratcliffe (ed.) *Proceedings of the Nuffield Foundation Seminars: Beyond 2000: Science Education and the Future*, Seminar 3, 8–9 November 1997, Centre for Science Education, King's College London.

Ogborn, J., Kress, G., Martins, I. and McGillicuddy, K. (1996) *Explaining Science in the Classroom*, Buckingham: Open University Press.

Thompson, J.J. (ed.) (1975) *Practical Work in Sixth Form Science*, Department of Educational Studies, University of Oxford.

Wellington, J.J. (1981) '"What's supposed to happen, sir?" – some problems with discovery learning', *School Science Review*, 63(222): 167–73.

White, R.T. (1988) *Learning Science*, Oxford: Blackwell.

Wittgenstein, L. (1953) *Philosophical Investigations*, Oxford: Oxford University Press.

Part II

PERSPECTIVES ON PRACTICAL WORK IN SCHOOL SCIENCE

School practical work can be seen from a number of different perspectives. Later in the book we look at its authenticity – in what respects does, and should, school science relate to so-called real science? In this part of the book we examine practical science from three different perspectives: an historical perspective; the viewpoint of the pupils or students of science; and the perspective of the science teacher.

Jenkins begins by considering the rationale for practical chemistry in the early nineteenth century when it was seen as a vehicle for 'training the mind' and developing the skills of observing, reasoning and so on deemed to be of general value. How interesting that the statements of 1818 and 1847 which Jenkins considers are so similar to the rhetoric of the 1970s' Manpower Services Commission on 'generic' or 'transferable skills', the 1980s' TVEI and Enterprise projects, and now the 1990s' core or 'key' skills which pervade educational discourse (though it is worth noting that any mention of scientific method or skill is noticeably absent in the new era of key skills). Jenkins shows how the persuasive arguments of the nineteenth century, based on science as 'mental training' were used to support practical work in the century's last quarter when there was a huge growth of labs, resources and equipment in the public and grammar schools. As the twentieth century came in, the place of practical work in science was secured by legislation, whilst set, standard experiments began to develop and were passed on by lab books and manuals. At the end of this century, after nearly 200 years of evolution, we now have the domination of the school lab and its resources over school science and its complete control of the expectations of pupils, parents and teachers of what a science lesson should look like. Jenkins' view is that school practical work is too much a 'prisoner of its past': what if this domination and these expectations were broken? His chapter thus sets the scene and the tone for the rest of the book.

Leach takes up the theme of expectations and viewpoints by considering the perspective of the learner of science. He argues that, in the school laboratory, a number of different cultures meet. Students and teachers both have views about the nature of science and scientific activity which may be at odds. Neither party may have a clear or well-formulated view of what science is. This is hardly surprising since the world of science is itself so diverse. As Leach argues, there is no *one* culture of science – scientists may range from biochemists to geologists and astrophysicists. Hence practical work in school science cannot model all the practices of professional science – but Leach argues that it should at least teach something about the nature of science. Leach reports that young people are likely to have an image of science which has certain features, for example: data collected by scientists are seen as untainted or undetermined by theory; knowledge claims – that is, laws and theories – are seen to emerge from data in an unproblematic way; and data collected in science can actually confirm or verify these claims. In some ways, of course, these images of science have been reinforced by the kind of practical work which has occurred in schools, as later authors point out. Leach's persuasive argument is that we should be aware of learners' assumptions and views about science so that it may be possible to teach accordingly, and successfully convey important messages about the nature of science.

Finally, Gough provides a third perspective in his usual unorthodox style and invites us to reconceive labwork. He likens the lab to a theatre, and suggests – using a fictional extract from a lesson – that it is often the 'theatre of the absurd'. All labs in schools are theatres of representation but they currently bear little resemblance to the sites where contemporary science takes place (nor, as earlier writers in this field have pointed out, do their contents bear any likeness to any other objects ever seen outside the walls of a school lab). But, Gough argues, there is at least one kind of educationally worthwhile activity to which they *are* materially suited, namely, object-orientated play and exploration. School laboratories are places where students can experiment with objects in the pre-Baconian sense of 'experimental' – based on experience. Rather than conceiving school laboratories as a replica of 'modern science', teachers should reconceive them as extensions of the material and mythic space of the playground.

Later in the book, Solomon takes up the same theme of 'play' and shows its importance in learning science.

3

THE SCHOOLING OF LABORATORY SCIENCE

Edgar Jenkins

Although laboratories for the conduct of scientific research have existed since at least the seventeenth century, the science teaching laboratory, designed and equipped to teach classes of students, is a much later development. Like other aspects of the history of science education, it is essentially a nineteenth-century phenomenon that is intimately linked with the growing professionalisation of science and the vigorous assertion of its educational claims. This chapter examines the case made for the practical teaching of science in school laboratories and outlines the growth of laboratory teaching since the late nineteenth century. Attention is also given to the role attributed to the laboratory in the science curriculum projects of the 1960s and in the science component of the National Curriculum introduced in England and Wales following the passage of the Education Reform Act 1988. It is suggested that there is now a pressing need to re-examine critically the contribution that the practical teaching of science in the laboratory can make to scientific education at school level.

Constructing a case for laboratory teaching

The obstacles to the development of student teaching laboratories were considerable. Apart from practical concerns such as cost and design, such science teaching as existed in universities was commonly by means of lectures, often enlivened by demonstrations intended to capture the interest of as many students as possible since it was the students' fees which generated most or all of the lecturer's income. A more fundamental issue, however, was the question of the purpose which the necessarily expensive teaching of practical science to undergraduates should serve. Answers to this question began to be constructed as a number of institutions, notably King's College and University College London in 1845, followed the pioneering example of Thomas Thomson, who established the first undergraduate course in practical chemistry at Glasgow in 1818 (Duff 1997). In essence, the case for the practical teaching of chemistry to undergraduates was constructed in terms which paralleled those associated with longer-established components of the undergraduate curriculum such as mathematics and the classics. Laboratory teaching, in particular, was used to help rebut the claim that the study of chemistry could not provide a liberal education. Such a claim rested on the belief that chemistry was essentially concerned with facts and laws – that is, with information, the acquisition of which had no power to develop the mind. By emphasising that practical chemistry, especially systematic qualitative analysis, engaged students in observation and reasoning, advocates of laboratory teaching to undergraduates were able to argue that the subject could be taught in ways that met the essential condition of *training the mind*. As John Gardner put it, 'He who has become an expert analyst has obtained a power capable of application in any direction for advancing his own knowledge' (Gardner 1846: 296). It also, of course, met another essential condition; namely, that of ensuring a supply of well-trained students, some of whom could make their contribution to the advancement of chemical knowledge.

Laboratories for teaching undergraduate physics presented different problems from chemistry and they developed somewhat later in the nineteenth century. Compared with chemistry, physics embraced a wider variety of experimental activities that were not readily accommodated within a single laboratory. Physics equipment was often both delicate and expensive, and physics was a mathematical and quantitative discipline which required deductive and inductive reasoning based upon accurate observation and precise measurement. Designing a laboratory, constructing equipment and devising courses which accommodated these concerns and matched the intellectual and practical capabilities of the students was a far from straightforward task, and it was not until the closing decade of the nineteenth century that practical classes in physics secured a place in the undergraduate curriculum (Shepherd 1979). The courses placed a heavy emphasis upon measurement, especially of physical constants.

The arguments made for scientific education and for the practical teaching of science within universities in the mid-nineteenth century were readily transferred to, although not readily accepted by, the public and endowed grammar schools. These arguments were set out with particular clarity in a seminal report published in 1867 by the British Association for the Advancement of Science and entitled *On the Best Means of Promoting Scientific Education in Schools* (BAAS 1868). The report suggested that the case for teaching science rested upon several distinct grounds. First, science offered an excellent means of mental training. Second, the incorporation of science within the curriculum could appeal to those boys (*sic*) on whom the usual 'non-scientific studies produced very slight effect'. Third, the methods and result of science had 'so profoundly affected all the philosophical thought of the age' that an 'educated man was under a very great disadvantage' if he remained unacquainted with them. Additionally, it was claimed that the teaching of science could be justified on the grounds that even a 'moderate acquaintance' led to a 'very great intellectual pleasure' in after life. Finally, science should be taught because it affected materially 'the present position and future of civilization'; that is, because scientific knowledge was useful. This five-point rationale was underpinned by a sharp distinction drawn between scientific *information* and scientific *training*, a distinction presented in the report as that between general 'literary acquaintance' with scientific facts and the knowledge of method that may be gained by studying the facts at first hand under the guidance of a competent teacher. While both of these aspects were recognised as important, the principal benefit of a scientific education was the development of a 'scientific habit of mind'. Such a 'habit of mind' required the 'systematic teaching of experimental physics, elementary chemistry, or botany, with the last of these, because of its direct relationship with everyday experience, admitting pre-eminently of being taught in the true scientific manner'. The reference to the educational value of botany is to be understood in terms of the mental training afforded by the study of plant morphology and taxonomy, although it should be noted that, for a variety of reasons, including its relatively low cost, the subject came to assume a particular importance in the scientific education of girls.

Promoting the laboratory teaching of science

The reference in the report to 'studying the facts at first hand' was a clear endorsement of the practical teaching of science in the laboratory or, where appropriate, in the field. In the mid-nineteenth century, the importance of such teaching was highlighted by the experience of the science examiners acting on behalf of the Department of Science and Art or the Oxford and Cambridge Local Examination Boards. Time after time, the examiners reported on the limitations of candidates' 'bookish knowledge' of science, an outcome which, in the case of the Department of Science and Art, was much encouraged by the system of 'payment by results'. Memorising the textbook was common, and, when textbooks were not available, the teaching frequently involved students in no more than copying down verbatim notes dictated slowly by the class teacher (Ministry of Education 1960). In 1871, candidates preparing for the examinations set by the Department were warned that they should not attempt to grapple with the more advanced forms of science until they had received sound and practical instruction in those subjects which constitute the groundwork of all the physical sciences. In the following year, Frankland, the examiner in inorganic chemistry, reported that 'the unsatisfactory results of the examinations in the elementary stage [were] obviously due to the want of sufficient experimental illustrations in the classes' (Science and Art Department 1872). The Department's response to these serious shortcomings was a 'vigorous onslaught against teaching unillustrated by experiment', a policy supported by means of grants to help finance the building of laboratories and the purchase of equipment (Abney 1904: 868). The Department offered building grants at the rate of 2s. 6d. per square foot of internal area and attached strict conditions to the use of any facilities provided in this way. For example, the grant to be given towards the cost of building a chemistry laboratory was allowed only if the laboratory constituted 'a room or part of a room set apart for the study of Practical Chemistry'. Such accommodation could not be used to teach other subjects, although it could be made available for 'practical work in other experimental sciences' when not required for chemistry. Grants for the purchase of apparatus were available for up to 50 per cent of the cost and those for the purchase of laboratory fittings could not exceed one-third of the capital outlay. None the less, the total grant for science instruction paid by the Department of Science and Art rose from £20,228 in 1879 to £240,822 by the end of the century (Abney 1904: 875).

Following the publication of the British Association report in 1867, the public schools, which had nothing to do with the work of the Department of Science and Art, also began to provide for the practical teaching of science. When the Public School Commissioners reported in 1864, Rugby School was the exception among the nine public schools they had investigated, most of which 'altogether omitted' physical science from their curricula. The Taunton Commissioners, reporting four years later, found a similar lack of laboratory accommodation in the endowed schools, very few of which took advantage of the permission given to them in 1868 to use part of the endowment of a school to provide funds with which to finance the building of laboratories. Of the 128 endowed grammar schools sufficiently interested to reply to an inquiry from the Devonshire Commission in the early 1870s, science was taught in sixty-three, of which only thirteen had a laboratory and eighteen 'scientific apparatus of any kind' (Devonshire Commission 1872). The Devonshire Commissioners were, however, able to record some progress in the leading public schools, partly because, by 1872, Harrow, Eton and Charterhouse were either building or planning new science laboratories. This example was followed by other schools such as Rossall, Wellington, Cheltenham, Dulwich, Christ's Hospital and the grammar schools at Bradford and Manchester. Almost all of these laboratories were equipped for the teaching of chemistry, rather than physics, although the pioneering work of A.M. Worthington at Clifton is a distinguished exception (Sutcliffe 1929a: 87–8).

After 1890, other means were available to encourage endowed grammar schools to build specialist accommodation for the teaching of science. In that year, surplus government funds, the so-called 'whisky money', arising from the abandonment of some provisions of a Local Taxation (Customs and Excise) Act, were made available to the newly created local authorities to be spent on technical education and/or the relief of the rates. Some authorities, such as the West Riding of Yorkshire, allocated all of the income to technical education, administering the money via a Technical Instruction Committee established under the Technical Instruction Act of 1899. Some of the 'whisky money' went to continuation schools, but funds were also made available to local grammar schools, sometimes in the form of an annual grant, and at other times, as a lump sum to build and equip science laboratories. Between 1890 and 1902, the Technical Instruction Committee of the West Riding County Council aided the provision of 341 physics laboratories, 13 chemical laboratories and 3 'combined laboratories' in those grammar schools to which it awarded scholarships. The Manchester Grammar School similarly received a grant from the Corporation to extend its facilities for the practical teaching of physics and chemistry.

During the last quarter of the nineteenth century, therefore, resources were provided in a somewhat haphazard and serendipitous way, but on a significant scale, to support the provision and equipping of school science laboratories. The outcome was a growth in the number of laboratories (see Table 3.1) on a scale which was not to be matched until the school building programme after the end of the Second World War, with perhaps as many as 1,100 school science laboratories being built between 1877 and 1902.

The design of laboratories and fittings to meet the specifications of the Department of Science and Art owed much to William de W. Abney who, after eight years of teaching 'some branches of physical science at the School of Military Engineering', was appointed a Departmental Inspector for Science in 1876 and became Director for Science in 1893. The earliest laboratories funded by the Department were described by Abney as having a 'sealed pattern efficiency' which, whatever its shortcomings, had the virtue of telling 'people what is the least that is expected of them' (Abney 1904: 868–9). By the beginning of the twentieth century, however, the substantial experience of laboratory design in both schools and universities led to some standardisation of form and size and to the publication of a number of important and influential treatises. Felix Clay's *Modern School Buildings*, which appeared in 1902, contains a lengthy chapter on rooms 'for the teaching of science and art', but T.H. Russell's *The Planning and Fitting*

Table 3.1 School laboratories recognised by the Department of Science and Art

Year	Chemistry	Physics	Biology
1880	133	—	—
1900	669	219	17
1901	772	291	26
1902	758	320	34

Source: Data from Abney (1904: 875)

of Chemical Laboratories (1903) is undoubtedly the most thorough survey of the state of development of laboratory design and fitting at the beginning of the century. Photographs of school chemistry laboratories in Russell's volume typically show the fume cupboards, central racks of reagents and the various items of equipment needed to undertake systematic qualitative analysis.

In 1904, the Regulations of the Board of Education governing the curricula of grant-aided secondary (that is, grammar) schools required that instruction in science 'include practical work done by the pupils' (Board of Education 1904a). In the early years of this century, therefore, the position of the laboratory in secondary school science teaching was secured by legislation and it has not been seriously challenged to this day. Solomon, for example, writing in 1994 claimed that 'Science teaching must take place in a laboratory; about that at least there is no controversy' (1994: 7). What, however, was also secured, although not by statute, was a clearer operational understanding of the purposes of laboratory teaching and kind of work that it was appropriate for different groups of students to undertake.

Inevitably, those purposes were reflective of the broader social functions attributed to the schools themselves. In the case of the grammar and public schools, with their long-standing and close connections with higher education, those functions were essentially academic, with school science courses, notably in physics and chemistry, laying the groundwork for more advanced study at the universities. That advanced study, in turn, was intended to ensure the production of a small number of graduates who could contribute to the advancement of science itself. To this extent, therefore, science teaching in the grammar and public schools can be described as pre-professional. In schools which served other social functions, notably the elementary schools which provided the education of the majority of the population of England and Wales until the passage of the 1944 Education Act, science education had a different purpose. No laboratories were required here, the Elementary School Regulations issued by the Board of Education in 1904 merely advising that 'a room suitably fitted for elementary practical work in science may be provided for the use of one large or several contributory schools'. Such a room, fitted with 'strong and plain tables, sinks, cupboards and shelves and, where necessary a fume closet' was not, as a rule, to exceed 600 square feet in area and had to be provided with 'a proper supply of gas' (Board of Education 1904b). The distinction in the laboratory provision required of secondary and elementary schools supported from public funds were eventually codified in a series of Building Regulations, first issued in 1907 and revised on a number of occasions, notably in 1914. In the grammar schools, there had to be not less than 30 square feet of floor space per pupil, any laboratory had to be large enough to accommodate a complete class, and the number of laboratories required in a secondary school of a given size was laid down. In the elementary schools, in contrast, the provision of a specialised room for teaching science required the approval of the Board of Education, and its construction, incorporating 'benches of a simple character', allowed for between 20 and 25 square feet of floor space per pupil. In these schools, the scientific education of the majority of the school population in England and Wales was confined to nature study, although practical classes, sometimes involving work in a laboratory, were developed in the inter-war years for older pupils attending senior schools. Significantly, when new Building Regulations were issued in 1939 for these senior schools, established following the Hadow Report of 1926, the reference was to a 'science room' rather than a laboratory, and the emphasis was once again upon 'simplicity' of design and fittings, the only feature regarded by the Board of Education as necessary being a demonstration bench 'at least eight feet long by about two feet' or, at most, 'two feet six inches wide' and 'two feet nine inches high'. It was not necessary for pupils' benches to be 'of an elaborate type', and ordinary solid tables, without sinks or fixed points for gas supply, were judged appropriate. The science room was to be equipped for the teaching of general science, although 'a small glass house', very close to this room and 'accessible from it', was regarded as useful for schools wishing to teach some biology. All equipment and apparatus for the teaching of science was to be regarded as part of the furnishing of the room so that where a separate preparation and storage room was provided, the science room itself could be reduced in size to a floor area of 900 square feet (Board of Education 1939: 40–5).

Practical science by the book

In the specialised laboratories found in increasing numbers in the grammar and public schools, the practical teaching of science, principally chemistry and physics, was, in large measure, already codified by the time of the 1904 Regulations. Such codification owed much to the development and publication of the laboratory manual which offered students and teachers alike clear guidelines about what was expected. Worthington's *An Elementary Course of Practical Physics*, derived from his experience of teaching at the Salt Schools in Shipley and, later, at Clifton College, where boys had worked in pairs from printed sheets giving details of the experiments. These experiments ranged widely to include mensuration, heat, hydrostatics and elasticity, and engaged pupils in exercises such as locating a centre of gravity of a solid, measuring the period of a simple pendulum, establishing the density of a range of solids or liquids, or determining the latent heat of freezing or boiling of water. Worthington subsequently authored a more fully developed practical physics course, published in 1896 as *A First Course of Physical Laboratory Practice*. According to Layton, this 'did for physics what qualitative analysis schemes had previously done for chemistry and became the

model for many subsequent courses, achieving a sixth edition by 1903'
(Layton 1990: 46).

Just how much of a model these early laboratory manuals became is
evident from a survey of the exercise and laboratory books of pupils over the
following half century. Notebooks used by pupils in grammar and public
schools in different parts of the country and at different times reveal a
marked similarity in the work done and in the manner in which such work
was recorded and presented. Many of the experiments in physics and
chemistry conducted by grammar schools pupils in the early years of the
century were repeated by their successors until at least the 1950s, and, for
the most part, the accounts of such experiments have been clearly derived
from a standard format: Test, Observation, Inference, or Title, Apparatus,
Method, Observation, Results and Conclusion. The requirements of the
Higher School Certificate Examination introduced in 1919 further consoli-
dated the work done. This was not simply a matter of the form and content
of the practical examinations. Written papers in physics and chemistry were
replete with questions which either asked candidates to describe how they
would determine some physical quantity such as the surface tension of water
using a capillary tube or the solubility of a sparingly soluble salt in water, or
required them to undertake calculations based upon the established laboratory exercises. When, in 1948, Tyler published his highly successful *A
Laboratory Manual of Physics*, he readily acknowledged the difficulty, if not
impossibility, of producing a book on practical physics without borrowing
from the 'various standard works available'. Those standard works often,
like Tyler's own volume, 'set out the results in each case in detail in blank
form, so that, if desired, the student can make direct entries of his observations' (Tyler 1948: 2).

It is thus perhaps not surprising that the practical teaching of science in
school laboratories was all too readily reduced to a set of routine 'cook-book'
exercises, sometimes involving little more than a lengthy elaboration of the
obvious. Worthington himself was aware of the risk that his own course
might degenerate into little more than mechanical manipulation. In 1896,
he commented that physics, 'like all scientific teaching', was to be taught
'not with a view of training up Physicists, but with the object of evoking in
the boys [sic] a genuine and generous interest in natural phenomena, and
with training them to habits of patient . . . study', adding that the 'first aim
was not to show pupils how measures of physical constants might be made
but what they mean' (Worthington 1896: 4). Regrettably, Worthington's
injunction was to be largely ignored.

Learning science by investigation

Others, however, attempted to redefine the role of the school science
teaching laboratory by aligning it more closely with the activities associated

with scientific research. In the case of physics, David Rintoul, Worthington's successor at Clifton, sought to emphasise 'the spirit of scientific curiosity' by presenting experiments in the form of problems which the student was required to solve (Rintoul 1898: vi). In the case of chemistry, the principal advocate of the view that the teaching laboratory was a place where students could learn by conducting investigations was Henry Armstrong, although he professed to dislike the word 'laboratory', preferring instead to refer to a 'workshop'. Armstrong went much further than Rintoul, campaigning vigorously from 1884 onwards for the teaching of 'scientific method', a term which he understood as the methodical, logical use of knowledge. Armstrong had no time for school science laboratories which were 'mere slavish copies' of those to be found in universities. Apart from a good chemical balance, Armstrong's preference was for 'simple contrivances', preferably made by the pupils themselves working under the guidance of their teachers. Armstrong's heuristic approach to science teaching has been well documented (for example, Brock 1973) and need not, therefore, be recounted here. Two points, however, need to be made in the present context. First, although heuristic teaching was adopted by relatively small numbers of teachers, Armstrong's emphasis upon 'finding out' as an objective of laboratory teaching was to endure, finding its later expression in the Nuffield Science Teaching Project of the 1960s and, subsequently, in the commitment to 'Experimental and Investigative Science' in the science component of the National Curriculum in England and Wales. Second, both the psychological and the philosophical underpinnings of heurism were to collapse in the early years of the century. 'The transfer of training' implicit in the teaching of scientific method did not withstand the scrutiny of the experimental psychologists, faculty psychology itself fell out of favour, and developments such as thermodynamics, relativity and quantum theory made it impossible to sustain the notion of scientific method as 'organised common sense'. When heurism re-emerged in the 1960s and 1980s, therefore, it had to call upon different supporting psychologies which allowed science to be presented as a set of 'processes' or skills (Wellington 1989), the latter having the inestimable (dis)advantage of seemingly lending themselves readily to assessment. As for philosophy, philosophical ideas have been called in aid, rather than served as determinants, of school science laboratory teaching practice. Their purpose has been to sustain the notion of the scientific community as the 'very paradigm of institutionalised rationality', a task that, in the second half of the twentieth century in particular, faces insuperable obstacles.

Marking time

In the inter-war years, partly in response to the alleged excesses of heurism (Natural Science in Education 1918) but principally to a desire to bring science 'into the homes of the people' (Smithells 1919), attempts were made to broaden the science courses provided in grammar and public schools. The most significant attempt was the development of courses of general science, although the growth of biology as a school subject during this period, particularly after 1930, should not be underestimated (Jenkins 1979). As far as laboratory teaching is concerned, little change took place at the sixth form level. In the main body of the school, however, the attempt to promote science for all and to illustrate the importance of science in everyday life led to something of a revival of the lecture demonstration, a teaching method that Armstrong had dismissed as 'dogmatic, not . . . heuristic' (Brock 1973: 143). The manipulation and mastery of the apparatus displayed by the teacher revealed the *sine qua non* of the search for scientific truth which the lecture demonstration sought to present, an approach to scientific education most clearly illustrated in Fowles's classic *Lecture Experiments in Chemistry*, first published in 1937.

For most of the inter-war years, laboratory building, along with other forms of school accommodation, was severely restricted by the economy measures introduced by successive governments. The elementary schools were badly affected as local education authorities delayed their building programmes, postponed Hadow reorganisation and implemented economies on buildings and staffing. Some secondary schools were able to take advantage of grants provided by the Board of Education to finance advanced courses at sixth form level, and the grants were usually sufficiently generous to allow some of the money to be spent on equipping a laboratory or on adapting existing accommodation for the practical teaching of science. The need to modify existing classrooms, under conditions of severe economic restraint when the secondary school population was expanding, does much to explain the size of many school science laboratories which, by the 1930s, became standardised at 960 square feet. The demolition of partition walls between classrooms 20 × 24 square feet arranged along a 6-foot-wide corridor allowed the space to be converted into two laboratories, each of 960 square feet, and a preparation room with dimensions of 20 by 18 feet. In the aftermath of the recommendation of the Hadow Committee that the 'construction and equipment of Modern Schools should approximate to the standard required from time to time by the Board' of Education for local authority secondary schools, the Board produced new *Suggestions for the Planning of New Buildings for Secondary Schools* (Board of Education 1931).

However, the detailed advice offered by the Board was to have little impact in the face of the economies imposed upon the school building programme in the inter-war years, and it is certain both that laboratory provision varied greatly from one secondary school to another and that, in many cases, the level of provision fell below that recommended by the Board of Education. This variation was matched by an equally great, if not greater, variation in the funding and technical assistance available to support the teaching of practical science. Managing school science laboratories in these circumstances, when the majority of science teachers were forced to struggle with the sole help of some students, who had received little or no instruction in the care of the laboratory and its apparatus, prompted the publication of a number of texts, of which Sutcliffe's *School Laboratory Management* was a pioneering volume (1929b). It supplemented more narrowly technical publications dealing with the laboratory arts, such as glass blowing, and it was widely used until at least the 1950s, passing out of print only as reformed school science curricula made different and increased demands on laboratory design, techniques, reagents and apparatus.

Despite the tripartite system of free secondary education for all created by the 1944 Education Act, and the replacement of the School Certificate Examination by the subject-based General Certificate of Education in 1951, the laboratory teaching of science in grammar and public schools in England and Wales in the early 1950s would have seemed strikingly familiar to someone teaching half a century earlier. School physics continued to emphasise measurement, and chemistry the preparation and properties of materials, with systematic wet qualitative analysis for the more senior pupils. Biology continued to make progress towards a secure place in the secondary curriculum, but real advance was not possible until its connection with medical education was finally severed in the following decade. At sixth form level, biology, like chemistry and physics, retained its pre-professional function, A-level courses requiring pupils to acquire a knowledge of anatomy and morphology by dissecting standard 'types' and of simple plant and animal physiology and biochemistry through suitable experiments. The new secondary modern schools, in contrast, struggled to establish a distinct identity in the face of inadequate resources, including a severe and chronic shortage of science teachers and a level of laboratory provision far below that found in most grammar schools.

The laboratory and science curriculum reform

By the late 1950s, however, a number of initiatives had already been taken which were to lead in England and Wales to the large-scale curriculum reform movements of the 1960s, funded, first, by the Nuffield Foundation and, later, by the Schools Council, set up in 1964. The origins of these developments are not the concern of this chapter (see Waring 1979, Layton 1984), but it is important to note that they closely reflected the then prevailing social structure of secondary schooling. The first projects to be undertaken were for the minority of able boys and girls preparing for examinations in physics, chemistry and biology at the Ordinary level of the GCE. The needs of the majority of the secondary school population were to be met by the Nuffield *Secondary Science* Project, structured not around the grammar and syntax of the scientific disciplines but in terms of themes such as movement, energy and using materials. The touchstone for the selection of content within these themes was its significance for the pupils, determined by reference to their presumed interests and needs as adolescents and future citizens. Rather different needs and interests were, of course, presumed in the case of those attending selective schools intended to produce the new technocrats, the scientifically literate captains of industry and the civil servants fit for the society which Harold Wilson, in the 1960s, was to claim would be forged in the white heat of technological revolution.

In all the Nuffield Projects pupils were, as far as possible, to engage in investigative activities and, thereby, gain vicarious experience of scientific discovery. They were, in short, once again to 'learn science by doing science', a doctrine that owed more, at least at the secondary level, to a reinvigoration of the historical commitment to laboratory work than it did to ideas about the importance of direct experience and discovery in children's intellectual development although these were of rhetorical significance. Pupils engaged in laboratory work so that they could 'become a scientist for a day' or engage with those intellectual and other processes offered as characteristic of scientific discovery. New apparatus intended to promote laboratory teaching through investigation was developed, much of it used as part of a teaching strategy that came to be known as 'guided discovery'. Such discovery, however, was fraught with tensions and contradictions, not least as pupils found themselves deflected from an inquisitive 'what ought to happen' towards gaining a secure knowledge of what they were required to know. There was further confusion between, on the one hand, the importance of direct experience and discovery in learning, and, on the other, an epistemology of science which, among much else, presented the relationship between observation and explanation as unproblematic. One enduring outcome of this confusion was the consolidation of a view of scientific method, naïve and inadequate in its own day and subsequently rendered antique by the more recent work of sociologists, historians and philosophers of science.

The impact of the Nuffield and Schools Council initiatives on the laboratory teaching of school science was significant. Pupils, although always a relatively small number, engaged in genuine investigations, especially at Advanced level. The projects lent important support to the idea that all science teaching should be laboratory-based, and thereby strengthened the hand of those arguing for improved levels of laboratory provision and for better technical assistance. Innovative ways of assessing pupils' practical competence were developed and the opportunity was taken to break free of the 'straitjacket of chronic success' by modernising the content of school science courses. Qualitative analysis disappeared from sixth form chemistry courses, and kinetic, thermodynamic and structural insights into chemical reactions were given some prominence. Aspects of modern physics, often illustrated by highly imaginative experimental techniques, were introduced to replace half a century or more of work with such items as the dip circle, the tangent galvanometer, Lees' disc or Fletcher's trolley. In biology, accommodation of some of the molecular, ecological and biochemical aspects of a rapidly changing field of scientific research allowed the subject to abandon its medical heritage and gain a secure and increasingly popular place in the secondary school curriculum.

In the early 1970s, the growing pace of the reorganisation of secondary education to establish a system of non-selective comprehensive schooling, allied with the raising of the school-leaving age to 16 in 1973, meant that schools were faced with the challenge of teaching science to more pupils and of a wider range of ability than hitherto. Driven principally by the demands of assessment, although earlier work associated with the Nuffield Science Teaching Project and with the Certificate of Secondary Education (CSE) introduced in 1965 was also significant, the rhetoric of the dominant, grammar-school tradition of laboratory teaching was recast. In a notable exercise of convenience, the teaching of practical science became a matter of promoting abilities, processes and so-called skills such as observing, hypothesising and deducing patterns, which, collectively, amounted to 'doing science'. This 'laboratory science for all' became an integral part of the examination for the General Certificate of Education (GCSE) introduced in 1988, when the general requirement that all GCSE subjects include an element of teacher-assessed coursework was translated, in the case of science, into the demand that 'All schemes of assessment must allocate not less than 20 per cent of the total marks to experimental and observational work in the laboratory or its equivalent' (DES 1985). The attempt by the Examination Boards and schools to implement this policy led to considerable confusion and difficulty. Science teachers were urged to undertake practical assessments in 'normal' classroom or laboratory settings and to involve pupils in 'open-ended investigations'. Such conditions rarely, if ever, prevailed. In practice, the assessment instruments were often focused, routinised, based on what is commonly termed 'scientific-content' and heavily mediated by pupils' literacy. In many cases, they were not in any real sense practical/experimental activities at all, and the outcomes were rarely used for diagnostic or formative purposes (Donnelly *et al.* 1993).

The science laboratory and the National Curriculum

The problems of assessing practical science for all pupils at GCSE level, however, were to pale into insignificance in the face of those arising from the introduction of the National Curriculum following the passage of the Education Reform Act 1988. Between 1988 and 1995 the science component of this curriculum took a number of forms. All, however, privileged the laboratory teaching of science and sought to define the role of the teacher in assessing pupils' practical competence. The first of the four

Attainment Targets of the 1991 curriculum, commonly referred to as 'Sc1', required that all pupils undertook, and were assessed in undertaking, individual investigations. Described by a leading science educator as 'outrageously ambitious . . . but right' (Black 1993), teachers' attempts to conduct whole class investigations within the statutory ten-point scale of assessment led to widespread frustration and anger. As one Head of Science expressed it, '[I feel] bitterness because I feel shoved around, bitterness because I can't believe that anybody who understood what I had to do would make me do it' (Donnelly *et al*. 1996: 1). The introduction of 'Sc1' also presented difficulties for the science teachers' professional organisation, the Association for Science Education, which found itself in public conflict with some of its own members as it sought to defend what might be called the 'official line' about the educational and other benefits claimed for engaging all pupils of compulsory school age in scientific investigations. Perhaps one of the most interesting features of the controversy over this Attainment Target was the claim of its supporters that teaching scientific investigation was a long-standing feature of science teachers' practice. If this was indeed the case, the bitterness referred to above becomes all the more puzzling. What seems more likely is that 'Sc1' became a large-scale and centrally directed attempt to reform science teachers' daily working practice. In the absence of a genuine dialogue with those most closely concerned, strife was almost inevitable.

Although 'Sc1' gave way to 'Experimental and Investigative Science' in yet another revision of the science component of the National Curriculum, many of the operational obstacles which it presented to teachers have not been overcome. In the present context, however, it is more important to draw attention to the issues which it has raised and which remain unresolved. Pupil laboratory work stands at the focus of two issues in the science curriculum. The first of these is its role as a pedagogic tool. This role, it can be argued, has come to dominate attempts to promote pupils' active involvement with learning. For some, such domination, sometimes buttressed by a naïve espousal of 'constructivist' ideas, is difficult, if not impossible, to justify. Teachers in other disciplines do not have access to a laboratory and its attendant paraphernalia as a means of engaging their pupils' interest and intellect. Yet it can hardly be argued that, as a result, the teaching of, say, the humanities is less effective than that of science. Beyond this, the laboratory often appears to dominate teachers' and pupils' notions of what a science lesson is, how it should be structured and what sorts of activities can legitimately occur there. This raises the question of what would happen if this domination were to be broken and some of the energy and resources devoted to laboratory teaching put into developing other pedagogic tools and strategies, including those involving information and communication technologies.

The second issue concerns laboratory work as a component of the science curriculum proper. It derives from the view that science is about the material world, that a key purpose of science education is to give pupils some access to human understanding of that world and that pupils need to engage with the world to understand what science is. It is hardly necessary to argue these points. However, it does not follow that pupils ought necessarily to spend a substantial part of their science education attempting to replicate the activities of professional scientists, an attempt which pre-supposes that it is possible to portray in the school context not only scientific concepts but also the social and institutional locations of science, and its specific modes of moral and ontological engagement with the material world.

Time for reform

The laboratory teaching of science has developed in England and Wales within the context of a selective system of secondary education that, until recent times, has had a close relationship with the academic science of higher education. Despite profound changes in secondary education, in the organisation of science itself (Gibbons *et al.* 1994) and in our under-standing of the scientific endeavour (Olby *et al.* 1990), the school science laboratory at the end of the twentieth century reflects an enduring commitment to understanding science in terms of its greatest mystery, 'scientific method'. The laboratory teaching of science in schools is too much a prisoner of the past and there is a need, no less pressing than that identified by Kerr a generation ago (Kerr 1963), to re-examine critically the role it can reasonably hope to play in assisting pupils to learn science. While school science teaching without laboratory work may be unthink-able, attributing to laboratory activities outcomes that cannot realistically be met, or that might be met more effectively in other ways, is no longer an option.

References

Abney, W. de W. (1904) Presidential Address to Section L, BAAS, *Report of the Annual Meeting, 1903,* London: Murray.
BAAS (1868) *Report of the (Dundee) Meeting, 1867,* London: Murray.
Black, P.J. (1993) Address at a conference organised by the Association for Science Education, June.
Board of Education (1904a) *Regulations for Secondary Schools,* London: HMSO.
—— (1904b) *Code of Regulations for Public Elementary Schools and Schedule,* London: HMSO.
—— (1931) 'Suggestions for the planning of new buildings for secondary schools', Pamphlet no. 86, London: HMSO.
—— (1939) 'Suggestions for the planning of buildings for public elementary schools, Pamphlet no.107, London: HMSO.

Brock, W.H. (ed.) (1973) *H.E. Armstrong and the Teaching of Science 1880–1930,* Cambridge: Cambridge University Press.

Clay, G.F.N. (1902) *Modern School Buildings, Elementary and Secondary: a Treatise on the Planning, Arrangement and Fitting of Day and Boarding Schools,* London: Batsford.

DES (1985) *General Certificate of Secondary Education: the National Criteria for Science,* London: HMSO.

Devonshire Commission (1872–75) *Report,* vol. VI, London: HMSO, p. 1.

Donnelly, J., Buchan, A.S., Jenkins, E.W. and Welford, A.G. (1993), *Policy, Practice and Professional Judgement: School-based Assessment of Practical Science,* Driffield: Studies in Education.

Donnelly, J., Buchan A., Jenkins, E.W., Laws, P. and Welford, A.G. (1996) *Investigations by Order: Policy, Curriculum and Science Teachers' Work under the Education Reform Act,* Driffield: Studies in Education.

Duff, D. (1997) 'The forgotten pioneer', *Chemistry in Britain* (May): 46–8.

Fowles, G. (1937) *Lecture Experiments in Chemistry,* London: Bell.

Gardner, J. (1846) 'An address delivered at the Royal College of Chemistry, June 1846', *The Chemist* 4: 294–301.

Gibbons, M., Limoges, C., Nowotny, H., Schwartzman, S., Scott, P. and Trow, M. (1994) *The New Production of Knowledge: the Dynamics of Science and Research in Contemporary Societies,* London: Sage.

Jenkins, E.W. (1979) *From Armstrong to Nuffield; Studies in Twentieth-century Science Education in England and Wales,* London: Murray.

Kerr, J.F. (1963) *Practical Work in School Science: an Account of an Inquiry into the Nature and Purpose of Practical Work in School Science teaching in England and Wales,* Leicester: Leicester University Press.

Layton, D. (1984) *Interpreters of Science: a History of the Association for Science Education,* London: Murray.

—— (1990) 'Student laboratory practice and the history and philosophy of science', in E. Hegarty-Hazel (ed.) *The Student Laboratory and the Science Curriculum,* London: Routledge, pp. 37–59.

Ministry of Education (1960) 'Science in secondary schools', Pamphlet no. 38, London: HMSO.

Natural Science in Education (1918) *Report of the Committee on the Position of Natural Science in the Educational System of Great Britain,* London: HMSO.

Olby, R.C., Cantor, G.N., Christie, J.R.R., Hodge, M.J.S. (eds) (1990) *A Companion to the History of Modern Science,* London: Routledge.

Rintoul, D. (1898) *An Introduction to Practical Physics for Use in Schools,* London: Macmillan.

Russell, T.H. (1903) *The Planning and Fitting of Chemical Laboratories,* London: Batsford.

Science and Art Department (1872) *Nineteenth Report,* pp. xxiv, 49.

Shepherd, R.E. (1979) 'Individual practical work in the teaching of physics in England: a study of its origins and rationale', unpublished M.Ed. thesis, University of Leeds.

Smithells, A. (1919) *School Science Review* 1(1): 29.

Solomon, J. (1994) 'The laboratory comes of age', in R. Levinson, (ed.) *Teaching Science,* London: Routledge/Open University, 1.

Sutcliffe, A. (1929a) 'Student laboratories in England: a historical sketch', *School Science Review*, xi(42): 81–90.

—— (1929b) *School Laboratory Management,* London: Murray.

Tyler, F. (1948) *A Laboratory Manual of Physics*, London: Edward Arnold.

Waring, M. (1979) *Social Pressures and Curriculum Innovation: the Nuffield Foundation Science Teaching Project,* London: Methuen.

Wellington, J.J. (ed.) (1989) *Skills and Processes in Science Education*, London: Routledge.

Worthington, A.M. (1881) *An Elementary Course of Practical Physics,* London: Rivingtons.

—— (1896) *A First Course of Physical Laboratory Practice*, London: Longmans, Green and Co.

4

TEACHING ABOUT THE
WORLD OF SCIENCE IN
THE LABORATORY
The influence of students' ideas

John Leach

One of the arguments put forward for practical work is that
it teaches students something about the world of science.
The idea is that students learn about the ways in which
scientists use knowledge to explain real phenomena and
events, the ways in which scientists investigate and so on.
But what do students think that science is all about, and
how might this influence their learning during practical
work? This chapter considers students' understandings of
the nature of science itself, and the implications of this for
the teaching of science through practical work.

Introduction

When teachers and students work together in the teaching laboratory, a
number of cultures meet. Perhaps the most obvious of these is the culture of
formal schooling, which defines, amongst other things, the relative status of
participants in the activity. Even in the most democratic teaching laboratories, all participants know the relative status of teachers and students.
Students and teachers also live in cultures outside of formal schooling, and
as a result have personal values and attitudes which may well influence their
actions in the teaching laboratory: negative attitudes towards the use of
animals in teaching is one example of this.

Another culture that influences activities in the teaching laboratory is the
culture of science itself. A recurring theme in this book is that the world of
science is diverse, encompassing vastly different activities which are carried
out for various purposes, and to this extent there are many cultures of
science. Indeed, the differences between activities performed by groups of
scientists are often more apparent than the similarities. For example, in

different disciplines of science the design and execution of investigations may be quite different. Sometimes, it is possible for scientists to do something to the natural world to see how it responds: clinical biochemists might put a patient on a particular diet and look for effects on the patient's metabolism, for example. Many geologists and astrophysicists investigate phenomena that have already happened, however, and it is not therefore possible to carry out experimental interventions. Groups of scientists also use theory in different ways for different purposes. Some theory is treated as reliable and unproblematic: clinical biochemists test for the disease phenylketonuria by measuring the concentration of phenylpyruvate in the urine of newborns using Iron III Chloride, and it is taken for granted that the test will give reliable results. In other cases, the application of accepted theory to real situations is much more problematic. Consider the recent disputes about the likely outcome of underground nuclear testing in the Pacific. Argument focused upon the influence of local factors on the long-term geological stability of the area, and hence the risk of leakage of radioactive species, rather than the theory of nuclear reactions and geological vitrification *per se*. In such cases, generating predictions about future outcomes is much more complex than a process of applying reliable scientific theories.

It is impossible for school practical work to model all the practices of professional science, and indeed school practical work would not set this as its aim. This issue is picked up elsewhere in this book. However, a case can be made that something about the practices of science can be taught through practical work. This chapter addresses the ways in which activities in the teaching laboratory might be used to teach students something about the world of science, and about how students' ideas about the world of science might influence the outcomes of laboratory teaching. The chapter has three main sections. The first relates to the world of the teaching laboratory, considering what is being taught and what is meant by 'the world of science'. The second section then considers what we know about students' ideas about science and how these might influence learning during practical work. In the final section, some thoughts are presented as to how practical work might be used more effectively to develop students' ideas about the world of science.

There is no single account of the world of science that enjoys broad support in the history, philosophy and sociology of science, and increasingly science is being portrayed as a multifaceted activity. This poses a dilemma for science education: how can students be taught about the world of science through formal science education, if there is no agreed understanding of how that world operates? As Matthews (1997) has pointed out, this is a moral question and there is a fine line between teaching about science and indoctrinating students into one particular view of science. For Matthews, a solution lies in explicit teaching of the philosophy of science to science teachers in order to facilitate a more explicit and better informed treatment of the epistemology of science in the curriculum. It is, however, rare for science teachers to undertake study of the history, philosophy and sociology of science as part of their training in the English-speaking world. In spite of this lack of philosophical training amongst science teachers, we will see later in this chapter that science teachers have basic knowledge about the world of science that may well not be shared by their students.

So far in this chapter, 'the world of science' has been treated as a 'black box', although there have been hints that scientific activity is probably best viewed as multifaceted, and taking place in many different worlds. Work in the history, philosophy and sociology of science has attempted to characterise the products of science and the activities of scientists around questions such as:

- What are the purposes of science and the questions addressed by science?
- How are scientific knowledge claims generated, and how do they relate to natural phenomena?
- What are the characteristics of enquiry as practised by scientists?
- How is the work of scientists related to broader social activities and concerns?
- How do scientists interact with each other in their work?

These questions relate to the *epistemology* of science – that is, the grounds on which scientific knowledge is believed – and the *sociology* of science – that is, the ways in which scientific activity is socially and institutionally organised, and relationships between communities of scientists and the broader society. In the remainder of this chapter, these kinds of epistemological and sociological issues about science will be referred to as *the nature of science*.

There is a marked absence of consensus about these questions in the literature. However, some very fundamental assumptions tend to be shared, by historians, philosophers and sociologists of science as well as scientists and science teachers. For example, there is broad agreement that scientific knowledge goes beyond providing descriptions of the material world. This can be illustrated by considering the case of the atom. Realists believe that atoms exist in the material world, and that the primary criterion for judging scientific accounts of the structure of matter is the extent to which they relate to atoms in the material world. Scientists' descriptions of atoms are none the less viewed as being underdetermined by data from the material world, that is, scientific descriptions of atoms are *models* of 'real' atoms, and it is not possible to 'prove' correspondence between scientific models and 'the real thing'. On the other hand, relativists would take a different position. Scientists' descriptions of atoms are viewed as human constructions which are particularly suitable for the job of explaining the behaviour of materials. According to this perspective, knowledge claims are judged in terms of their 'viability' – that is, their success in generating explanations and predictions – rather than the extent to which they reflect the world as it exists. So, although there are wide differences in perspective between realists and relativists about the relationship between knowledge claims and the material world, at a very fundamental level there is agreement that scientific knowledge is *not* a simple description of the material world.

Other examples of broad agreement within science studies are that one purpose of science is investigating natural phenomena, and that individual scientists work as members of communities and institutions. It must be emphasised, however, that such assumptions are only shared at a fundamental level.

For science educators, however, the significant issue is that science students may well not share these fundamental assumptions about the nature of science. In formal science education, science teachers might be viewed as representatives of the culture of science, portraying something about the culture of science to students (Driver *et al.* 1994). If teachers and students have different fundamental assumptions about the nature of science, what effect will this have on communication? The probability is that students and teachers will not understand each other and, from the teacher's point of view, learning will be unsuccessful. If teachers know something about their students' fundamental assumptions about the nature of science, however, it may be possible for them to structure their teaching to address the students' assumptions, thereby making learning more successful.

Teaching about science in the laboratory: aims and purposes

The aim of some practical work is to teach science content, whereas other practical work aims to teach something about the methods of science (see Millar in this book). Practical work is likely to place different emphasis on teaching content and method according the age of students and the type of course being studied. In primary schools, greater emphasis is usually placed upon providing students with experience of natural phenomena, than upon introducing students to scientific explanations of phenomena. In addition, some basic aspects of experimental design (such as controlling key variables to make a 'fair test') are typically introduced. During the secondary years, greater emphasis is placed upon introducing students to scientific explanations for phenomena, although practical work aiming to teach about scientific method is also common. Much 'illustrative practical work' (Woolnough 1985) is carried out, aiming to teach students how accepted scientific knowledge claims can be used to explain particular phenomena. Students are introduced to increasingly sophisticated scientific content as they progress through their science education. Illustrative practical work is therefore common at all stages of science education from the secondary years onwards.

In many countries, students have some choice as to the subjects studied at the upper end of secondary education (typically after the age of 15 or 16). Different students will study different amounts of science – or even no science at all. At this stage, an element of pre-professional training starts to appear in the practical work undertaken by students who have selected science as a major area of study. In the United Kingdom, for example, some upper secondary school courses in science are labelled 'vocational' and include teaching in specific professional contexts (see, for example, Hunt and Russell 1994). In many courses, students are introduced to instrumentation and techniques that might be encountered in professional scientific settings. In higher education, this element of pre-professional training is even more prominent. Practical work is often designed to introduce students to laboratory procedures and instruments, and students may well spend extended periods of time working in laboratories in universities or industry alongside professional scientists. The major purpose of such practical work is teaching students something about an area of professional scientific work.

The above description of the changing aims of practical work at different stages of science education is clearly over-simplistic, and there is no intention to suggest that this is the only way that practical work could be organised. Some sort of relationship between knowledge claims and data lies at the heart of most practical work, however, whether its focus is upon teaching science content or teaching about science itself. In practical work, some epistemological issues are particularly important. These include the relationship between knowledge claims and data, the status of knowledge claims within the scientific community, the purposes of investigative activities, and the norms used in the warranting of knowledge claims in terms of the available evidence. Such relationships are central both to illustrative practical work, and practical work teaching about aspects of methodology. However, although these relationships are important to most practical activities, they usually remain tacit during teaching.

In illustrative practical work, students are asked to model a phenomenon in terms of a scientific knowledge claim. The term 'knowledge claims' is used to indicate the laws, theories, hypotheses and generalisations that constitute scientific knowledge. The knowledge claims used in science differ considerably in their nature. Some are essentially descriptions of the behaviour of phenomena, constituted in terms of easily perceptable features of phenomena. For example, Hooke's Law states a relationship between load and extension over a particular range. Other knowledge claims draw upon formal, abstract entities: fields are an example of entities used in scientific explanation that are not simply perceptible.

In modelling phenomena in terms of knowledge claims, the students are required to know something about the epistemology of the knowledge claim in question. For example, upper secondary school chemistry students often carry out illustrative practical work in which the extent of a chemical reaction is explained in terms of entropy. Entropy is a formal concept in that it is explicitly defined in relation to other concepts, in terms of abstract ideas such as infinitely large energy sinks and infinitely small heat transfers. It is important that students are aware that the meaning of entropy cannot be inferred from observations of events in the material world (such as the behaviour of a chemical reaction), because entropy is not defined in terms of objects and events in the material world. So, although it is appropriate to model chemical change in terms of entropy for some purposes, it is inappropriate for students to think that entropy can be 'discovered' by careful observation of chemical changes. Students may also encounter situations in illustrative practical work when their own findings do not agree with accepted scientific knowledge. For example, students may 'show' that starch is produced in plant leaves in the dark, or that energy is not conserved. In such cases, epistemological issues about the status of knowledge within the scientific community are raised: should students reject textbook science on the grounds of their own empirical work, or should a different course of action be pursued? Other practical work focuses more upon teaching students how to investigate aspects of the material world, and how to interpret data from investigations in terms of theory. In such cases, students are required to make judgements about epistemological issues such as what counts as an explanation, what counts as data and what counts as a valid knowledge claim from the evidence available.

The case being made here is that the purpose of some activities undertaken in teaching laboratories is to portray something about the nature of science itself, and that what students learn during practical work will be influenced by their personal understandings about the nature of science. There is a good deal of evidence that students at all stages of science education hold views about the world of science that influence their science learning. In the next section, this evidence is reviewed and the implications for student learning during practical work are considered.

Science learners' understandings about the nature of science

There is now a sizeable research literature addressing students' understandings about the world of science (see Lederman, 1992; Arnold and Millar, 1993; and Driver *et al.* 1996 for reviews). In this section, findings from some studies will be reviewed as they relate to students' learning in practical work, and consequently the main focus will be upon relationships between knowledge claims and data. The first part of this review presents findings from studies addressing students' understandings of the nature of data, knowledge claims, and relationships between the two. The second part of the review addresses studies of students' understandings of the status and reliability of public scientific knowledge, to the extent that it influences students' practical work. There is now a body of work addressing students' understanding of the social contexts in which scientists work, the implications of this for scientific literacy and the public understanding of science, and approaches to teaching (reviewed by Lederman 1992; Driver *et al.* 1996). Generally speaking, the teaching approaches advocated in this literature involve methods other than practical work including, for example, case studies from history (Solomon *et al.* 1992; Hodson in this book, Sutton in this book).

Students' understanding of data, of knowledge claims and of relationships between the two in practical work

There is broad support in the history, philosophy and sociology of science that knowledge claims and data only have meaning in relation to each other: data are collected with a knowledge claim in mind, knowledge claims refer to data. To many readers, this point may seem too trivial to merit a mention. We shall see, however, that many students take a different view, assuming that the data collected in experiments are untainted by the theoretical commitments of the investigators. Rather than evaluating knowledge claims and data, the purpose of experimental work is reconceptualised as a process of description through careful data collection.

Views of the nature of data

Lubben and Millar (1996) report findings from a study addressing, amongst other things, the ways in which UK students in the 11–16 age range think it is appropriate to handle data in investigations of natural phenomena. Evidence is presented for different levels of understanding of the collection and evaluation of empirical data. At the lower levels, it is assumed by students that measured values are perfectly accurate: that is, they correspond to 'real' values. Procedures such as taking repeat measurements are viewed as allowing the experimenter to become familiar with the equipment in order to take a perfect measurement, if they are seen as necessary at all. Getting the same value twice is also seen as evidence of a perfect value. At the higher levels, it is assumed that averages of measurements should be taken, as you cannot be sure how close you are to a 'real' value from even the most careful measurements. For some students, the only method of judging a value is by reference to an authority source (such as a data book), whereas others assume that the spread of a set of measurements gives some indication. An age-related trend was reported, 45 per cent of 16-year-olds indicating that spread gives information about confidence, compared to 15 per cent of 11-year-olds.

Séré et al. (1993) report surprisingly similar reasoning amongst under-graduate physics students learning about the statistical analysis of measure-ment errors. Amongst these students, '[t]he general view is that, the more measurements one makes, the "better" the result is, without understanding the nature of this "better"' (p. 427).

Although there was a general view that the quality of an estimate from measurements depends upon the spread of the measured data, few students appeared to recognise the influence of systematic and random errors upon the accuracy and precision of the estimated value.

During practical work, students may have to make decisions about the amount of data that has to be collected and the conclusions that can be drawn from given data sets. It appears that, even at the undergraduate level, students may proceed as though perfectly accurate and precise values can be obtained in an unproblematic way from measured data. For example, students may select the mode from a set of measurements as the 'true' value, rather than making judgements about values from sets of data. Procedures such as drawing lines of best fit through data points may then be seen as routines leading to descriptions of relationships in the material world. Alternatively, lines of best fit may be viewed as hypotheses about relationships.

Views of the nature of knowledge claims

Students' approaches to data collection and data interpretation during practical work will be influenced by their views of the place and nature of theory in empirical investigation. They may not, for example, recognise the interplay between data and theory in the process of investigation, and as a result they may not accept that it is legitimate to develop the design of an experiment in the light of data already collected. In particular, students who see scientific models as simple descriptions of the material world may frame their data interpretation during practical work in terms of things that can be observed, rather than scientific theory.

There is a good deal of evidence that very young children may not differentiate knowledge claims from evidence that might support or refute them. Kuhn et al. (1988) presented students with data sets (such as infor-mation about the diet of children and whether they caught colds) and knowledge claims (such as 'eating X causes colds'). They show that many students aged 10–12 appear to treat the data set as a series of instances or non-instances of the knowledge claim, rather than as a set of evidence against which the knowledge claim might be evaluated. Similar findings are reported for students in this age range by Carey et al. (1989) and Leach (1997). However, Samarapungavan (1992a) presents evidence that students of this age are *able* to differentiate between knowledge claims that are and are not supported by data, although in practice this strategy is often not used. This would appear to suggest that many pupils in the lower secondary years may not spontaneously treat data sets as evidence against which knowledge claims can be evaluated. However, following explicit teaching, pupils are likely to be able to evaluate knowledge claims against data sets.

Older students do appear to differentiate knowledge claims from evidence against which they might be evaluated. However, many seem to see knowledge claims as 'emerging' from data in an unproblematic way. Larochelle and Désautels (1991a) asked twenty-five Francophone Canadian students aged 15–18 open-ended questions about the origins of scientific knowledge claims ('How do you think we can produce scientific knowledge?', 'What is an experiment?', 'What is an observation?'). Knowledge claims were seen as being revealed through data collection, more data resulting in more sureness about the knowledge claim. Similar findings are presented by Niedderer *et al.* (1992). Driver *et al.* (1996) report findings from a cross-sectional interview study of the images of science amongst UK students aged 9–16. A framework for characterising features of students' epistemological representations is presented, drawing upon interviews carried out with students on five different tasks. Three broad epistemological representations are presented, which are termed 'phenomenon-based reasoning', 'relation-based reasoning' and 'model-based reasoning'.

In phenomenon-based reasoning students view knowledge claims as descriptions of phenomena, making no distinction between description and explanation. For such students, the evaluation of knowledge claims in terms of data is unproblematic, as knowledge claims are viewed as simple descriptions. In relation-based reasoning, knowledge claims are seen as relationships between observable or taken-for-granted features of phenomena (for example, the size and orientation of an inflated balloon). Theoretical entities (such as air pressure within the balloon) are not postulated or drawn upon in explanation. Correlations are assumed to be causal, and empirical evaluation of knowledge claims therefore involves establishing correlations between observable or taken-for-granted features of phenomena. In model-based reasoning, explanation is taken as involving 'coherent stories involving posited theoretical entities' (1996: 114). The process of empirical evaluation was viewed by such students as involving conjecture and uncertainty. Individual students typically drew upon more than one of these epistemological representations, though model-based reasoning was rarely seen in students in the 9–16 age range. Many students of secondary school age assumed that explanation in practical tasks involved relating taken-for-granted variables, rather than evaluating theoretical knowledge claims.

The above evidence suggests that students are likely to need support in recognising relationships between knowledge claims and data during secondary school practical work, whether the purpose of the practical work is to illustrate scientific concepts or to teach about scientific investigation. There is some evidence that the situation may be similar for students at the undergraduate level. Ryder and Leach (1997) report findings from an interview study with twelve UK undergraduate science students, in which scientific knowledge claims were overwhelmingly portrayed as provable through straightforward empirical processes.

Although the history of science is littered with examples where theories are retained in spite of apparently contrary evidence, there is a logical asymmetry between the implications of evidence that supports a knowledge claim, and that which does not support it. To use a famous example, it is logical to conclude that all swans are *not* white as soon as a black swan is sighted, though it is *not* logical to conclude that all swans are white no matter how many white swans are seen. During practical work, and particularly open-ended investigations, students' approaches to data collection and data processing will be influenced by their implicit beliefs about the logic of proof and falsification. How do students treat evidence that apparently supports or contradicts knowledge claims?

It is now reasonably well established that many students up to adolescence and beyond may exhibit a confirmatory bias when considering the implications of data for knowledge claims (for example, Kuhn *et al*. 1988; Carey *et al*. 1989; Driver *et al*. 1996; Leach 1997). That is, students evaluate knowledge claims against data differently, according to whether they believe the knowledge claim or not. Knowledge claims that are believed are less likely to be rejected in the light of contradictory evidence than knowledge claims that are not believed. Older students are less likely to exhibit this confirmatory bias (Kuhn *et al*. 1988; Driver *et al*. 1996).

For many students, it appears that tasks presented to them as problems of evaluating knowledge claims against data are actually interpreted as having a different purpose. A number of studies of students' approaches to tasks involving the coordination of knowledge claims and data suggest that pre-adolescent students assume that the purpose of the task is to achieve a particular outcome rather than to evaluate a knowledge claim (for example, Metz 1991; Schauble *et al*. 1991; Solomon *et al*. 1994; Millar *et al*. 1995). Older students are more likely to view the purpose of such tasks in terms of evaluating knowledge claims, and make decisions about actions to be taken in terms of explicit models of phenomena. For example, Millar *et al*. (1995) describe the actions taken by students asked to investigate the effects of various materials as thermal insulators to keep a drink cool. Older students drew upon a model of the phenomenon to make predictions which were then evaluated empirically, sometimes resulting in modification of the model. By contrast, younger students tended to manipulate apparatus with no apparent purpose in mind, or alternatively use the materials to produce and optimise a desired effect.

The processes by which students become able to use new concepts are complex, and certainly involve more than rational evaluation of empirical examples and counter-examples (Rowell and Dawson 1983; Chinn and Brewer 1993; O'Loughlin 1992). It appears, however, that some students may not recognise that the purpose of some tasks in practical work is to consider the relationship between knowledge claims and data, and it may well be necessary for this to be made more explicit in teaching.

Students' understanding of the status of knowledge claims within the scientific community, and possible implications for practical work

It has already been noted that theory change in science does not happen solely on the basis of empirical evidence. If evidence is collected which does not support a knowledge claim, subsequent action depends upon the status of the knowledge claim within the scientific community. An extreme situation might involve theories A and B being proposed to explain a novel phenomenon. If the data that are collected support theory A rather than theory B, the likely future of theory B is bleak. Another extreme situation might involve evidence being presented that does not support theory C, a theory widely believed within the scientific community upon which many other theories rest. Although theory change may well occur in this case, well-established theories do not tend to be abandoned lightly.

If students believe that all knowledge claims in science are of equal status, this will affect their actions during practical work. If the data collected are not consistent with established scientific knowledge, a number of options are open to the investigator. One option is to reject established knowledge. The option that is pursued will depend upon the investigators' beliefs about the status of the scientific knowledge in question.

How do students see the implications of the status of knowledge claims for action during empirical work? Little attention has been paid to this question in existing research, though Driver et al. (1996) present evidence that many 16-year-old students are not particularly sensitive to the status of knowledge claims within the community of scientists when evaluating empirical evidence. Students were presented with different interpretations of evidence about the safety of food irradiation as a means of preservation. Some students suggested that policy decisions relating to the legality of food irradiation ought to be made by a process of adjudication where an 'unbiased' figure (such as the government!) made an impartial decision based on empirical evidence. Little mention was made of the role of the scientific community in establishing knowledge claims as reliable.

Practical work may well have a fairly minor role in teaching about the social functioning of the scientific community. However, it may well be appropriate to raise issues with students about how public knowledge is warranted as reliable, and the roles of social and empirical processes in that warranting. Indeed, discussions amongst students within a class or group could be used as a vehicle for the introduction of ideas about the warranting of knowledge in communities of professional scientists.

A footnote about methodology

The studies described above provide insights into students' performance when responding verbally or in writing to questions. The extent to which students draw upon similar ideas about the world of science during practical work is, however, open to question and few studies have taken this focus explicitly. There is some evidence, however, that although many research scientists give apparently naïve responses to interview questions about the nature of science, their accounts of their own practice as research scientists are more sophisticated (Samarapungavan 1992b). A similar increase in sophistication amongst students when working on investigations, compared to answering questions, is suggested by Rowell and Dawson (1983). Munby's (1982) warning about the 'doctrine of immaculate perception' is still pertinent: researchers cannot assume that their interview questions are understood by students in the way that was originally intended, nor that they themselves infer perfectly students' meanings from their responses. Little emphasis has been placed upon methodological issues underpinning the studies reported in this chapter: more detailed treatments can be found in Lucas (1975), Aikenhead (1973) and Leach (1997).

The issue of performance on tasks, as opposed to innate ability, has already been raised: there is no reason to assume that students with apparently naïve ideas could not be introduced to different viewpoints through teaching, and come to use those viewpoints in their practical work. In the next section, some issues are considered relating to how students' understanding of the world of science might be developed through practical work.

Some challenges for teaching science through practical work

It is important to be aware of the strengths and limitations of any teaching approach, and practical work is no exception. Although the aims for practical work are often stated in an over-ambitious way, practical work does have a place in teaching about the nature of science, because it can be designed to draw students' attention to epistemological issues about data and knowledge claims. Practical work whose primary focus is to teach specific science concepts also has an epistemological focus. What are realistic aims for practical work as a method of teaching about the world of science to students, bearing in mind what is known about students' likely ways of reasoning?

Teaching scientific content: illustrative practical work

The traditional purpose of illustrative practical work is to help students to understand a knowledge claim. Unproblematic contexts are selected, and the status of the knowledge being taught is never discussed or questioned. The practical work is often presented to students as an unproblematic process of explaining the material world in terms of true knowledge. A case might be made for adopting this approach if students' understanding is judged in terms of their ability to produce right answers to questions about content. However, as we have seen, students' epistemological understanding may result in unintended learning outcomes from such illustrative practical work, and it may well be necessary for teachers to be more explicit to students about how the practical 'illustrates' the knowledge claim. The notion of 'didactical transposition' (Chevellard, cited in Tiberghien 1997) describes how subject-matter knowledge is transformed for the purpose of teaching. Part of this process involves deciding the level of complexity at which students might be introduced to scientific models. Another aspect involves making explicit to students the phenomena and events modelled by particular theories, the boundary conditions, the problems and so on. Some approaches to practical work have adopted this approach. Tiberghien (1997) drew upon research findings about students' understanding of energy to inform decisions about how to present scientific accounts of electric circuits to students. Students were encouraged to model simple series circuits in terms of energy chains and reservoirs, in order to introduce the notion that energy can be characterised as a fundamental principle of conservation. During teaching, explicit emphasis was placed upon epistemological issues such as the limitations of students' existing models for electric circuits, and the difference between statements about knowledge claims and statements about objects and events in the material world.

Larochelle and Désautels (1991b) describe a computer model of a phenomenon designed to raise epistemological issues about knowledge claims and data with students. An unfamiliar phenomenon involving objects moving is presented to students, who have to generate explanations to account for the observed behaviour. Traces from the objects are seen to move under an opaque object: when they emerge, their trajectory has changed. How can this be explained? No authority source (for example, textbook or teacher) can be drawn upon to provide an answer. Students then work to generate knowledge claims, which are then subjected to critical comment by their peers. In describing the same simulation, Nadeau and Désautels (1984) suggest a number of questions that teachers might use to turn students' attention to epistemological issues during practical work. For example, when using equations to account for the data students might be asked whether they think that the equation constitutes valid knowledge of the phenomenon, whether this knowledge corresponds to reality, whether it is necessary to know what lies beneath the opaque object in order to predict the behaviour of the phenomenon (if there really is something underneath!).

Although this simulation is not illustrative practical work in the sense that no established concept is being illustrated, it does bring to the surface for students what is involved in modelling the material world in terms of scientific knowledge. An approach using a simulation of modelling based on a game is reported by CLIS (1987), to teach lower secondary students about the nature of modelling. Subsequently, students are taught a particulate account of matter, which the students then use to explain a number of simple phenomena presented through practical work.

Teaching about the world of science itself

If the purpose of practical work is to teach about the conditions under which knowledge claims can be used to model phenomena, or indeed the reasons why knowledge claims are thought to be reliable, then it is necessary to focus upon the ways in which knowledge claims can be applied to real problems and the reasons why knowledge claims are believed to be reliable. The problems of relating knowledge claims to phenomena that are often disguised by teachers in illustrative practical work then become the focus of attention. Teaching approaches such as using historical episodes, television programmes and data handling exercises are likely to be useful (see Osborne later in this book), though practical work may also have a place. Strategies might include students in having to justify the knowledge claims that they put forward following practical work (or, indeed, other activities). Some attention has been given to the skills that students need in order to do this. For example, Cross and Price (1992) describe the relevant skills as skills for understanding the argument, for judging the expert, for making independent investigations in the literature or in the field, and for participation in democratic ways of influencing decision-making. Driver *et al.* (1996) suggest strategies for developing such skills, including systematic and careful data collection, producing and justifying inductive generalisations, testing theories or comparing competing theories, and making and communicating knowledge claims from investigations carried out in collaborative groups. Little attention has been given to developing pedagogical strategies for developing students' abilities to construct and appraise scientific arguments, however (Driver and Newton 1997).

Many university departments in the United Kingdom require undergraduate students to undertake open-ended investigative projects in the laboratory alongside professional researchers, with the aim of teaching something about the world of professional science. For example, Ryder and Leach (1997) describe the ways in which students are drawn into cultures of professional scientific research in universities, by working within active research groups during their undergraduate education. The practice of involving students in authentic enquiry is also gaining prominence in some high schools (see, for example, Albone 1993; Roth 1995; Woolnough in this book).

The job that remains to be done

In this chapter, I have presented a case that science students in schools and universities hold views about the world of science that may well influence their science learning during practical work. Some brief comments have been made about how practical work (and other teaching approaches) might be used to teach about the world of science. Although a good deal is now known about how students think about the world of science, much less attention has been paid to the influence that this might have on their learning of science, and even less is known about the effectiveness of teaching approaches. Major challenges for the future involve finding out more about the influence of students' views of science on their learning, finding manageable ways of dealing with epistemological issues in the science curriculum, and promoting better communication between science teachers and their students about epistemological issues, in practical work and elsewhere.

Acknowledgement

The work described in this chapter was partly supported by the European Commission project *Improving Labwork in Science Education* (ref. PL95 2005). The author thanks Phil Scott and Jim Ryder for helpful comments on earlier drafts of the chapter.

References

Aikenhead, G. (1973) 'The measurement of high school students' knowledge about science and scientists', *Science Education* 57(4): 539–49.

Albone, E. (1993) 'Pupils as scientists', *Science and Public Affairs* (Summer): 45–9.

Arnold, M. and Millar, R. (1993) 'Students' understanding of the nature of science: annotated bibliography', Working Paper 11, Leeds/York: Centre for Studies in Science and Mathematics Education, University of Leeds/Science Education Group, University of York.

Carey, S., Evans, R., Honda, M., Jay, E. and Unger, C. (1989) 'An experiment is when you try it and see if it works: a study of grade 7 students' understanding of the construction of scientific knowledge', *International Journal of Science Education* 11(5): 514–29.

Chinn, C. and Brewer, W. (1993) 'The role of anomalous data in knowledge acquisition: a theoretical framework and implications for science instruction', *Review of Educational Research* 63(1): 1–49.

CLIS (1987) *Approaches to Teaching the Particulate Nature of Matter*, Leeds: Centre for Studies in Science and Mathematics Education.

Cross, R. and Price, R. (1992) *Teaching Science for Social Responsibility*, Sydney: St Louis Press.

Driver, R., Asoko, H., Leach, J., Mortimer, E. and Scott, P. (1994) 'Constructing scientific knowledge in the classroom', *Educational Researcher* 23(7): 5–12.

Driver, R., Leach, J., Millar, R. and Scott, P. (1996) *Young People's Images of Science*, Buckingham: Open University Press.

Driver, R. and Newton, P. (1997) 'Establishing the norms of scientific argumentation in classrooms', paper presented at the meeting of the European Science Education Research Association, Rome.

Hunt, A. and Russell, N. (1994) *GNVQ Science: Your Questions Answered – an Introduction and Guide to GNVQ Science*, London: Heinemann Educational.

Kuhn, D. (1997) 'Constraints or guideposts? Developmental psychology and science education', *Review of Educational Research* 67(1): 141–50.

Kuhn, D., Amsell, E. and O'Loughlin, M. (1988) *The Development of Scientific Thinking Skills*, London: Academic Press.

Larochelle, M. and Désautels, J. (1991a) '"Of course, it's just obvious": adolescents' ideas of scientific knowledge', *International Journal of Science Education* 13(4): 373–89.

—— (1991b) 'The epistemological turn in science education: the return of the actor', in R. Duit, F. Goldberg and H. Niedderer (eds) *Research in Physics Learning: Theoretical Issues and Empirical Studies*, Keil, Germany: IPN.

Leach, J. (1997a) 'Students' understanding of the nature of science', in G. Welford, P. Scott and J. Osborne (eds) *Research in Science Education in Europe: Current Issues and Themes*, London: Falmer Press.

—— (1997b) 'Students' understanding of the co-ordination of theory and evidence', paper presented at the annual meeting of the American Educational Research Association, Chicago, IL.

Lederman, N. (1992) 'Students' and teachers' conceptions of the nature of science: a review of the research', *Journal of Research in Science Teaching* 29(4): 331–59.

Lubben, F. and Millar, R. (1996) 'Children's ideas about the reliability of experimental data', *International Journal of Science Education* 18(8): 955–68.

Lucas, A. (1975) 'Hidden assumptions in measures of "knowledge about science and scientists"', *Science Education* 59(4): 481–5.

Matthews, M. (1997) 'James T. Robinson's account of the philosophy of science and science teaching: some lessons for today from the 1960s', *Science Education* 81(3): 295–316.

Metz, K. (1991) 'Development of explanation: incremental and fundamental change in children's physics knowledge', *Journal of Research in Science Teaching* 28(9): 785–98.

—— (1997) 'On the complex relation between cognitive developmental research and children's science curricula', *Review of Educational Research* 67(1): 151–63.

Millar, R., Gott, R., Lubben, F. and Duggan, S. (1995) 'Children's performance of investigative tasks in science: a framework for considering progression', in M. Hughes (ed.) *Progression in Learning*, Cleveland, Avon: Multilingual Matters.

Munby, H. (1982) 'The place of teachers' beliefs in research on teacher thinking and decision making, and an alternative methodology', *Instructional Science* 11: 201–25.

Nadeau, R. and Désautels, J. (1984) *Epistemology and the Teaching of Science*, Ottawa: Science Council of Canada.

Niedderer, H., Bethge, T., Meyling, H. and Schecker, H. (1992) 'Epistemological beliefs of students in high school physics', paper presented at the annual meeting of the National Association for Research in Science Teaching, Boston, MA.

O'Loughlin, M. (1992) 'Rethinking science education: beyond Piagetian constructivism towards a sociocultural model of teaching and learning', *Journal of Research in Science Teaching* 29(8): 791–820.

Roth, W-M. (1995) *Authentic School Science: Knowing and Learning in Open-inquiry Science*, Dordrecht. London: Kluwer.

Rowell, J. and Dawson, C. (1983) 'Laboratory counterexamples and the growth of understanding in science', *International Journal of Science Education* 5: 203–15.

Ryder, J. and Leach, J. (1997) 'Research projects in the undergraduate science course: students' learning about science through enculturation', in C. Rust, and G. Gibbs, (eds) *Improving Student Learning through Course Design*, Proceedings of the Fourth International Student Learning Symposium, Bath 1996: Oxford Centre for Staff and Learning Development, pp. 246–53.

Ryder, J., Leach, J. and Driver, R. (in press) 'Undergraduate science and students' images of the nature of science', *Journal of Research in Science Teaching*.

Samarapungavan, A. (1992a) 'Children's judgements in theory choice tasks: scientific rationality in childhood', *Cognition* 45: 1–32.

—— (1992b) 'Scientists' conceptions of science: a study of epistemic beliefs', paper presented at the annual meeting of the American Educational Research Association, San Francisco.

Schauble, L., Klopfer, L.E. and Raghavan, K. (1991) 'Students' transition from an engineering model to a science model of experimentation', *Journal of Research in Science Teaching* 28(9): 859–82.

Séré, M-G., Journeaux, R. and Larcher, C. (1993) 'Learning the statistical analysis of measurement errors', *International Journal of Science Education* 15(4): 427–38.

Solomon, J., Duveen, J., Scott, L. and McCarthy, S. (1992) 'Teaching about the nature of science through history: action research in the classroom', *Journal of Research in Science Teaching* 29(4): 409–21.

Solomon, J., Scott, L. and Duveen, J. (1994) 'Pupils' images of scientific epistemology', *International Journal of Science Education* 16(3): 361–73.

Tiberghien, A. (1997) 'Construction of prototypical situations in teaching the concept of energy', in G. Welford, P. Scott and J. Osborne (eds) *Research in Science Education in Europe: Current Issues and Themes*, London: Falmer Press.

Woolnough, B. (1985) *Practical Work in Science*, Cambridge: Cambridge University Press.

5

'IF THIS WERE PLAYED UPON A STAGE'

School laboratory work as a theatre of representation

Noel Gough

If this were played upon a stage now, I could condemn it as
an improbable fiction.
(William Shakespeare, *Twelfth Night,* Act 3, Scene 4)

ACT 1

SCENE 1

*A science classroom in a government secondary school in one of Melbourne's outer
eastern suburbs in May 1997. The upstage wall has a large, triple-hung chalkboard
at its centre with a fume cupboard at stage left and a half-glass door open at stage
right leading to a prep room where we glimpse steel shelves cluttered with apparatus
and chemical containers. A demonstration bench on a slightly raised platform is
centred about 1 metre downstage from the chalkboard. On it is a retort stand to which
a single pulley is clamped at the highest position. Alongside the stand are a number of
masses, including a 1 kg and 200 g mass, some string and a spring balance. A
laboratory bench, with cupboards underneath, runs the entire length of the left side
wall over which there are large exterior windows. At regular intervals there are work
areas that can be identified by gas taps, power points, and sinks with gooseneck
faucets. An identical bench runs along the right side wall but stops about 2 metres
from the stagefront, at which point there is a large half-glass sliding door open to a
corridor lined with banks of lockers. There are also windows to the corridor above this
bench but most of them are filled with posters on science topics: birds of south-eastern
Australia, the human muscular system, etc. On the side bench near the prep room door
is a stack of metre rulers. The centre stage area is filled with several rows of writing
benches, each with four chairs under, arranged in two columns facing the chalkboard.*

*A bell signalling a period change is ringing as MS FRASER enters from the prep
room carrying a large tray which she puts down on the side bench next to the stack of*

metre rulers. The tray contains a number of spring balances, lengths of string, large wooden blocks, single pulleys, 200 g masses, various smaller masses and sticks of chalk. She then moves to a position behind the demonstration bench. At the same time, around thirty students – a mixture of boys and girls aged around 13 to 14 years – are entering from the corridor. All of the students are wearing at least one item of what is obviously school uniform, although it is equally obvious that the school does not enforce a strict uniform policy. The students are ethnically diverse – Anglo/ European, Mediterranean/Middle Eastern, Asian – and are talking noisily among themselves as they take their seats. Among the students are NATALIE, IRENA, MARK *and a Japanese boy* DASUKE.

MS FRASER: [*Voice raised*] OK, sit down quickly please and get out your books . . . come on, we've only got one period and I'm sure you don't want to be working into your lunchtime. [*Pause; students become quieter, though there are still some subdued murmurs;* MS FRASER *continues in more conversational tone.*] Yes, Irena, both your textbook and your workbook. [*Pause*] Get your bag out of the aisle please Mark, somebody could fall over it. [*Pause*] All right, we're doing the second part of Prac 6.5 today – on measuring work – it's on page 179.[1] [*Pauses as students find the page.*] Natalie, would you come out here for a moment, please?

NATALIE: [*Rising from her seat*] What for, miz?

MS FRASER: I just want you to help me demonstrate something. You were in the shotput at the House sports, weren't you?

NATALIE: [*Quizzically*] Yeah . . . so?

MS FRASER: [*Picks up 1 kg mass and hands it to* NATALIE.] Could you just stand facing the class holding that mass out in front of you at arm's length *without moving* please? See how long you can hold it. [NATALIE *holds out the mass for about 10 seconds and then gives up with a grimace; there is some giggling and bantering from the students*].

MARK: [*In a sarcastic undertone meant to be heard.*] Piss weak!

MS FRASER: No need for that Mark . . . perhaps you can tell the class if you thought Natalie was doing any work while she was holding that weight, um, mass out in front of her?

MARK: Ah, yeah, um . . . yeah I s'pose so . . . but not much! [*Laughs*]

MS FRASER: What about you Natalie, did you think you were doing any work? You can go back to your seat now.

NATALIE: [*Returning to her seat, pulling a face at* MARK] Yeah, for sure, it was hard to hold it still.

MS FRASER: What do other people think? [*Pause*] Well, I can see that not many of you have done the reading I set . . . the handout on work and energy?[2]

IRENA: I did miz but I didn't understand it . . .

MS FRASER: Is that what others thought? What about you, Dasuke?

DASUKE: [*Quietly, hesitating over choice of words*] There is no . . . work done if the . . . if it does not move. . . . Work is force on . . . is the force over . . . is the force that it takes to move something . . . so it's force multiplied by distance.

MS FRASER: That's right Dasuke. Work is really force times distance. [*Turns and writes 'W = F × d' on the chalkboard.*] Natalie may have thought that she was doing a lot of hard work to hold the weight, um, mass up, but this isn't actually the case. In science, work is defined as the product of the force applied to an object and the distance it moves. So since the weight wasn't moving, the distance is zero, so the amount of work done is zero.

NATALIE: [*Rolling her eyes, in an undertone*] That's *so* stupid . . .

MS FRASER: It's not stupid, Natalie, it's just that scientists have very clear definitions of terms like work and in science when you use a force to move something, you are working. [*Pause*] OK, so look at the prac instructions on page 179. You'll see that the hypothesis we're testing is that work can be measured if force and distance are known. The aim is to actually measure the work done by moving various objects. The equipment's listed there. You'll need to get the retort stands and clamps out of the cupboards under your benches and you can collect the rest of it from the bench over there. [*Points to the tray she brought in and the metre rulers.*] When you get to step 7, set up the pulley like I've got it here. [*The last sentence is almost drowned out by the noise of scraping chairs as the students start moving around the room to collect and set up the equipment.* DASUKE *collects the equipment quickly and purposefully, with* MARK *dawdling behind him with hands in pockets. While they are collecting the equipment,* NATALIE *and* IRENA *chatter to each other about a new CD they would like to buy, but this is frequently interspersed by their asking each other if this is what they are supposed to be doing. They usually resolve this by looking at what* DASUKE *is doing and copying him rather than referring to their textbooks.*]

If the above script 'were played upon a stage now', few science teachers could condemn it as an 'improbable fiction'. Similar scenes will be familiar to anyone – student, teacher, researcher – who has had more than a passing acquaintance with science classrooms. But if we agree that school science should represent the reality of out-of-school science in some intellectually and morally defensible fashion, then the above scene is not only an 'improbable' fiction but a rather dangerous one. As I will argue in this chapter, if we assume that routines like those played out above are relatively harmless, then we are in effect constituting science education as a theatre of the absurd in which the actors are aware of neither its theatricality nor its absurdity.

My argument is constructed around two key ideas. First, I will use the concept of *simulation* to analyse and question some of the ways in which school science mediates our understandings of 'reality' and its representation.

I will then argue that considering school laboratory work as a *theatre of representation*, with particular reference to the multiple meanings of 'play', may provide us with some generative ways of rethinking school science and the place of practical work within it.

School science as simulacrum

Jean Baudrillard's (1983) concept of simulations and *simulacra* – simulated representations – provides a useful register for questioning assumptions about the extent to which laboratory work in school science brings students closer to understandings of the 'real', whether this be 'real' science or the 'reality' that scientists study. Baudrillard (1988: 170) outlines four successive historical phases of a sign or image:

1 It is the reflection of a basic reality,
2 It masks and perverts basic reality,
3 It masks the *absence* of a basic reality,
4 It bears no relation to any reality whatever: it is its own pure simulacrum.

Let us examine the above scene in terms of its representation of any reality other than that of school laboratory work itself. I will argue that, in at least four significant ways, this scene fails to reflect any 'basic reality' but, rather, exemplifies the ways in which school laboratory work 'masks and perverts' the 'reality' of science, and either 'masks the *absence* of' or 'bears no relation to any reality whatever'.

First, like most school laboratories, Ms Fraser's classroom with its fume-cupboard, gooseneck faucets and gas taps is a stereotyped gesture towards the diverse sites in which scientists pursue their labours. The activities that take place in such classrooms – indeed, the activities that *can* take place in them – bear little or no resemblance to contemporary scientific practice. For many years, the physical sciences especially have been characterised by the types of highly industrialised and technologised 'Big Science' which require very different facilities from those on which school laboratories are modelled. More recently, virtually all of the sciences – mathematical, physical, biological, cosmological and so on – have moved away from studying the simple systems that have been the object of mainstream science since Newton's day towards studies of complex systems; for recent accounts of this shift see, for example, Cohen and Stewart (1994); Favre *et al.* (1995); Kauffman (1995). Whether they are furnished with optical or electron microscopes, Bunsen burners or multimillion-dollar particle accelerators, most laboratories are equipped for studying the *material* structures of simple systems. But in the study of complex systems – protein folding in cell nuclei, task switching in ant colonies, the nonlinear dynamics of the earth's atmosphere and far-from-equilibrium chemical reactions – the emphasis is on modelling their *informational* structure through computer simulations (see, for example, Casti 1997). Little of what now counts as 'progress' among communities of working scientists is accomplished by the sort of individualistic, small-scale, low-tech 'bench work' to which school laboratories are suited.

A second way in which the activities initiated by Ms Fraser 'mask and distort' the 'reality' of scientific work is that they reproduce stereotyped and mythologised versions of science and its methods. During the last two decades, a number of studies of scientists at work – see, for example, Charlesworth *et al.* (1989); Haraway (1989); Latour (1987); Latour and Woolgar (1979) – have explored the differences between what is actually done in sites of scientific labour and the stereotypical image of science constructed from what scientists say they do and what society at large believes they do. For example, Charlesworth *et al.* (1989: 271) conclude that: 'What strikes one forcefully as one looks at the way scientists carry on in reality, is the enormous disparity between that reality and the idealized or mythical accounts of it that are given by . . . scientists themselves'. Thus, when she refers to 'the hypothesis we're testing', Ms Fraser is gesturing towards the pervasive myth that scientific work is characterised by a special kind of method. But as Latour writes:

> Now that field studies of laboratory practices are starting to pour in, we are beginning to have a better picture of what scientists do inside the walls of these strange places called 'laboratories'. . . . The result, to summarise it in one sentence, was that nothing extraordinary and nothing 'scientific' was happening inside the sacred walls of these temples.
>
> (1983: 141)

Charlesworth *et al.* reached similar conclusions:

> the neat classical picture of deductions being made from theories and then tested by observation and experiment (the so-called hypothetico-deductive method) scarcely ever corresponds to the reality of the scientific process. Much of scientific investigation relies on a pragmatic 'let's try it and see what happens' approach, and the getting of data is all important.
>
> (1989: 271)

Thus, much science education distorts the interrelationships between theory, method and data by representing data generation as part of an invariable sequence of activities that can be rationalised as 'the scientific method' of producing 'scientific knowledge'. This not only ignores the pragmatics and social determinants of data production but, as Charlesworth *et al.* (1989: 271) observe, 'irrational and uncontrollable factors – lucky breaks, playing one's hunches, being in the right place at the right time – also play a disconcertingly large part in scientific discovery'.

A third way in which school science 'masks and perverts' scientific work is by trivialising the myth of scientific method itself (that is, it adds another layer of distortion to what is already a distortion). To refer to the proposition that 'work can be measured if force and distance are known' as 'the hypothesis we're testing' is a ludicrous perversion of even the 'neat classical picture' of experimental method. Yet both of the science textbooks that Ms Fraser is using (like every other school science textbook I have seen) seriously distorts – and therefore impedes learners' understanding of – the history of experimental science by calling any and every 'practical' activity conducted in a school laboratory an 'experiment'. Most often they are not experiments at all in the hypothetico-deductive sense, but recipes for demonstrating the propositional knowledge that students are expected to reproduce in tests. For example, labelling an activity designed to estimate the average braking force on a bicycle an 'experiment' (see Parsons 1996: 153) trivialises the role of experimental method in scientific inquiry and diminishes the imagination, skill and ingenuity which scientists need to design the kinds of experiments that do, in fact, advance scientific knowledge.

The fourth way in which Ms Fraser's class approaches Baudrillard's 'pure simulacrum' is signalled by her insistence that Natalie's commonsense understanding of work is wrong and that it is the mission of science education, supported by the intellectual authority of textbooks and the material weight ('um, mass') of the laboratory, to replace this commonsense understanding with another, 'correct', 'scientific' understanding. It is worth examining Ms Fraser's handout from Parsons (1996: 150) in some detail. The topic of 'Work and energy' is introduced by a half-page freehand illustration of a girl pushing hard against a brick wall. She is grimacing with the effort and beads of sweat are bursting from her brow. She is watched from their perch on overhead wires by two puzzled birds (both are wide-eyed and one has a question mark over its head) with the characteristic colours and features of galahs (this is a nice local touch: among white Australians the galah is an emblem of extreme foolishness – the village idiot of birdland). Its caption indicates that this drawing is no mere decoration but a substantial component of the text: 'Figure 8.1: Considerable force is being applied here. How much work is being done?'

Occupying a narrow but very prominent column on the left hand side of the page (bold black print over a bright yellow box) is a so-called 'Fact File' (a regular feature of this particular text) which reads, in part:

A scientist considers that no work has been done on an object if the object has not moved through a distance. For example, if you spend all day pushing hard against a wall, but the wall does not move, then no work has been done on it!

Consider the cumulative effect of the exclamation mark, the positioning of the above sentences in a 'Fact File', the illustration I have described (a girl, two galahs) and its caption. All of these are part of a commonplace rhetorical strategy of science textbooks which Ms Fraser reinforces by co-opting Natalie for her own little demonstration. Both the textbook and the teacher appeal to commonsense understandings of an everyday word, reject this understanding, then replace the meaning of the word with a formula, in this case by claiming that 'work is *really* force times distance'. Ms Fraser's use of the word 'really', and all of the textbook's graphic and semantic ploys, are directed towards establishing their claims to having authoritative knowledge of what 'work' means. They are claiming that any other meanings for 'work' are deficient, unscientific, intuitive, even foolish (clinging to your commonsense understandings makes you a bit of a galah).

Such stipulative definitions are not, and cannot ever be, 'scientific' truth claims. The assertion that 'no work has been done' if we try but fail to move an object does not belong in a 'Fact File'. There is and cannot be one privileged 'fact' informing what 'work' means. Words *in fact* mean whatever they are used to mean, and 'work' is used to mean 'force multiplied by distance' only in very restricted circumstances. As David Chapman (1992) writes:

> The intellectually honest way to present this concept would be to invent a new word for it, say 'woozle'. Woozle is the product of force and distance. Actually, we are going to need new words for those too, so woozle is the product of frizzle and drizzle. We could go through a physics book and systematically substitute these new words in and we'd get a new book that wouldn't be making claims to ownership of any ordinary-language words. I believe that students would have a much easier time with such a book; it would be much easier to learn the new words than to deal with the cognitive dissonance involved in abandoning old ones.[3]

Many science educators might say that this is not done because relating a physics concept, such as woozle, to an everyday concept, such as work, allows learners to use their commonsense understanding of this phenomenon as a stepping stone to understanding the 'correct' scientific concept. However, as the proposed rewritten text entry above would make clear, work has very little to do with woozle, and saying that woozle is 'work' is confusing. If this was no more than a recycling of the word, students could understand that 'work' has two meanings, which would present them with little or no difficulty; but the claim that is imposed on the students by the textbook, the teacher and the planned laboratory activities is that woozle is the *true* meaning of 'work' and that they must abandon other meanings. Chapman concludes:

> I believe the actual reason physics continues to claim 'work' for its own can be seen if we imagine the fully-renamed physics book about woozle and frizzle. The problem with this book is that it never makes contact with reality. It's a nice consistent mathematical system that isn't about anything. If it is going to describe the world, it either has to have some ordinary words in it to ground it, or else we need to have instruments that measure woozle and frizzle rather than work and force.

But, as most physicists will acknowledge if the point is pressed, this cannot be done. The real world is not programmed to run according to the rules of Newtonian mechanics or any of the other representations that western scientists, in their astonishing arrogance, have come to call 'laws'.

At this stage I must emphasise that I am neither seeking to diminish the significance of Newtonian mechanics in the history of western science nor suggesting that Newton's work should be ignored in science education. The point at issue here is that if students perceive an incoherence between their commonsense understandings of reality and a scientific representation of it, science educators should not assume that the 'fault' lies with students or that it is their sacred duty to coerce students towards an orthodox belief. On the contrary, science educators should be helping students to *understand the incoherence* rather than to fudge it – to *demonstrate* that gaps between reality and representation are inevitable rather than to deploy all sorts of rhetorical tricks (including laboratory work) in an effort to persuade students that it all makes sense.

For example, the textbook used by Ms Fraser asserts that: '*All masses attract each other.* No one has yet discovered why'; yet the very next paragraph states that:

> The force of attraction between masses is known as *gravitational force*. The larger and closer the masses, the greater is the pull between them.
> The gravitational force between the earth and the sun holds the earth in orbit around the sun. The gravitational force between the moon and the earth holds the moon in orbit around the earth.
> (Cooper et al. 1988: 160; emphasis in original)

This is blatantly self-contradictory, and if students don't recognise the contradiction teachers should draw attention to it. If 'no one has yet discovered why' all masses attract each other, how can the attraction be attributed to 'gravitational force'? This example demonstrates the tendency of science educators to naturalise what is socially constructed by referring to a representation as a phenomenon and, further, to privilege one representation as an explanation for that phenomenon. Here, 'gravitational force' is accorded the status of a natural phenomenon for which Newton's 'law' of gravitation is the privileged explanation.[4] Yet, as Katherine Hayles (1993: 33) notes: 'Gravity, like any other concept, is always and inevitably a representation'. Thoughtful science educators are unlikely to disagree with Hayles, although they are more likely to refer to 'constructions' than to 'representations'. However, science educators cannot avoid questions about which of many possible constructions/representations they should choose to privilege. For example, Fensham et al. (1994: 6) assert that constructivist teaching 'does not give students licence to claim that their meaning is as good as scientists' meaning, no matter what its form': constructivism 'does not mean "anything goes"; some meanings are better than others. Means for determining what is better are then significant'. They then endorse criteria for explaining a natural phenomenon that are very familiar in the rhetoric of western science, namely, that an explanation should be 'elegant and parsimonious and connected with other phenomena, as well as having . . . intelligibility, plausibility and fruitfulness . . . and be testable'. The defensibility of these criteria is not questioned. But why should an aesthetic criterion like elegance apply to scientific explanations? Why should an arbitrary criterion such as parsimony be applied? Like all of the other criteria that Fensham et al. (1994) recommend, their meanings are embedded in the historically specific practices of interpretation and testimony that characterise the narrative traditions of western science.

Rather than trying to determine that 'some meanings are *better* than others', Hayles (1993: 33) suggests that 'within the representations we construct, some are ruled out by constraints, others are not'. In Hayles's terms, 'by ruling out some possibilities . . . constraints enable scientific inquiry to tell us something about reality and not only about ourselves':

> Consider how conceptions of gravity have changed over the last three hundred years. In the Newtonian paradigm, gravity is conceived very differently than in the general theory of relativity. For Newton, gravity resulted from the mutual attraction between masses; for Einstein, from the curvature of space. One might imagine still other kinds of explanations, for example a Native American belief that objects fall to earth because the spirit of Mother Earth calls out to kindred spirits in other bodies. No matter how gravity is conceived, no viable model could predict that when someone steps off a cliff on earth, she will remain suspended in midair. This possibility is ruled out by the nature

of physical reality. Although the constraints that lead to this result are interpreted differently in different paradigms, they operate universally to eliminate certain configurations from the range of possible answers.

(1993: 32–3)

Hayles (1993: 33) emphasises that constraints do not – indeed cannot – tell us what reality *is* but, rather, that constraints enable us to distinguish which representations are consistent with reality and which are not. For example, the limit on how fast information can be transmitted with today's silicon technology is usually explained as a function of how fast electrons move through a semiconductor. 'Electron' and 'semiconductor' are social constructions, but the limit is observed no matter what representation is used. If atomic theories had been formulated around the concept of waves rather than particles, then we might now explain the limit in terms of indices of resistance and patterns of refraction rather than electrons and semiconductors. Hayles notes that for any given phenomenon, there will always be other representations, unknown or unimaginable, that are consistent with reality: 'The representations we present for falsification are limited by what we can imagine, which is to say, by the prevailing modes of representation within our culture, history, and species'.[5] Hayles calls this position 'constrained constructivism':

> Neither cut free from reality nor existing independent of human perception, the world as constrained constructivism sees it is the result of active and complex engagements between reality and human beings. Constrained constructivism invites – indeed cries out for – cultural readings of science, since the representations presented for disconfirmation have everything to do with prevailing cultural and disciplinary assumptions.
>
> (1993: 33–4)

Constrained constructivism suggests alternative approaches to representing 'reality' in the science education curriculum that do not collapse into antirealist language games. Constrained constructivism is not 'anything goes', but neither does it fall into the trap of disallowing representations that fail to match current orthodoxies. This suggests to me a rather different role for school laboratory work than it has fulfilled to date. Instead of using school laboratory work as a strategy for persuading students to *accept* scientists' social constructions of reality, we could use school laboratories as 'theatres of representation' in which these constructions are both tested for their consistency with reality and also for their continuities and discontinuities with other (not necessarily 'scientific') representations.

School science as theatre of representation

In an earlier publication, *Laboratories in Fiction: Science Education and Popular Media* (Gough 1993a), I argued that it would be preferable for much routine practical work to be replaced by activities that involve a close analysis of the 'cultural texts' of scientific production, including primary sources (such as scientific reports), historical accounts of scientific work, the biographies and autobiographies of scientists, scientific journalism in print and electronic media, and images of science in the fine arts and popular media. In regard to the latter, I emphasised the significance of using science fiction in its many and various forms as a 'laboratory of ideas' in which meanings are subjected to experimentation (see also Gough 1993b). While I would still argue that such activities are essential, I will offer here another alternative that arises from thinking of school laboratories as theatres of material representations.

The concept of 'play' provides several metaphors that might be generative in rethinking school laboratory work. First, while the artefacts and apparatus assembled in school science laboratories are most often used as props for staging tightly scripted (re)enactments of mythologised versions of scientific practices, these same props could perhaps be material resources for improvised play – for object-orientated 'experiments' in the pre-Baconian sense (as in the Latin *experimentalis*, based on experience, not authority or conjecture). A difficulty with this proposal is that I can only imagine children of primary school age (or younger) being motivated to play with many of the objects available in secondary school laboratories (such as the blocks, masses, pulleys and spring balances provided in Ms Fraser's class). Nevertheless, the question of what types of materials and apparatus are likely to stimulate exploratory play among secondary school students could, at least in some circumstances, be a worthwhile focus for classroom-based action research. Apart from some stereotypical assumptions about boys tinkering with computers and/or cars, I suspect that we have very little understanding of what kinds of *things* teenagers are genuinely curious about. Donald Winnicott's (1971) analysis of 'transitional objects' – cultural materials that may function interchangeably as toys, tools and/or symbols in various phases of our personal and social development – provides one way of thinking about the educative potential of material objects that may help us to ask new questions about how best to furnish and equip science laboratories (see also Hodgkin 1985: 39–61).

Second, the 'plays' we stage in school laboratories can be scripted in many different ways, so that they not only simulate (however crudely) the work of professional scientists in producing and inscribing data, but also draw attention to the material contributions this work makes to the production and circulation of culturally privileged knowledge – to represent some of the ways in which, as Latour (1984: 257) puts it, 'science is politics continued by other means'. For example, in the scene that opens this chapter, science provides Ms Fraser with the authority to exercise her power over the meaning of production processes in her classroom, and she is thus able to dismiss Natalie's quite reasonable response ('that's *so* stupid') to being force-fed nonsense simply by asserting that authority. But what is Natalie supposed to do when she is asked to learn something that makes no sense to her? Let us rehearse some possibilities:

- She could conclude that, because she cannot make sense of what she is told, she must be deficient in some way – that she is the kind of person who 'can't do science'.
- She could conclude that, since this particular bit of science makes no sense, science writ large is nonsensical and that she might as well ignore it.
- She could decide that, appearances notwithstanding, science *must* make sense, since textbooks and people like Ms Fraser say so. She might then revise her understanding of 'understanding' and learn how to perform socially rewarded forms of intellectual activity regardless of whether or not they are meaningful to her. She may even become a science teacher.
- She could decide that science makes no sense, but that since there are social rewards for displaying an 'understanding' of it, she might as well learn to do that.

With the resources currently available to schools and science teachers, actively encouraging students towards taking up the latter position may be the best that they can do. Like much of what is authorised as 'scientific knowledge', Newtonian mechanics makes most sense if it is understood within its specific social, cultural and historical context. If science educators cannot explain this in a way that makes sense to students, they should either stop trying or simply come clean about the social rewards of pretending to do so.

This leads directly to my third suggestion about the generative possibilities of 'play' in rethinking school science education; namely, that imagining school laboratories as 'theatres of representation' may help teachers and learners to discern the 'play' in the operations, relations and conditions that constitute science as a cultural practice – using 'play' here in a Derridean sense that likens the play of power across discursive fields to 'play' in a machine: a relative freedom of movement within limits (see, for example, McGowan 1991: 103–5). Many of Jay Lemke's (1990) recommendations for 'teaching against the mystique of science' are pertinent here. Drawing on his studies of communication in science classrooms, Lemke (1990: 167–81) summarises his recommendations into four major groups as follows:

Teaching students to talk science:
- give students more practice talking science
- teach students how to combine science terms in complex sentences
- discuss students' commonsense theories on each topic
- teach students the minor and major genres of science writing

Bridging between colloquial and scientific language:
- have students translate back and forth between scientific and colloquial statements or questions
- discuss formal scientific style and use informal, humanizing language in teaching scientific thematics

Teaching about science and scientific method:
- describe the actual relation between observation and theory
- describe science as a fallible, human social activity
- emphasize that science is just another way of talking about the world, no more difficult than any other

Helping all students use science in their own interests:
- adapt teaching and testing to students' language and culture
- acknowledge and work to resolve conflicts of interest between the curriculum and students' values
- give students practice using science to decide policy issues according to their own values and interests.

Lemke's detailed justification for these recommendations is worth reading in full (I will also leave it to readers to identify for themselves the ways in which Ms Fraser explicitly or implicitly violates these recommendations). But here I want to focus attention on the specific implications of Lemke's recommendations for laboratory work. Much of Lemke's research consists of systematic analyses of teacher and student talk in 'regular' science classes – when teachers are doing demonstrations or talking theory.[6] Indeed, he asserts that 'science in the laboratory . . . is as much different from science in the classroom as it is from the teaching of other subjects':

> In the laboratory, students talk science to each other to guide themselves through prescribed experimental procedures, to decide what to do when something seems to have gone wrong, and to write up notes on what they have done. They talk science with their teacher when he or she comes around to see how they are doing, asking a question when they have initiated the contact, or answering one when the teacher has. This is often a lively use of the language of science, integrated with nonverbal activity. Unfortunately, too often, students don't seem to have enough command

of the language they need to be able to figure out what's really going on in lab while it's happening. At best, some of them construct it later. This is why I am skeptical about how much science students actually learn from lab work itself, though of course lab work is necessary and valuable as one part of a good science curriculum.

(Lemke 1990: 156–7)

I share Lemke's scepticism, but cannot agree that it is a matter 'of course' that laboratory work (as we now know it) 'is necessary and valuable' in a science curriculum. I also do not agree with another possible reading of Lemke's words, which carry the implication that current school laboratory routines (such as guiding students through 'prescribed experimental procedures') are acceptable in principle and that all we need to do to make laboratory work more meaningful to students is to give them a better 'command of the language'. But, rather than simply implementing Lemke's recommendations on talking science as a means to improve what students 'actually learn from lab work', I would like to suggest that we should also be attempting to change the laboratory practices so that they too become a means of helping students to improve their command of language. Thus, for example, recipes for 'experimental procedures' should not only be couched in terms of the 'minor and major genres of science writing' but also *invite* students to 'translate back and forth between scientific and colloquial statements or questions'. In some instances, the encouragement (or discouragement) for students to do this sort of translation may be as much a function of the activities themselves as of the language in which the procedures are presented by a teacher or textbook.

For example, the 'prac' that Ms Fraser's students are about to undertake is framed in terms of a major genre of science writing ('the hypothesis we're testing is . . .') and her justification of her assertion that 'work is really force times distance' is couched in two of the minor genres of science writing; namely, the stipulative definition (work is 'the product of the force applied to an object and the distance it moves') and syllogism ('since the weight wasn't moving, the distance is zero, so the amount of work done is zero'). The procedures that the students are expected to follow involve measuring (with a Newton spring balance) the work done by moving various objects – masses and wooden blocks. These objects are presented – and, I suspect, experienced by students – almost as abstractions and therefore do not invite being talked about in colloquial terms. A comparable exercise in Parsons (1996: 153) provides students with procedures for estimating the average braking force on a bicycle. While students are still asked to measure and interpret 'work' by reference to the same definition and syllogism, using an everyday object like a bicycle invites more colloquial representations of what is going on. Terms like 'work' and 'force' now have to be negotiated by reference to the brakes operated by a real human rider rather than to anonymous blocks, masses and Newton meters.

Although I think it would be easier for students to 'translate back and forth between scientific and colloquial statements or questions' if they were working with bicycles rather than blocks, I would extend a further invitation to students, namely, to compare these two 'pracs' as a form of 'theatre' in which they themselves and various objects – brakes, bicycles, blocks, masses – have been (con)scripted as 'actors'.[7] We need to ask, and encourage students to ask, just what Cooper *et al.* (1988) and Parsons (1996) are each trying to achieve by 'staging' these particular interactions among learners and objects.[8]

If we draw attention to the ways in which scripts for practical work manipulate actors to achieve specific audience effects, students might begin to understand these scripts as fictions – which may be the most truthful and responsible way in which school laboratory work can represent science as a cultural practice.[9]

If the fiction that follows were played upon a stage now, I could defend it.

ACT 1

SCENE 1 (revised)

Same as previous except that the demonstration bench is cluttered with many different objects – one each of everything mentioned in the earlier version of this scene plus anything else that might conceivably have been supplied to a school during the last thirty years and that could conceivably be used in teaching about Newtonian mechanics: a miniature runway and trolley, ticker tape and timer, stop watch, various balls, a measuring tape, trundle wheel, elastic, bits of Meccano and Lego, and so on. MS FRASER is distributing textbooks of various ages and conditions to the workstations down each side of the laboratory. Of course, having read this chapter, MS FRASER is now a different person.

MS FRASER: [*Voice raised*] OK, settle down quickly please and get out your books . . . [*Pause; students become quieter; MS FRASER continues in more conversational tone.*] Yes, Irena, chapter 8 . . .[10] [*Pause*] Now, as usual when we start a new unit, we need to sort out who's going to do what. You'll see at the front of your book that the main CSF[11] outcome for this chapter is to 'report on an investigation into the forces and energy transformations involved in using everyday equipment'. So, as far as I'm concerned the minimum work requirement[12] is that you'll all do at least one investigation and I hope some of you do more. You don't have to stick with the investigations in the book but the reason I asked you to look at chapter 8 for homework was to give you some ideas. Could I just have a show of hands to see how many of you are interested in the ones in the book? [*Leafs through book calling out brief descriptions of investigations. Students respond as indicated.*] Braking force on a bicycle? OK, hands down, that's just about everyone –

NATALIE: Could we do that with roller blades too miz? Or instead?

MS FRASER: Um, yeah, sure . . . I guess . . . do you actually *have* a brake on blades?

NATALIE: Yeah . . . you know, under the heel.

MS FRASER: OK . . . um, where was I? Energy changes in a pendulum? No one? What about spring constant of a rubber band? No? I guess they do both look a bit boring . . . Building and testing a windmill? 1, 2, 3, 4 . . . plenty of takers for that one. . . . Power of a photovoltaic cell? Just you, Dasuke? OK . . . Electric motors? 2, 4, 6 . . . OK, lots of you doing that one. . . . Rebounding of sports balls? Just about everybody for that one too. Yes, Irena?

IRENA: Could we do something with the last section, coping with collisions? The stuff about seatbelts and airbags? There's no experiment there but there's some activities and maybe we could make something up?

MARK: [*Laughing*] Hey, miss, can we crash some cars?! [*Laughter from other students*]

MS FRASER: [*Dryly*] I don't think so Mark . . . but yes, Irena, I'm sure you –

MARK: [Excitedly] Hey, do you remember crash test dummies?

NATALIE AND IRENA: [*They catch each other's eye, grin, and sing in unison.*] Mmm, mmm, mmm, mmm . . . !

MARK: [*Laughs too but tries to suppress it quickly.*] Nah, not the band *dummies* . . . . I mean the toys? Remember? [*Some nods and 'yeahs' from others*] I had 'em about four years ago –

MS FRASER: [*Rolling her eyes*] Yes, my son had them too. What's your point, Mark?

MARK: Ah, I dunno, but I thought . . . um, maybe we could –

IRENA: [*Butting in, impatiently*] Yeah, for the stuff on collisions, you know, miz? We could –

MARK: – make some models or something –

MS FRASER: Sure, that could be interesting . . . do you two want to try to design some sort of test or demonstration or something? [*Some other students express interest too.*] Yes, OK, well, see what you can come up with . . . does anyone else have any other ideas at the moment? Yes, Dasuke?

DASUKE: [*Quietly, hesitant*] I . . . would it be possible to – I looked at the force-distance graphs and . . . and . . . thought they might work better on computer. I tried – I made the chart with Microsoft Graph. . . . You can work out answers without counting squares –

MS FRASER: So would you like to try modelling some kind of force and energy transformations as one of your investigations, Dasuke? That would be good. . . . OK, one thing I'd like you all to do is a bit of revision on things like force, mass, acceleration. . . . I think you did some of that last year? [*Some groans from students*] What's the problem?

NATALIE: Oh, you know, like that stuff about work at the beginning of the chapter and it only being work if you're moving something . . . it just seems *so* stupid . . . [*Mutters of agreement from other students*]

MS FRASER: I actually agree with you, Natalie. And that's why I think a bit of revision might be useful. I know that some teachers and books try to make it sound reasonable but I can see why it mightn't make sense to you. But I don't think you should worry too much about that. I didn't understand it until I learned a lot more about the history of science than I did when I was in school or even when I was doing my teacher training. I think that probably many people who write the textbooks don't understand it either – including the author of yours. With all due respect to Mr Parsons, I think that the first page of the chapter you're reading, where he writes things like 'when *you* use a force to move something, *you* are working', I think that's all a bit pointless. And that so-called 'fact file' really annoys me . . . but, look, I'll come back to that later. I actually think it helps if you remember that most of these definitions and equations to do with forces and work and things were invented by one man – Isaac Newton – back in the seventeenth century. He assumed that God had created the universe like building a gigantic machine and set it running – like a huge bit of clockwork – and Newton was trying to figure out the rules it ran by, like trying to figure out how God had programmed it. . . . And people then – and for the next couple of hundred years – thought Newton had come up with the right answers. For a lot of purposes, he'd come up with some pretty *good* answers, they seemed to work, but – yes, Mark?

MARK: Ah . . . well, it's probably nothing . . . but that album, Crash Test Dummies, you know, what was it called . . . ?

NATALIE: *God Shuffled His Feet* . . .

MARK: That's it – well, I was just . . . nah, I'll listen to it tonight – haven't played it for ages – there was something – I'll let you know tomorrow if I find what I'm thinking of.

MS FRASER: OK, now, about the revision – it looks like most of you want to do the bicycle braking exercise? [*Nods, murmurs of assent from class*] We can do that tomorrow – if as many as possible of you bring your bikes tomorrow that would be great – we're going to have to do a lot of that outside – but in the time we've got today I thought we could do something in here. What I've done is to put some old textbooks at your workstations – they're all open at pracs that try to get you to understand relationships between force and mass and energy and things like that. Some are the books you used last year, some are older – there's even my old Form 3 science textbook. All the equipment you might need is on the front bench. Now, what I want you to do is – well, first, I just want you to do what the book says you should do – but that's not all. What I really want to find out from you is which bits of it make sense and which bits don't. If anything the book says you should do doesn't make sense, jot down why you think that. But also try to make a note of the things that *do* make sense. I guess what I really want you to do is try to figure out what the person who wrote the textbook wants you to learn from doing what they say – and I want you to tell me, *with reasons*, how good a job you think they are doing. . . . OK? So, you can start on that now. . . . [*The last sentence is almost drowned out by the noise of scraping chairs as the students start moving around the room to look at the books at their workstation and then collect and set up the equipment.* IRENA *lingers.*]

IRENA: Miz? Is that like – well, my mum's an architect and I asked her about this forces stuff and she said she'd sort of learned it when she was at uni but that the only people she knew who really understood it were the – what did she call them? The building – no, the structural engineers – but she said that they never really used it either 'cos mostly they had tables and things they looked up or it was just, like, well, they just tried it out to see what happened . . . [*To Dasuke, who is nearby and has been listening*] Your dad's an engineer or something isn't he?

DASUKE: Yes. But he – oh . . . no, I don't think I can explain. . . .

IRENA: What?

MS FRASER: It's OK if you can't explain, Dasuke, but we'd be – well I know I'd be interested. . . .

DASUKE: I . . . I showed my father. [*Holds up textbook.*] He is mechanical engineer – or really designer. He designs, not cars, but machines for *building* cars. He . . . he said that when he is designing machines, physics is not so important as *shibusa* . . . . [*Laughs*] I don't believe him!

MS FRASER: [*Puzzled*] Sorry Dasuke, I don't quite understand . . . but if, well, if your father designs machinery and he thinks something's more important than physics – then I'd like to know more about whatever it is – did you say 'shibusa'?

DASUKE: [*A little embarrassed*] It doesn't matter – yes, *shibusa*, he says things work best if they are *shibui* – but . . . I don't know, I still think he knows this mechanics, you know, forces and things. . . . [*Shrugs*]

MS FRASER: Well, if you'd like to find out more from your dad and tell us . . . ? [*Dasuke nods; he has had enough for now.*][13]

Notes

1 The textbook being used by the class is Cooper *et al.* (1988).
2 The handout is a photocopy of two pages from Parsons (1996: 150–1).
3 Quoted from an email message posted to the list-server <postech@weber.ucsd.edu>

on Friday 13 March 1992. The subject of Chapman's message is: 'Science is stupid, part nineteen.'

4 Cooper *et al.* (1988: 164) leave the reader with no doubt about their faith in Newton's explanations: 'There are all sorts of forces acting on things which move on the surface of the earth. Since ancient Greek times this has caused confusion among some scientists. In 1687 Sir Isaac Newton sorted out most of the problems.'

5 It should be noted that an analysis of the consistency between reality and a representation is different from applying Karl Popper's (1965) doctrine of falsification, since Popper maintained that congruence is a conceptual possibility. But as Hayles (1993: 35) explains, the most we can say is that a representation is 'consistent with reality as it is experienced by someone with our sensory equipment and previous contextual experience. Congruence cannot be achieved because it implies perception without a perceiver.'

6 Lemke's book covers some of the same thematic territory that is explored, somewhat more speculatively, by Clive Sutton (1992). However, Lemke's research is more empirical (he includes examples of transcripts and detailed structural analyses of classroom conversations) and more explicitly positioned as socially critical educational inquiry.

7 This approach would provide another meaning for the 'prac crit' – a commonplace of English teaching and assessment in which students are asked to compare critically two literary works (such as two poems on a similar theme) with each other.

8 In some ways this suggestion can be seen as a logical extension (from the sociology of science to education) of what Latour (1988, 1993) calls 'actor network theory', which assumes that nonhuman 'things' as well as humans must be regarded as actors in any socio-technological assemblage or network.

9 For arguments about the place of fiction in curriculum inquiry and research methology, and examples of its uses, see also Gough (1994, 1995, 1996, 1997).

10 The textbook being used by the class is Parsons (1996).

11 The 'CSF' is Victoria's (1995) *Curriculum and Standards Framework*, which provides the broad policy framework within which Victorian schools are expected to design their curricula. The 'standards' are expressed as statements of learning outcomes which students are expected to achieve at different levels of their schooling. The textbook by Parsons (1996) is in a series deliberately designed to fit the National Science Statement and Profiles and adaptations of it such as the CSF.

12 Subjects in the Victorian Certificate of Education (years 11 and 12 of secondary school) are designed around 'work requirements' and 'common assessment tasks' (CATs). Work requirements specify broad learning processes and outcomes that may have a wide range of local variations. For example, in VCE Environmental Studies, one of the six work requirements specified for year 11 is a systems analysis of a local environment. Many schools have adopted work requirements as a curriculum structuring principle in years 9 and 10.

13 The Japanese word 'shibusa' refers to aesthetic values. For something to be *shibui* means that it has qualities that imbue it with the most valued expressions of aesthetic attainment in Japan. These qualities include simplicity, implicitness, modesty, silence, naturalness and roughness (see, for example, Yanagi 1972). A key principle is that of the *unfinished*: if something is *shibui* it invites participation by the observer – it opens up new possibilities because it is unfinished. That is why I have stopped writing the revised playlet at this point. It is intended to be an invitation of the unfinished.

References

Baudrillard, Jean (1983) *Simulations* (trans., Paul Foss, Paul Patton, Philip Beitchman), New York: Semiotext(e).

—— (1988) *Selected Writings* (trans., Mark Poster). Cambridge: Polity Press.

Casti, John L. (1997) *Would-be Worlds: How Simulation is Changing the Frontiers of Science*, New York: John Wiley & Sons.

Charlesworth, Max, Farrall, Lyndsay, Stokes, Terry and Turnbull, David (1989) *Life among the Scientists: an Anthropological Study of an Australian Scientific Community*, Melbourne: Oxford University Press.

Cohen, Jack and Stewart, Ian (1994) *The Collapse of Chaos: Discovering Simplicity in a Complex World*, New York: Viking Penguin.

Cooper, Viv, Pople, Stephen, Ray, Bryan, Seidel, Pam and Williams, Michael (1988) *Science to Sixteen 1*, revised Australian edn, Melbourne: Oxford University Press.

Favre, Alexandre, Guitton, Henri, Guitton, Jean, Lichnerowicz, André and Wolff, Etienne (1995) *Chaos and Determinism: Turbulence as a Paradigm for Complex Systems Converging toward Final States* (trans., Bertram Eugene Schwarzbach), Baltimore and London: Johns Hopkins University Press.

Fensham, Peter J., Gunstone, Richard F. and White, Richard T. (eds) (1994) *The Content of Science: a Constructivist Approach to its Teaching and Learning*, London: Falmer Press.

Gough, Noel (1993a) *Laboratories in Fiction: Science Education and Popular Media*, Geelong: Deakin University Press.

—— (1993b) 'Environmental education, narrative complexity and postmodern science/fiction', *International Journal of Science Education* 15(5): 607–25.

—— (1994) 'Narration, reflection, diffraction: aspects of fiction in educational inquiry', *Australian Educational Researcher* 21(3): 47–76.

—— (1995) 'Manifesting cyborgs in curriculum inquiry', *Melbourne Studies in Education* 29(1): 71–83.

—— (1996) 'Textual authority in Bram Stoker's *Dracula*; or, what's really at stake in action research?' *Educational Action Research* 4(2): 257–65.

—— (1997) 'Weather™ Incorporated: environmental education, postmodern identities, and technocultural constructions of nature', *Canadian Journal of Environmental Education* 2: 145–62.

Haraway, Donna J. (1989) *Primate Visions: Gender, Race, and Nature in the World of Modern Science*, New York: Routledge.

Hayles, N. Katherine (1993) 'Constrained constructivism: locating scientific inquiry in the theater of representation', in George Levine (ed.) *Realism and Representation: Essays on the Problem of Realism in Relation to Science, Literature and Culture*, Madison, WI: University of Wisconsin Press, pp. 27–43.

Hodgkin, R.A. (1985) *Playing and Exploring: Education through the Discovery of Order*, London and New York: Methuen.

Kauffman, Stuart (1995) *At Home in the Universe: the Search for the Laws of Self-Organization and Complexity*, New York and Oxford: Oxford University Press.

Latour, Bruno (1983) 'Give me a laboratory and I will raise the world', in K.D. Knorr-Cetina and M. Mulkay (eds) *Science Observed: Perspectives on the Social Study of Science*, New York: Sage Publications, pp. 141–70.

—— (1984) *Les Microbes, Guerre et Paix, Suivi de Irreductions*, Paris: Metaillie.

—— (1987) *Science in Action: How to Follow Scientists and Engineers through Society* (trans., Catherine Porter), Milton Keynes: Open University Press.

—— (1988) *The Pasteurization of France* (trans., Alan Sheridan and John Law,), Cambridge, MA: Harvard University Press.

—— (1993) *We Have Never Been Modern* (trans., Catherine Porter), Cambridge, MA: Harvard University Press.

Latour, Bruno and Woolgar, Steve (1979) *Laboratory Life: the Social Construction of Scientific Facts*, Beverly Hills, CA: Sage.

Lemke, Jay L. (1990) *Talking Science: Language, Learning, and Values*, Norwood, NJ: Ablex Publishing Corporation.

McGowan, John (1991) *Postmodernism and its Critics*, Ithaca, NY: Cornell University Press.

Parsons, Malcolm (1996) *Science 4*, Melbourne: Heinemann.

Popper, Karl (1965) *Conjectures and Refutations: the Growth of Scientific Knowledge*, 2nd edn, New York: Basic Books.

Sutton, Clive (1992) *Words, Science and Learning*, Buckingham and Philadelphia: Open University Press.

Victoria, Board of Studies (1995) *Curriculum and Standards Framework*, Carlton, Victoria: Board of Studies.

Winnicott, D.W. (1971) *Playing and Reality*, London: Tavistock.

Yanagi, Muneyoshi (1972) *The Unknown Craftsman: a Japanese Insight into Beauty*, Tokyo: Kodansha International.

Part III

THE SEARCH FOR AUTHENTICITY

One of the recurring themes of practical work over the last century or more has been its quest to mirror, model or mimic real scientific activity. In some ways this is rather like the search for the holy grail – however, as Leach has already argued, science education has a large responsibility to teach people about the nature of science, scientific methods and how scientists work. This responsibility has an *intrinsic* justification; that is, to know about the activity of science is an essential part of scientific literacy and the public understanding of science, and it is often given a two-fold *extrinsic* justification. First, it is required as part of education for citizenship and the ability to be a decision maker and voter in a democracy imbued with science; and second, the activity of working like a scientist and the skills of scientific method are said to be valued by employers (a point argued by Woolnough in this section of the book).

This part of the book begins with the clear analysis which readers have come to expect from Hodson. He begins by considering existing attempts at creating 'authentic' school science, and identifies nine common myths which have been promoted (wittingly and unwittingly) not only by practical work but also by science textbooks and published schemes. He examines each one in detail and shows (in a similar way to Gough earlier) how they create a mythologised version of science in education. Hodson talks about some of the features of authentic science and describes how some of the myths about science can be dispelled. He describes three teaching strategies in some detail: practical exercises, historical case studies and student-led inquiries. These can all help to convey a more authentic view of science. Hodson also stresses the important role of ICT for the future of practical work, and describes particularly how the use of simulations in science education can develop some of the authentic skills of doing science. This theme on the value of ICT is taken up by three short chapters later in the book which illustrate the value, or indeed the added-value, of the use of ICT.

Hodson also signals another theme which is taken up by Sutton and Osborne later in the book: the importance of allowing learners to practise the language of science.

Hodson's belief in student-led inquiries is the starting point for Woolnough's chapter, the second in this section. Like Hodson, Woolnough's writing on practical work over the last decade and more is well known. Here he argues that school science should prepare students to live in a scientific democracy and also prepare them for work in a scientific, technological world. In common with all the authors in this book (we do have some solid ground) Woolnough begins from the premise that scientists do not work to one scientific method. One of the facets of the work of scientists neglected in curricula is the personal or tacit knowledge which can be developed but which is often neglected in the sanitised world of school science (the same theme of implicit knowledge is taken up in a later chapter, from a different angle, by Nott and Masters). Using a number of illustrations, Woolnough describes 'authentic science activity of a practical problem-solving nature'. He argues for the importance of doing messy, problem-solving research projects which can develop personal knowledge as well as some of the skills and attitudes which employers say they require.

Finally, room is given to Jenifer Helms to give a full and extensive account of a real-life project undertaken by school pupils in the wetlands of the West Coast of the USA. Her case study needs to be published and read in full in order to appreciate the many facets of authentic science involved in community-based practical work of this nature. Helms puts forward a useful working definition of the 'activity of science' which has a number of different dimensions. These dimensions are concerned with the methods, the questions, the context, the objects of study, and the goals and purposes of science. She focuses on these dimensions in describing her study of the wetlands project, and shows how they can be applied in considering the authenticity of practical work. Helms describes some of the perceived gains (cognitive and affective) in a project of this kind – and with commendable honesty she also points out the limitations and problems associated with this kind of practical science work in the community.

6

IS THIS REALLY WHAT
SCIENTISTS DO?

Seeking a more authentic science in
and beyond the school laboratory

Derek Hodson

> The laboratory sets science apart from most school subjects
> . . . communicating understanding of, and the skills asso-
> ciated with, scientific method. Without the laboratory, it
> could be difficult for students to comprehend what scientists
> do.
>
> (White 1988: 186)

As Millar (Chapter 2 in this volume) illustrates, practical work in school
science has a range of educational purposes. Prominent among them is a
concern to teach students about the methods of scientific inquiry. It
follows that practical activities devised for this purpose should be
grounded in a view of science that is philosophically sound and that
opportunities should be provided for students to undertake authentic
scientific inquiries for themselves and by themselves. Sadly, in most
schools, these requirements are only rarely met (Hodson 1993a). In
many schools there is an almost unrelieved diet of worksheet-driven
'cookbook exercises' in which students slavishly follow teacher directions
and only very occasionally engage in serious thought about what they are
doing or why they are doing it. Moreover, science is presented as a fixed,
algorithmic process in which a successful outcome (namely, the 'right
answer') is virtually guaranteed if the sub-processes are carried out
'correctly'. By implication, scientists are portrayed as possessed of a
superior rationality and an all-purpose method for arriving at the truth.
This chapter employs perspectives deriving from the philosophy and sociology of science to articulate a more authentic view of scientific inquiry and to
shed light on the twin tasks of learning about scientific inquiry and learning
to conduct scientific inquiries.

Some problems of authenticity

Despite a major effort in recent years to direct the attention of teachers and curriculum developers to the importance of considerations in the history, philosophy and sociology of science (Matthews 1992), many school science curricula (and practical work activities, in particular) continue to promote deficient or distorted views of science. Apart from concern that a significant aspect of humankind's cultural achievement should be so poorly understood by students, there are very clear indications that these distortions and falsehoods serve to exclude many girls and members of ethnic minorities from crossing the border into the culture of science (Hodson 1998).

One of the fundamental assumptions of much practical work in schools is that observation and experiment can provide secure and certain knowledge about the universe. Because observations are regarded as independent of theory and independent of the particular life experiences of the observer, there is little incentive for teachers to look closely at the theoretical framework within which a practical lesson is designed. Because knowledge is assumed to derive directly from observation, emphasis becomes concentrated on *doing* rather than on *thinking*, and little or no time is set aside for discussion, argument and negotiation of meaning. Increasing emphasis on the sub-processes and procedures of science and the 'proper' and careful collection of data diverts attention away from questions of what the data might mean. Evidence is considered unproblematic and the possibility of alternative interpretations is given scant attention. This culture of school science 'experiments' is beautifully captured by Nadeau and Désautels.

> The work done in the laboratory by students can be no more than a *simulation* of the method followed by scientists. The hypothesis is established by the teacher, and the students' task consists of manoeuvring to arrive at the predicted results. As a rule, most students are uncertain as to what is involved and they merely carry out the directions in the laboratory guide step by step, as though following a recipe. The validity of the results obtained is seldom questioned, and if by chance the experiment fails, the teacher imposes a conclusion. The students are asked to write a laboratory report, which will be corrected, but the results are rarely used in class.
>
> (1984: 33)

As a consequence, experiments are regarded as decisive tests of the validity of hypotheses and conjectures. This myth is reinforced by insistence on a third person, passive voice, emotionally neutral style of laboratory report in which the experimentally determined factual evidence supposedly 'speaks for itself', and any suggestion that the experimenter/inquirer is engaged in the active construction of meaning is carefully excised.

Embedded in this brief characterisation of school practical work are a number of myths about science and science education that are transmitted, consciously or unconsciously, by teachers and curriculum materials. I am certainly not claiming that all nine myths are promoted by all science curricula; rather, that most curricula promote one or more of them and that, across the range of curricular provision, all nine are in evidence.

1   Observation provides direct and reliable access to secure knowledge.
2   Science starts with observation.
3   Science proceeds via induction.
4   Experiments are decisive.
5   Science comprises discrete, generic processes.
6   Scientific inquiry is a simple, algorithmic procedure.
7   Science is a value-free activity.
8   The so-called 'scientific attitudes' are essential to the effective practice of science.
9   All scientists possess these attitudes.

Space does not permit a detailed rebuttal of each of these misunderstandings about science and scientific inquiry. Suffice it to say that, in practice, every experiment is designed, conducted and interpreted within a theoretical matrix (an agreed way of conceptualising events and phenomena), a procedural matrix (a current 'method' or 'practice' underpinned by theories and conventions about how to conduct, record and report experiments) and an instrumental matrix (involving various theories of instrumentation). It is this theoretical understanding that gives both purpose and form to experiments. Further, if theories are incommensurable, a point on which many philosophers of science agree, there can be no crucial experiment to decide between them. Such experiments would require competing theories to make mutually exclusive predictions about the same events. In practice, competing theories address the world in different ways (often using different concepts) and, therefore, make different kinds of predictions about observable phenomena. Usually, therefore, it is possible only to provide an experimental evaluation of a theory *on its own terms*.

We seriously mislead students when we pretend that the kinds of experiments they perform in class constitute a straightforward and reliable means of choosing between rival theories. Because of the theory dependence of experiments, considerable judgement is involved in appraising the significance of apparently falsifying evidence. Experimental testing of theories is not, therefore, an infallible, single step, but a multi-step decision-making process monitored and validated by the community. Experiment and theory have an interdependent and interactive relationship: experiments assist theory building (by giving feedback concerning theoretical speculations), and theory, in turn, determines the kinds of experiments that can and should be carried out, and determines how experimentally acquired data should be interpreted. Both experiment and theory, then, are *tools for thinking* in the quest for satisfactory and convincing explanations.

Nor is experimentation the simple application of an all-purpose algorithm comprising a series of content-free, generalisable and transferable steps, as advocates of the so-called Process Approach to science education allege (Wellington 1989). Real science is an untidy, unpredictable activity that requires each scientist to devise their own course of action. In that sense, there is *no* method. In approaching a particular situation, scientists choose an approach they consider to be appropriate to the particular task-in-hand by making a selection of processes and procedures from the range of those available and approved by the community of practitioners. Further, scientists refine their approach to a problem, develop greater understanding of it and devise more appropriate and productive ways of proceeding *all at the same time*. As soon as an idea is developed, it is subjected to evaluation (by observation, experiment, comparison with other theories and so on). Sometimes that evaluation leads to new ideas, to further and different experiments, or even to a complete re-casting of the original idea or reformulation of the problem. Thus, almost every move that a scientist makes during an inquiry changes the situation in some way, so that the next decisions and moves are made in an altered context. Consequently, scientific inquiry is holistic, fluid, reflexive, context-dependent and idiosyncratic, not a matter of following a set of rules that requires particular behaviours at particular times (Hodson 1992, 1993b). It is best summed up by Percy Bridgman's (1950) remark that 'scientific method, as far as it is a method, is nothing more than doing one's damnedest with one's mind, no holds barred'.

It follows that real scientific inquiry is characterised by frequent false starts and blind alleys; it can be, and often is, re-directed by unexpected events and by unanticipated technical problems; it can be profoundly influenced by the availability (or not) of particular laboratory equipment or its unexpected malfunctioning, by the publication of a research paper in the same field or chance conversation with another researcher.

Demythologising the science curriculum

The various myths about science can be dispelled by a combination of practically based exercises, historical case studies and student-directed inquiries. For example, the theory-laden nature of observation and its dependence on the prior knowledge and experience of the observer can be addressed via optical, tactile and auditory illusions, puzzle pictures, and the kind of observation exercises described by Nadeau and Désautels (1984). Classification tasks, use of puzzle boxes, feely bags and scavenger hunts (Hodson 1986) can help students recognise the theory dependence of classification, measurement, hypothesising, inferring, and all the other activities involved in doing science. The essential point is that, without a bold assumption of previously validated theories, observation and experiment – and the theory building that they inform and validate – would be impossible. A thoughtful discussion of some of the theory assumed in the design of common laboratory instruments can help students to appreciate that the supposed distinction between objective observation and theoretical inference is less clear than some science textbooks would assert, and is more a characteristic of their own stage of conceptual understanding (and their confidence in it) than a fundamental demarcation. When an observational exercise or an experiment from earlier in the course is repeated, the new observational language and the new interpretation of the results can be shown to include theoretical notions that were previously unknown. That new theoretical understanding may subsequently lead to the design of quite different experiments and the focus of attention on different aspects of a phenomenon or event.

Historical case studies can challenge myths about science being value-free and dependent on a particular cluster of so-called 'scientific attitudes' (objectivity, open-mindedness, intellectual integrity, communality and the like) and can help students to recognise that science and technology (like art, music, literature and politics) are human endeavours that influence, and are influenced by, the sociocultural context in which they are located. At the simplest level, studies of the societal impact of inventions such as the steam engine, the printing press or the computer can be used to bring about an awareness that science and technology are powerful forces that shape the lives of people and other species, and impact significantly on the environment as a whole. They can also be used to show that scientific and technological development are both culturally dependent and culturally transforming. In other words, science is a product of its time and place, and can sometimes change quite radically the ways in which people think and act. The science of Galileo, Newton, Darwin and Einstein, for example, profoundly changed our perception of humanity's place in the universe and precipitated enormous changes in the way people address issues in politics, economics and history.

As Young (1987) says, 'Science is practice. There is no other science than the science that gets done.' What we do – that is, the questions we ask, the kind of problems we perceive and try to solve, and so on – depends on who we are and where we are. Science and technology are driven by the needs, interests, values and aspirations of the society that sustains them. This is well illustrated by a study of such scientific curiosities as phlogiston theory, transmutation of the elements and theories of spontaneous generation, and by consideration of contemporary 'alternative' or pseudosciences. Why, for example, is acupuncture dismissed by Western scientists, despite its widespread and successful use in the East? The work of Wilhelm Reich, once widely respected but now totally discredited, might make an interesting study. So, too, the history of the notion of continental drift, now the basis of plate tectonics, but once dismissed as fanciful. The ways in which social and cultural influences can lead to distortion and misuse of science for political goals can be highlighted by studies of phrenology and its role in under-pinning the unjust social system of nineteenth-century England (Hodson and Prophet 1986) and the Soviet suppression of Mendelian genetics in favour of Lamarckism during the 1950s. In similar vein, articles by Arnold (1990,1992) reveal the extent to which some German archaeologists colla-borated with the Nazi regime in promoting the claim that the Germanic culture of Northern Europe had been responsible for virtually every major achievement of Western civilisation, and that the Greeks were really Germans who had migrated south during Neolithic times to avoid a natural catastrophe. From here it is but a short step to consideration of scientific racism: the misuse of the notion of 'race' to perpetuate stereotyping, legitimise discrimination and institutionalise injustice (Hodson 1993c; Hodson and Dennick 1994).

Of course, a full appreciation of the impact of sociocultural factors on the development of scientific ideas cannot be gained by a simple chronological survey. To gain proper insight, students need to understand the nature of the issues and problems as they appeared at the time; they need to see the false starts and unproductive lines of speculation that were sometimes followed; they need to appreciate the part played by individual creativity, personal ambition, and social and economic pressure. In other words, historical studies must enable learners to immerse themselves in the cultural and intellectual milieu of the time. Drama, literature, music and art can play a key role in establishing the appropriate context – a somewhat different interpretation of 'practical work' in school science than is usual.

If science and technology are driven by sociocultural factors, it follows that different societies will define and organise science differently and so produce different science. It may be profitable to ask, 'How much could be changed (aims, values, methods, criteria of validity, content and so on) and it still be considered science?' It is intriguing to ask, for example, whether it is meaningful to recognise a distinctive 'African science' – a style of inquiry in which priorities, practices and criteria of judgement are more in sym-pathy with traditional values and beliefs (Jegede 1995, 1998). Christie (1991) asks similar questions with respect to the 'science' (knowledge of the natural world) developed and practised by the Aboriginal people of Australia. Others might ask whether it is legitimate to talk of 'feminist science'. In my view, there is much to be gained from confronting students with such questions (Hodson 1993c, 1997), but see Loving (1997) for a counter view.

The final cluster of myths concerning scientific method is best addressed by student-driven practical work and, necessarily, careful reflection on it. While scientists are engaged in a constant struggle to make sense of the often ill-defined problem situation in which they are working, school science students are presented with problems that are often very clearly defined and have clearly articulated procedures that lead to successful outcomes. 'Years of effort have produced foolproof "experiments" where the right answer is certain to emerge for everyone in the class if the laboratory instructions are followed. Science is presented as a body of information which is (and can be) verified and certain' (Kirschner 1992: 278). Authenticity requires that students struggle to frame their own problems, devise their own strategies, look for ways to interpret and make sense of their findings. In traditional laboratory work, all theorising (identifying the area of concern, stating the problem to be investigated, designing the inquiry, planning the inquiry strategies and techniques, interpreting the data, designing the report or communication) is the responsibility of the teacher, with periodic but rather cursory consultation with the more vocal students. Teachers decide what to study, how to study it and how to explain, or explain away, discrepant events and unanticipated results (Masters and Nott, Chapter 12 in this volume); students act in a predominantly technician's role of carrying out the lab operations. The major shift I am advocating is from 'student as technician' to 'student as creative scientist', with sole responsibility for the inquiry. While students will necessarily be constrained in their approach by what they currently know and by the laboratory skills they currently possess, it is ownership of and sole responsibility for the inquiry that provides the stimulus for the extension and development of both their conceptual and procedural knowledge.

Further learning occurs when students are encouraged to write about their inquiries in less formal ways. An investigator's logbook is an ideal vehicle for encouraging students to reflect on questions such as: What am I going to do? Why am I doing it? What difficulties do I anticipate? Is the investigation proceeding as planned? Do I need to re-think? Could anything be improved? What is being acknowledged here is that one of the key elements in doing science, and a consequence of the dynamism discussed earlier, is *changing one's mind* – going back to an earlier stage in order to try something different.

Working in this relatively unstructured way is the only way in which students can experience what it is like to conduct a scientific inquiry. Of course, poor design, unexpected difficulties and just plain bad luck will sometimes intervene and render the inquiry inconclusive. But much will have been learned about the vagaries and uncertainties of scientific inquiry, and much will have been done to combat the myths that currently surround the curriculum portrayal of scientific practice.

As part of the 'myth reduction' exercise, it should be emphasised that not all scientific inquiries are experimental in nature. Many fields of scientific endeavour deal with events that are remote and inaccessible in time and space, and so make little or no use of experiments. In some fields, experimentation may be possible in principle but is ruled inadmissible for ethical reasons, or is too difficult, dangerous or expensive. It is here that correlational studies play a crucial role. In a sense, studies seeking correlations among variables are more faithful than experimental inquiry to the supposed open-mindedness of science because they make fewer assumptions about the nature of the interactions. They also provide opportunities to study phenomena and events in natural settings rather than the contrived situation of the laboratory. It is also the case that many field settings are simply unsuitable for experimental inquiry because they are too complex or too fragile and uncertain. Making science experiences in school more authentic necessitates a shift away from the current preoccupation with experimentation and the 'illusion of certainty' (Hodson and Bencze 1998) that accompanies it. Bencze (1996) provides a detailed argument for the adoption of correlational studies in science education and a critical discussion of their distinctive features, including systematic inquiry via statistical control.

Creating opportunities for doing science

Because the ways in which scientists work are not fixed and not entirely predictable, and because they involve a component that is experience-dependent in a very personal sense, they are not teachable by conventional didactic methods. That is, one cannot learn to do science by learning a prescription or set of processes to be applied in all situations. The only effective way to learn to do science is by doing science, alongside a skilled and experienced practitioner who can provide on-the-job support, criticism and advice. It is here that the notion of *apprenticeship* is useful. As Jean Lave (1988) says: 'Apprentices learn to think, argue, act, and interact in increasingly knowledgable ways with people who do something well, by doing it with them as legitimate, peripheral participants.' For Lave, apprenticeship is not just a process of internalising knowledge and skills, it is the process of becoming a member of a community of practice. Developing an identity as a member of the community and becoming more knowledgeable and skilful are part of the same process, with the former motivating, shaping and giving meaning to the latter. 'Newcomers become oldtimers through a social process of increasingly centripetal participation, which depends on legitimate access to ongoing community practice' (Lave: 1991: 68). When they are given opportunities to participate peripherally in the activities of the community, newcomers pick up the relevant social language, imitate the behaviour of skilled and knowledgeable members, and gradually start to act in accordance with the community norms. In an apprenticeship model of learning, both the nature and timing of teacher intervention are crucial: deciding how to attend to each learner in a way that is appropriate to them, taking into account their unique personal framework of understanding, including its affective and social components; and deciding when to encourage and support, when to direct or instruct, and when to involve others. Knowing when, where, how much and what type of guidance, critical feedback and support are needed to facilitate effective learning, and the development of good learning behaviours and inquiry skills, is a matter of professional judgement, deriving from experience and thoughtful reflection on it. Too much guidance can interfere with students' thought processes, act to frustrate problem solving and lead to premature closure; too little guidance can leave students unable to make satisfactory progress and can lead to feelings of frustration, and even alienation. To be effective, teacher guidance and assistance needs to be pitched slightly beyond the current level of unaided performance – that is, in what Vygotsky (1978) refers to as the 'zone of proximal development'.

Constant dialogue between teachers and students is, of course, essential if good intervention decisions are to be made. It is the nature of the language used by the teacher during these exchanges that establishes the interpretive framework within which students are able to make scientific sense of whatever is being studied. Again, there is an issue of fine professional judgement: neither imposing meaning nor permitting students to construct whatever meaning happens to suit them, for whatever reasons. Rather, teachers should seek to create a dialogic context in which meaning is *co-constructed*.

> The teacher remains in charge, but his or her exercise of control is manifested not in a once-and-for-all choice between intervening with the 'correct' answer or standing back and leaving the students to find their own solution, but in the making of moment-by-moment decisions about how to proceed, based on knowledge of the topic, understanding of the dynamics of classroom interaction, intentions with respect to the task, and a continuous monitoring of the ongoing talk.
>
> (Wells and Chang-Wells 1992: 46–7)

Clear and skilful demonstration of expert practice ('modelling') and the provision of opportunities for critical questioning, interspersed with opportunities for guided participation by the 'novice', provided they are informed by critical feedback from the 'expert', comprise the stock-in-trade of the apprenticeship approach to the teaching and learning of complex tasks in 'real life' practical situations (Lave and Wenger 1991). For the more formal situation of school-based learning, the following three-phase approach may be relatively easily implemented.

- *Modelling*, where the teacher exhibits the desired behaviour;
- *Guided practice*, where students perform with help from the teacher;
- *Application*, where students perform independently of the teacher.

Hodson and Hodson (1998a,b) discuss the key elements of modelling, and little is to be gained by reiterating that discussion here. To achieve intellectual independence, however, students must take responsibility for their own learning and for the planning, executing and reporting of their own inquiries. In other words, learning as assisted performance must enable students, eventually, to go beyond what they have learned and to use knowledge in creative ways in solving novel problems and building new understanding. Consequently, alongside the modelled investigations, students should work through a carefully sequenced programme of (1) investigative exercises, during which the teacher acts as learning resource, facilitator, consultant and critic, and (2) simple holistic investigations conducted independently of the teacher. Investigative exercises provide opportunities for students to learn through a cycle of practice and reflection, and to achieve, with the careful assistance of the teacher, a level of performance they could not achieve unaided. Eventually, students will be able to proceed autonomously: choosing their own topics and problems, and approaching them in their own way. By this stage, they are responsible for the whole process, from initial problem identification to final evaluation and communication to others.

Of course, that communication needs to be in a language and form that make sense to the inquirer, and little is to be gained by too early an insistence on formal write-ups. Much can be achieved by creating opportunities for students to justify their choice of topic, design and interpretation to an audience of peers and experts. Conferencing and public presentation has three important learning outcomes: it assists and develops conceptual and procedural understanding; it mirrors authentic scientific practice; it contributes to the establishment of a learning community. It also gives students a valuable opportunity to practise the language of science, an aspect of science education that is much neglected (Lemke 1990).

In any scientific inquiry, students achieve three kinds of learning. First, enhanced conceptual understanding of whatever is being studied or investigated. Second, enhanced procedural knowledge – that is, learning more about experiments and correlational studies, and acquiring a more sophisticated understanding of observation, experiment and theory. Third, enhanced investigative expertise, which may eventually develop into scientific connoisseurship. Providing opportunities for students to report and debate their findings, and supporting them in reflecting critically on personal progress made during the inquiry, are key elements in achieving this integrative understanding. However, because of the idiosyncratic nature of scientific investigation, and the highly specialised but necessarily limited range of conceptual issues involved in any particular inquiry, doing science is insufficient in itself to bring about the breadth of conceptual development that a curriculum seeks (Hodson 1996).

Beyond conventional benchwork

While laboratory benchwork is the usual stock-in-trade of the science teacher, many valuable opportunities for learning about science and doing science can be provided by fieldwork. Killerman's (1996) study shows that well-planned fieldwork not only raises students' levels of attainment in tests of conceptual understanding but also has a beneficial impact on their environmental attitudes and attitudes towards conservation. Because they don't disturb, violate or destroy (as experimental inquiries often do), field-based correlational studies are more in keeping with non-exploitative environmental values, and so might be regarded as education *for* the environment, as well as education *about* and *in* the environment.

While fieldwork usually conjures up images of groups of students involved in time-consuming and expensive visits to distant field centres, with consequent large-scale disruption of the regular curriculum and potential alienation of other teachers, it doesn't have to be that way. As Lock (1998) points out, quality fieldwork is possible at low cost and minimal disruption by more imaginative use of sites within the school grounds and by the construction and utilisation of 'model environments', often using cheap and readily available materials. In the context of the foregoing discussion of learning through apprenticeship, it is worth noting that fieldwork sometimes provides opportunities for students to work alongside practising scientists, as in the Wetlands Project described by Helms (Chapter 8 in this volume) and the extensive study of the impact of water pollution and farming methods on insect-eating birds outlined by Cunniff and McMillen (1996), both of which are US ventures. In a British context, Albone *et al.* (1995) list twenty-eight projects, half of which are field-based activities, involving cooperative research between practising scientists and school students. Similar opportunities may arise in zoos, botanic gardens and museums (Griffin 1998).

The use of computer simulations is a particularly powerful technique for enabling students to engage in the more creative aspects of scientific inquiry. In many laboratory-based lessons, students do not have opportunities to engage in hypothesis generation and experimental design because teachers are unwilling to provide the time, meet the cost, or run the risk of students adopting inappropriate, inefficient or potentially hazardous experimental strategies. Consequently, teachers tend to design all the experiments, usually in advance of the lesson, and students merely follow their instructions. With a computer simulation, poor designs can go ahead and any problems can be discovered by the students and modified, or eliminated, quickly and safely. In this way, students learn from their mistakes and are led to investigate more thoroughly and more thoughtfully. More importantly, they learn that designing experiments is not a specialised and difficult business carried out by white-coated experts in sophisticated laboratories. Anyone can do it, including them. Too often, experiments in class are presented as the *only* way of proceeding; by contrast, computer simulations enable different groups of students to come up with different procedures, some of which will work well, some less well, some not at all. This is more like real science. There are at least three learning goals embedded in such experiences. First, students learn much more about the phenomena under investigation and the concepts that can be used in accounting for them, because they have more time and opportunity to manipulate those concepts. Second, they acquire some of the thinking and strategic planning skills of the creative scientist. Third, they learn that science is about people thinking, guessing and trying things that sometimes work and sometimes fail.

Interrogation of computerised databases enables students to explore ideas, to make predictions and speculate about relationships, and to check them against the facts quickly and reliably without the restrictions of worksheets and teacher directions, and without the attendant 'noise' of benchwork. These methods have made it possible for learners to investigate thoroughly their own questions about a whole range of things without the constraints imposed by inadequate laboratory facilities, underdeveloped practical skills, insufficient time, lack of materials or considerations of personal safety. Although there is no benchwork involved, these activities constitute *doing science* in a very real sense. By using the computer as a tool to find answers to their own questions, students develop real problem-solving and inquiry skills. Problem situations have to be analysed, questions formulated and searches planned. Through such activities students learn to identify problems that are significant, worth investigating, and susceptible of systematic inquiry. At the same time, they learn that not all questions and problems have a unique solution or a right answer, and that many solutions are tentative, and in need of refinement through further inquiry. In other words, doing science often generates as many questions as it answers. As noted earlier, scientific inquiry is not always experimental. Many investigations involve a search for correlations; the systematic search for cause and effect, and the theory building that constitutes an explanation, may follow later. Computerised data management systems are invaluable in facilitating and supporting the sophisticated interrogation, manipulation and presentation of data essential to correlational studies.

It should also be noted that computers have a major role in enhancing benchwork. By displaying data in a variety of ways, plotting graphs, performing calculations, analysing data, collecting data, and even monitoring and controlling experiments, computers can eliminate much of the 'noise' associated with complex apparatus, the boredom of long waiting times and the mathematical problems caused by lengthy and sometimes difficult calculations. Computer-enhanced experimentation enables the student's attention to be focused on the creative phases of scientific inquiry, leaving the technician's role to the computer. In addition, because of the 'stamina' and versatility of the computer, students can investigate a much wider range of phenomena and events, and can utilise techniques that would be otherwise unavailable. In many ways, computer-assisted laboratory work (and computer-assisted fieldwork using portable computerised probes) is more like real scientific research than most conventional school practical activities, so it may be expected to have a beneficial effect on students' image of science, and possibly on their interest in and attitudes towards science.

Effecting change

Arguments abound for the inclusion of history, philosophy and sociology of science issues in pre-service and in-service teacher education courses as a way of ensuring a more authentic presentation of scientific practice in school (Matthews 1992, 1994). However, it seems that teachers' views about the nature of science are not always the principal influence on their design of learning experiences, even for those experiences involving an extensive hands-on component (Hodson 1993d; Lederman 1995; Mellado 1997). Even those teachers who hold clear and coherent views about scientific inquiry do not plan laboratory-based activities consistently in relation to those views, concentrating instead on the immediate concerns of classroom management and on concept acquisition and development. Consequently, there is little prospect of effecting the kind of changes in practical work advocated here by exhorting teachers to change. Even less by mandating change!

Significant change will only result when teachers are able to work through both the philosophical and pedagogical issues for themselves. Authenticity and philosophical validity have to be translated into classroom practice that conforms with other aspects of teachers' classroom practice (including their views of learning), is compatible with the educational climate of the school (the 'school culture') and, to an extent, meets the expectations of the students (Lakin and Wellington 1994). These conditions are most likely to be met when teachers work with a facilitator/researcher/change agent in an action research mode (Hodson and Bencze 1998). Action research is an approach to curriculum development and teacher education that takes account of the uniqueness of each educational situation, acknowledges and builds on the personal professional knowledge of teachers (Connelly and Clandinin 1988), and ensures that all aspects of the curriculum are subject to rigorous critical scrutiny. By giving teachers a substantial measure of control of the curriculum, action research creates the sense of ownership of the curriculum essential to effective and long-lasting change.

References

Albone, A., Collins, N. and Hill, T. (1995) *Scientific Research in Schools: a Compendium of Practical Experience*, Bristol: Clifton Scientific Trust.

Arnold, B. (1990) 'The past as propaganda: totalitarian archaeology in Nazi Germany', *Antiquity* 64: 464–78.

—— (1992) 'The past as propaganda', *Archaeology* 45: 30–7.

Bencze, J.L. (1996) 'Correlational studies in school science: breaking the science-experiment-certainty connection', *School Science Review* 78 (282): 95–101.

Bridgman, P.W. (1950) *The Reflections of a Physicist*, New York: Philosophical Library.

Christie, M. (1991) 'Aboriginal science for the ecologically sustainable future', *Australian Science Teachers Journal* 37: 26–31.

Connelly, F.M. and Clandinin, D.J. (1988) *Teachers as Curriculum Planners*, New York: Teachers College Press.

Cunniff, P. and McMillen, J. (1996) 'Field studies: hands-on, real-science research', *The Science Teacher* 63: 48–51.

Griffin, J. (1998) 'Learning science through practical experiences in museums', *International Journal of Science Education* 20(6).

Hodson, D. (1986) 'Rethinking the role and status of observation in science education', *Journal of Curriculum Studies* 18: 381–96.

—— (1992) 'Assessment of practical work: some considerations in philosophy of science', *Science & Education* 1: 115–44.

—— (1993a) 'Re-thinking old ways: towards a more critical approach to practical work in school science', *Studies in Science Education* 22: 85–142.

—— (1993b) 'Against skills-based testing in science', *Curriculum Studies* 1(1): 127–48.

—— (1993c) 'In search of a rationale for multicultural science education', *Science Education* 77(6): 685–711.

—— (1993d) 'Philosophic stance of secondary school teachers, curriculum experiences, and children's understanding of science: some preliminary findings', *Interchange* 1 and 2: 41–52.

—— (1996) 'Laboratory work as scientific method: three decades of confusion and distortion', *Journal of Curriculum Studies* 28: 115–35.

—— (1998) 'Personalizing, de-mythologizing and politicizing: critical multiculturalism in science and technology education', in S. May (ed.) *Critical Multiculturalism: Rethinking Multicultural and Antiracist Education*, Lewes: Falmer Press.

Hodson, D. and Bencze, L. (1998) 'Becoming critical about practical work: changing views and changing practice through action research', *International Journal of Science Education* 20(6).

Hodson, D. and Dennick, R. (1994) 'Antiracist education: a special role for the history of science and technology', *School Science & Mathematics* 94(5): 255–62.

Hodson, D. and Hodson, J. (1998a) 'From constructivism to social constructivism: a Vygotskian perspective on teaching and learning science', *School Science Review* (June).

—— (1998b) 'Science education as enculturation: Some implications for practice', *School Science Review* (Sept.).

Hodson, D. and Prophet, B. (1986) 'A bumpy start to science education', *New Scientist* 1521: 25–8.

Jegede, O.J. (1995) 'Collateral learning and the eco-cultural paradigm in science and mathematics education in Africa', *Studies in Science Education* 25: 97–137.

—— (1998) 'Worldview presuppositions and science and technology education', in D. Hodson (ed.) *Science and Technology Education and Ethnicity: An Aotearoa/New Zealand Perspective*, Wellington: The Royal Society of New Zealand, pp. 76–88.

Killerman, W. (1996) 'Biology education in Germany: research into the effectiveness of different teaching methods', *International Journal of Science Education* 18: 333–46.

Kirschner, P.A. (1992) 'Epistemology, practical work and academic skills in science education', *Science & Education* 1(3): 273–99.

Lakin, S. and Wellington, J. (1994) 'Who will teach the "nature of science"? Teachers' views of science and their implications for science education', *International Journal of Science Education* 16: 175–90.

Lave, J. (1988) *Cognition in Practice: Mind, Mathematics and Culture in Everyday Life*, New York: Cambridge University Press.

—— (1991) 'Situating learning in communities of practice', in L.B. Resnick, J.M. Levine and S.D. Teasley (eds) *Perspectives on Socially Shared Cognition*, Washington, DC: American Psychological Association.

Lave, J. and Wenger, E. (1991) *Situated Learning: Legitimate Peripheral Participation*, New York: Cambridge University Press.

Lederman, N.G. (1995) 'The influence of teachers' conceptions of the nature of science on classroom practice: the story of five teachers', in F. Finley, D. Allchin, D. Rhees and S. Fifield (eds) *Proceedings: Third International History, Philosophy, and Science Teaching Conference*, vol. 1, Minneapolis, MN: University of Minnesota, pp. 656–63.

Lemke, J.L. (1990) *Talking Science: Language, Learning and Values*, Norwood, NJ: Ablex.

Lock, R. (1998) 'Fieldwork in the life sciences', *International Journal of Science Education* 20(6).

Loving, C.C. (1997) 'From the summit of truth to its slippery slopes: science education's journey through positivist-postmodern territory', *American Educational Research Journal* 34: 421–52.

Matthews, M.R. (1992) 'History, philosophy and science teaching: the present rapprochement', *Science & Education* 1: 11–47.

—— (1994) *Science Teaching: the Role of History and Philosophy of Science*, New York: Routledge.

Mellado, V. (1997) 'Preservice teachers' classroom practice and their conceptions of the nature of science', *Science & Education* 6: 331–54.

Nadeau, R. and Désautels, J.F. (1984) *Epistemology and the Teaching of Science: a Discussion Paper*, Ottawa: Science Council of Canada.

Vygotsky, L.S. (1978) *Mind in Society: the Development of Higher Psychological Processes*, Cambridge, MA: Harvard University Press.

Wellington, J.J. (1989) 'Skills and processes in science education: an introduction', in J.J. Wellington (ed.) *Skills and Processes in Science Education*, London: Routledge.

Wells, G. and Chang-Wells, G.L. (1992) *Constructing Knowledge Together: Classrooms as Centers of Inquiry and Literacy*, Portsmouth, NH: Heinemann.
White, R.T. (1988) *Learning Science*, Oxford: Basil Blackwell.
Young, R.M. (1987) 'Racist society, racist science', in D. Gill and L. Levidow (eds) *Anti-racist Science Teaching*, London: Free Association Books.

7

AUTHENTIC SCIENCE IN SCHOOLS, TO DEVELOP PERSONAL KNOWLEDGE

Brian E. Woolnough

Much of school science is devoted to helping students understand the principles and theories of science. Much of educational research into school science has been devoted to trying to understand how children learn the principles and theories of science. And yet we do not seem to be very successful in achieving this goal (Adey *et al.*, 1994). Are we, perhaps, aiming at the wrong goal in school science? Ought we not to be aiming at something more appropriate, more useful to our students, whether potential scientists and engineers or just (*sic*!) potential citizens, and to employers? Ought we not to be taking more note of helping our students to build up their skills, their attitudes and their personal knowledge in such a way that it will be useful to them in their future life and employment? David Boud and his colleagues (1993), when reflecting about the learning in higher education, said: 'Most of what is written about learning makes us uneasy, as it neither reflects our felt experience as learners nor the issues that we have come to see as important in our lives and work'. I have the same sense of unease about the learning, and the theories of learning, that purport to be going on in schools. Learning science is not as objective, detached, clinically cognitive as we pretend. It is much more messy, much more individualistic and has much more untapped potential than we are currently realising. It involves much more commitment, much more of the personality of the individual learner. In Boud's words again: 'We have come to recognise that ideas are not separate from experience, learning is not unrelated to relationships and personal interests, and emotion and feelings have a vital role to play in what we may later come to identify as intellectual learning.'

In this chapter I want to explore how far we can go in school science to relate to such learning, to encourage and develop such personal learning, and in so doing will be exploring how far we can go in exposing students to authentic science in school and thus produce the sort of knowledge, attitudes and skills that are really useful to each individual student and their potential employers. I will argue that it is possible, desirable and, indeed, necessary that we should introduce some such authentic science into our school science courses if we are to keep them alive.

Public knowledge – personal knowledge

Scientific knowledge comes in two forms, public knowledge and personal knowledge. Knowledge that is public is written down in books and journals, is described in syllabuses and provides a basis for public examinations. Public knowledge is explicit and can be shared between individuals through written and spoken language, language which both communicates and disguises differences in the individuals' understanding of the words. The community of scientists will share common meanings for the words used.

But there is another type of knowledge which is personal, personal to each individual and which is less easy to define. It is the type of knowledge which the individual has absorbed, through experience and practice, and which is useful to that person as he or she seeks to make sense of the world and to solve problems in it. It relates both to understanding aspects of the physical world and also to the procedures required to tackle problems in it. It is tacit, and involves our senses as well as our intellect, our emotional commitment as well as our intelligence. In Polanyi's words (1958) in his seminal book on personal knowledge, 'We know more than we can tell.' We assert that a piece of music is by Bach even though we have never heard it before, we know how to ride a bicycle even though we cannot explain its stability and why we don't fall off, we recognise a suitable substance and a sensible course of action in tackling a scientific problem even though we cannot always explain why. These all rely upon personal knowledge.

Scientists in their professional life rely both on public knowledge and, especially, personal knowledge to solve their problems. Indeed, it is only as the public knowledge has become personalised that it can be used. But personal knowledge is more than just personalised public knowledge, it is deeper, more sensual, more inarticulate and yet most useful. One aspect of authentic scientific activity utilises such personal, tacit knowledge to solve problems.

School science in most countries is increasingly dominated by accountability and assessment, and thus the form of science which is taught, so that it can be assessed, is predominantly public knowledge. Personal knowledge, because the individual cannot make it reliably explicit, gains little credit or status. But I will argue that unless school science teaching allows some place for the development and expression of personal knowledge in science, we will be betraying our students' education in misleading them about the authentic nature of scientific activity. I believe that we need also to stress the difference between the two types of knowledge in our teaching, and stress that both have value and importance. Of course we need to teach, and

110

assess, an understanding of that scientific knowledge which can be publicly made explicit. But such public knowledge alone is arid and useless; we need also to encourage personal knowledge. Ravetz (1971) spoke of science as 'a craft activity, depending on a personal knowledge of particular things and a subtle judgement of their properties'. Roth (1995) described learning in science as 'an enculturation into scientific practices'. Brown and Palinscar (1989) view learning as 'an apprenticeship in the (linguistic and tool-use) practices of a culture'. Millar (1996) asserts that 'learning science is a process of coming to see phenomena and events through a particular set of spectacles, and the intention of science education is to bring the learners "inside" the particular, and peculiar, view of things which scientists, by and large, share'. The personal, craft nature of doing science is fundamental and should be included in our portrayal of science in school.

I will be arguing that there is a place in school science for including authentic science activity of a practical, problem-solving nature for a number of reasons;

- to enable students to develop and use their personal knowledge through experience;
- to enable them to experience doing authentic science (and thus partake in one of our principal cultural activities);
- to provide students with the skills and attitudes (the personal knowledge) that are useful to employers; and
- to motivate students towards science and hence increase their propensity to learn public knowledge of science too.

Authentic science, if we define it as the way that scientists work, comes in many different forms. At times a scientist will be meticulously recording a series of results or mapping an environmental terrain, another scientist will be making precise calculations or computer simulations to predict likely weather patterns or the path of a satellite. Some scientists work alone, far more work in teams. Some do 'blue skies' research, many more work to tight industrial briefs. Some sit and think, others present reports synthesising the work of others, some argue and persuade in the political arena. The picture of all scientists as working rationally to some 'scientific method' is, and always was, a myth. Jenkins (1996) quotes Seigel describing a scientist as:

> one who is driven by personal convictions and commitments; who is guided by group loyalties and sometimes personal squabbles; who is frequently quite unable to recognise evidence for what it is; and whose personal career motivations give the lie to the idea that the scientist yearns only or even mainly for the truth.

It is an untidy picture, but one which links the personality with the intellect, and stresses the need to take a holistic approach to the learning and exemplification of science. It is a picture that we should bear in mind when we hope to give our students in school a picture of the nature of science, and will drive us away from a pseudo-exemplification through standard practicals in school science. It will encourage us towards a more realistic model of science through investigational projects, linked as widely as possible to the real world.

In this chapter I will use the term 'authentic science' to mean that type of doing science typified by problem-solving practical projects, in which the problem is in some way related to the real world of the student. The student will take ownership of the problem, it will be open-ended and have a significant degree of freedom about how the task is tackled. There will also be sufficient time available for genuine exploration and, where possible, the involvement of people, resources and ideas from outside the confines of the school. In such a research project, students follow their interests, and develop themselves as social-minded, self-governing persons exhibiting self-respect, self-direction, initiative, self-criticism and persistence. In the words of Hofstein and Rosenfeld (1996), 'The intended goal of the independent research project is to develop a more independent and autonomous learner.'

I am not arguing that 'practical problem solving' is the only form of authentic method of scientific activity. Different types of scientist work in quite different ways (and indeed Bridgeman's definition of the scientific method as 'doing one's damnedest to understand nature, no holds barred!' may be the only defensible definition of the scientific method!). But I would argue that it is one very important and very common way that professional scientists work and far more authentic than the closed, convergent, hypothesis-testing type of experiments so often done in school science practical classes. Of course, we also need to stress the appropriate language that scientists use in communicating their public knowledge, and to realise the importance of language in science to convey meaning too. Doing science is not the same as understanding science. As Sutton (1992, and in this book) stresses 'practical experience can never "speak for itself", but the words we use are necessary interpretative instruments of understanding'. But in stressing the importance of a shared public knowledge of science, we should not ignore the importance of personal knowledge.

A confusion of aims in school practical work

In the United Kingdom especially, and in many other countries too there is a strong tradition of doing practical work in school science (see Jenkins' chapter in this book). There is, however, a growing body of evidence that despite (or because of) this emphasis on practical work much school science teaching is unsuccessful in giving pupils an understanding of the ideas of science (OFSTED 1994; Adey *et al.* 1994; Clarkson and Wright 1992; Hodson 1992), is ineffective at exciting pupils with science so that they wish to continue with it into the sixth form and beyond (DfEE statistics, and Smithers and Robinson 1994; Woolnough 1994a, b), and, I would contend, is not giving students experience of doing authentic science.

Derek Hodson (1996) has made a perceptive analysis of the development of practical work in school science over the last three decades, which he describes as 'decades of confusion and distortion'. I welcome and agree with his arguments, both in his assertion that one of the major elements in science education is 'doing science – engaging in and developing expertise in scientific inquiry and problem solving' and that the practical work in the major curriculum developments over that period 'has seriously misrepresented the nature of scientific inquiry'. As I have said elsewhere,

> much practical work is ineffective, unscientific and a positive deterrent for many students to continue with their science. It is ineffective in helping students understand the concepts and theories of science. It is unscientific in that it is quite unlike real scientific activity. And it is boring and time-wasting for many students who find it unnecessary and unstimulating.
>
> (Woolnough 1995a)

I would argue that much of this ineffectiveness has been caused by a fundamental, and long-lasting, confusion and conflict between aims for doing practical work. We could argue that there are two main aims for teaching science – to know *what* and to know *how* – helping students understand the concepts of science and the processes of science. Science teaching should help students know and understand the principles and theories of science and also understand and appreciate the way that scientists work. The problems arise when practical work is used with the hope of meeting both of these aims – *at the same time.* I would contend that trying to fulfil both aims in the same experiment will prevent the achievement of either – if we so tightly structure the practical that it clarifies the theory we will not allow the student to experiment freely; if we encourage the student to investigate a problem independently it is unlikely that they will discover 'the right theory'. Layton (1973) pointed out this danger twenty-five years ago when he stated that 'it is difficult to see how both objectives, an understanding of the mature concepts and theories of science *and* an understanding of the processes by which scientific knowledge grows, *can be achieved simultaneously*' (my italics).

And yet this debilitating confusion still survives in our schools and educational thinking. Various surveys have been conducted over the last three decades into the reasons why teachers do practical work and the type of practical that they do (Kerr 1963; Thompson 1975; Beatty *et al.* 1982) and all of them come up with very similar findings. The latter surveys done at Oxford used some of the structure of the Kerr report of the early 1960s to enable a comparison to be made.

When asked to rate the reasons for doing practical work, teachers consistently over these thirty years rated those aims related to developing practical skills and attitudes most highly and those related to discovering or elucidating theory much lower (see Table 7.1).

Table 7.1 Teachers' perception of the role of practical work in science, 1962–96

(a) Aims (for students aged 16–18)	Kerr 1962	Oxford 1975	1996
To make phenomena more real through experience	7,9,6	2,2,3	4
To practise seeing problems and seeking ways to solve them	8,7,9	7,6,4	3
To promote a logical, reasoning method of thought	4,4,4	3,3,2	2
To encourage accurate observation and description	1,1,1	1,1,1	1
For finding facts and arriving at new principles*	3,3,3	8,7,8	10
To elucidate theoretical work as an aid to comprehension*	2,2,2	6,7,8	5
To arouse and maintain interest	9,10,10	4,5,5	6
To develop specific manipulative skills	6,5,5	5,4,6	7
To verify facts and principles already taught*	5,6,7	10,10,10	8
To satisfy National Curriculum and GCSE requirements	10,8,8	9,9,7	9

The numbers record the order of importance according to the rating the teachers gave to the different aims for teaching practical work in science. For the Kerr and the Oxford results the three numbers record the rating given by the physics, chemistry and biology teachers taken separately. The 1996 teachers are not differentiated.

And yet, the type of practical that teachers consistently say that they do most frequently is 'Structured Experiments linked to Theory'.

(b) Aims (for pre-16 students)	Kerr 1962	Oxford 1982	1996
To make phenomena more real through experience	2	4	3
To practise seeing problems and seeking ways to solve them	9	6	4
To promote a logical, reasoning method of thought	4	3	6
To encourage accurate observation and description	3	1	1
For finding facts and arriving at new principles*	5	7	8
To elucidate theoretical work as an aid to comprehension*	9	4	6
To arouse and maintain interest	1	2	2
To develop specific manipulative skills	7	5	7
To verify facts and principles already taught*	8	9	9
To satisfy National Curriculum and GCSE requirements	10	10	10

* these three aims specifically link the practical to the theory

Again, teachers of students pre-16 years of age respond similarly. They rate the aims related to practical skills more highly than those related to developing theoretical work, and yet, when asked what type of practical they do most frequently, they too consistently rate 'structured experiments linked to theory' the highest! Much of the recent pedagogy based on the theories of constructivism is also predicated on the assumption that the principal function of practicals is to clarify theory.

This confusion has lead to much inappropriate practical work being done, with consequent waste of time, money and resources and little gain in understanding of either the theories or the way of working of science. And yet there has been a 'thin red line' of teachers and educators who have advocated and propagated a more authentic type of practical science in schools which have demonstrated a more appropriate way forward (for example, Nuffield 1985; Woolnough 1994a; Roth 1995). Normally, though not exclusively, this authentic science has been represented by investigational, problem-solving projects. For the purpose of this chapter, I will take that as my meaning too. The problem to be solved will be owned by the student. It will relate to a topic of interest and will most likely be open-ended. It will take an extended period of time, will involve trials and researches, will allow for different approaches and different routes, will allow space for mistakes and dead-ends, and will lead to a solution which will be evaluated against the original problem and constraints. The planning, the execution and the evaluation will usually be intermixed in an iterative process. The time available, the problem and the resources will enable each student to succeed (at the appropriate level) and finish with a personal sense of achievement.

This sense of achievement is of central importance, as it bonds together the learning with the development of the personality in a way which Vygotsky (Davydov 1995) stresses is central to all meaningful learning. Hodson (1988), in discussing the claims for transferable skills from one context to another is sceptical of any significant transfer of cognitive or psycho-motor skills from one context to another, but asserts that:

> What may be transferable are certain attitudes and feelings of self worth . . . successful experience in one experiment may make children more determined and more interested in performing another experiment. The confidence arising from successfully designing an experiment might be a factor in helping children to stay on task long enough to design a new experiment successfully.

Though we can learn much from problems and failures, we – and especially schoolchildren – need enough success to build up our self-image, our motivation and our personal expertise.

I will argue that such authentic science is important in developing the student's *personal* knowledge of scientific phenomena and the way a scientist works, but not in increasing their *public* knowledge of the theories and principles of science. To suggest that any such authentic science practical work is not effective in increasing the students' public knowledge of scientific principles is to miss the point. This is not the aim of such practical work. In a recent, excellent article by Adey (1997), on the context dependency of learning, he questions the efficacy of authentic science. Unfortunately, he equates authentic science too closely to 'cognitive apprenticeship' and 'situated cognition' (of, for example, Lave 1988), and infers that the aim is to develop in the student a public, transferable understanding of science. The purpose of doing authentic science is to experience authentic science and to enjoy and become increasingly competent in it. Competence will develop by practice, in an increasingly wide range of contexts and problems. Through experience, correction, and reinforcing achievement the student will develop a store of personal knowledge including habits and procedures, brain-storming and creativity, commitment and self-confidence, and a range of personal, tacit knowledge of the properties and behaviour of materials and phenomena.

The needs of employment – a rationale for the future?

It is easy for those inside the educational system to produce answers to our own questions, irrespective of whether these are important questions or appropriate solutions to those 'outside'. It is good, periodically, to look outside the school system and ask what it is that the employers of our students would want them to bring with them from their school education. We should take note of this in regard to our science teaching and, in particular, in seeking a rationale for our practical work for the future. When employers are surveyed we find that they rarely stress that students should bring with them a large amount of public knowledge, but their requirements are much more related to the personal knowledge which the students can use.

Over the last few years different employers have produced reports outlining what they are looking for in their future employees (for example, CBI 1995; BT 1993; RAE 1996; CRQ 1997). Coles (1996), in making a survey of the requirements of a range of science-based industries, concluded that 'there are striking similarities in the lists', and with the requirements of 'scientists in other companies, services and HE institutions'. He consolidates a single generalised description of the qualities required in recruits for science-based work thus:

- Commitment and interest (the most important criteria),
- Core skill capabilities such as communication, numeracy and IT capability,

- Personal effectiveness, relationships and team work,
- Self reliance, resourcefulness,
- Initiative, creativity,
- The skill of analysis,
- Good general knowledge including understanding of the world of work,
- Professional integrity.

(After Coles 1996)

These qualities are rated more highly than paper qualifications (though the acquisition of these may have been inferred having been used as a preliminary filter in the selection process). Paper qualifications, at degree or A level, are seen primarily 'as an indicator of commitment to subject area'.

If these are the qualities that employers require, how can schools help their students develop them? I would argue that traditional practicals in school, tightly structured and prescribed so as to illuminate the underlying theory, will do little to promote them. (Indeed, research done by the Engineering Industry Training Board (1977) showed a *negative* correlation between the skills of apprentices to do projects and their skill in school practical work the previous year!) On the other hand, involving students in authentic, problem-solving science investigations, either individually or in groups, will develop these skills and attitudes that employers are asking for.

It is interesting to note that the qualities listed in Cole's list are not public and explicit in the readily assessable form, but are more personal and intangible, relying on broader professional judgement to assess. Qualities such as commitment, interest, initiative, self-reliance, resourcefulness, creativity and personal integrity are not easily measured but can be demonstrated through the student's previous experience and achievements, such as will have been demonstrated through involvement in authentic science, and the report of a problem-solving scientific investigation.

The feasibility of authentic science in schools

Having advocated the incorporation of authentic science into school science the questions remain 'Is it feasible?' and 'Is it effective?' The answer to both is 'yes', though, as we shall see, the place for authentic science investigations in schools may in some cases be extra-curricular while in other cases it may form part of the main science curriculum.

Practical problem-solving investigations and projects might be done as part of the school science curriculum or as extra-curricular activities. I have described many ways that they are being done in my book on *Effective Science Teaching* (Woolnough 1994a). A comprehensive compendium of practical experience of scientific research in schools has been put together by the Clifton Scientific Trust (Albone 1995). Some A-level courses such as Nuffield A-level courses in physics and biology have extended investigations as part of their assessed course work. Most A-level biology students would do projects as part of their fieldwork; many younger science students would also have experience of fieldwork. GNVQ science courses need to do such projects. It is possible to do extended projects as part of National Curriculum Science, in the Attainment Target Science 1: Experimental and Investigative Sciences. The Pupil Researcher Initiative (PRI) supports project work in the 14–16 age range through linked science research students, funded by EPSRC and PPARC. Many teachers will do investigational projects of an open-ended kind throughout their science courses, though inevitably these have to be relatively constrained. Many primary schools have good traditions of doing authentic science through, perhaps, environmental studies in the locality of their school. Nationally supported award schemes, such as CREST (CREativity in Science and Technology), BA's Young Investigator scheme, and Engineering Enterprise Scheme (EES), also support authentic science in schools.

Many science teachers, however, find that the pressures and constraints of the normal science curriculum encourage them to do their authentic science in extra-curricular time, through science clubs, through science and technology competitions, or through project weeks. Some utilise a mixture of timings, with projects being started and concluded in normal curriculum time and students encouraged to continue and develop them in their own time. There are ways of teaching authentic science in schools' science, and many science teachers have indeed found it feasible, and most rewarding.

The efficacy of authentic science

Surprisingly, little research seems to have been done to see how effective the teaching of authentic science is. Indeed, as Hofstein and Rosenfeld (1996) have commented, 'one of the biggest problems regarding student projects is the difficulty of reliable assessment', and that leads to difficulty of evaluation. Most of those who have been involved with students doing such independent research projects are nevertheless thoroughly convinced of their value to the students from their first-hand experience, despite the extra amount of work required to organise them. My own experience over many years, as a teacher and observer of such students' projects and as a moderator for the student investigations in the Nuffield A-level physics course, has convinced me beyond doubt of their unparalleled value. However, three specific pieces of research will illustrate less anecdotally the efficacy of students doing authentic science.

Recently we have had the opportunity of doing an evaluation of the

CREST award scheme and its associated GETSET (Girls Entering Tomorrow's Science Engineering and Technology) (McIntyre and Woolnough 1996; Woolnough 1997a). CREST is a national award scheme, with bronze, silver and gold awards for students who accomplish good investigational project work in science or technology. Its aim is to stimulate, encourage and excite young people about science, technology and engineering through task-centred project work. It stimulates and supports industry/community-linked projects which draw on students' creativity, perseverance and application of scientific and technological challenges. Typically, the bronze projects will be done by 13-year-olds and take about twenty hours' work; the silver will be done by 16-year-olds and take about forty hours; and the gold awards will be gained by 18-year-olds and will take about one hundred hours of work. The silver and gold award projects will always involve the students working with scientists or engineers from industry on a real-world problem. In the evaluation it quickly became apparent, through the response of both the teachers who organised it and the students who took part in it, that it was immensely impressive and highly successful in fulfilling its aims. It was highly motivating for the students who produced work for the CREST award of a very high standard, and, through the success achieved in completing work of this standard, it built up a high level of self-confidence.

Teachers were asked about eleven of the intended outcomes of CREST work, and asked to rate whether they felt they had had 'a large effect', 'a small effect', 'no effect' or 'a negative effect'. The vast majority of the teachers felt that all of the intended outcomes had been positively achieved, with the top three being as shown in Table 7.2.

Table 7.2 The top three intended outcomes of CREST work

	Large effect (%)	Small effect (%)
Ownership of and commitment to project work	67	30
A greater involvement with team work	67	23
A greater confidence in their own ability to do practical work	54	36

All of these are developing the personal knowledge of ways of working which industrial employers are explicitly looking for.

These personal ways of working were reinforced by the teachers in response to another question, when 97 per cent of them agreed, or strongly agreed, with the statement that 'Pupils gain personal development through taking part in the CREST award scheme'.

When the students who had been involved with CREST were asked how they felt about being involved with such authentic science in school, they too were very positive. In particular, when asked whether they agreed or disagreed with sixteen statements about the effect of CREST, they responded most positively to the following (Table 7.3):

Table 7.3 Student agreement with statements about the effect of CREST

	Agreed or strongly agreed (%)
I would like to take a further CREST award	87
I have enjoyed doing a CREST award	80
CREST allows me to experience real science and technology	79
Having a CREST award will be useful when I apply for a job or college	79
CREST has given me confidence in doing practical work	71
CREST has helped me communicate better	71

Again, the students felt that doing authentic science through CREST had not only been enjoyable but had also increased the sorts of skills that employers would find useful.

When employers, HE, the DfEE and OFSTED were asked about their reaction to students doing CREST, or CREST-type projects, they were all very positive. Clearly, those outside schools, as well as those directly involved with CREST, saw the value of involving students in extended project work related to real-life problems.

The evaluation of CREST was both qualitative and quantitative. In a typical year, about 12,000 students would be working on CREST awards (80 per cent on the bronze awards, 12 per cent silver and 8 per cent gold). Over half of those involved were girls. As to the practicalities of CREST type work, 37 per cent of CREST work was done in lesson time, with 44 per cent in club time and 19 per cent as a special activity. That not done in normal curriculum time was done in lunchtime or after school. Of the teachers involved 51 per cent were scientists, 41 per cent were teachers of technology. Of the CREST activities 30 per cent were based in the science department, 50 per cent in the technology department, with 20 per cent shared.

It is always difficult to test and to demonstrate that being involved in authentic science, of the CREST or GETSET type, makes students more likely to enter careers in science or technology. There are so many other factors influencing a student's choice (Woolnough 1994b, 1996). However, the evaluation of GETSET did show that the girls who had attended a two-day GETSET industry linked, problem-solving workshop when they were 13 or 14 had chosen to study the sciences and maths at A level three years later at a far greater rate than those girls who had not. They were more than three times as likely to be taking A-level physics, twice as likely to be taking chemistry, and one and a half times as likely to be taking A levels in biology, mathematics or technology (Woolnough 1997a). Caution should be taken in interpreting these data too literally. Nevertheless, both the qualitative and the quantitative evaluations of CREST and GETSET indicate that not only do students, girls as well as boys, enjoy doing authentic science, but also that their involvement has a very positive effect on their attitudes towards, and understanding of, science and careers in science.

A second in-depth study of the efficacy of students doing authentic science was carried out by Tytler (1992). He interviewed students and studied the reports of their independent research projects in the Student Talent Search (STS) in the state of Victoria, Australia. These students, aged between 10 and 15, carried out their own projects, largely, though not exclusively, in their own time. Their projects covered a very wide range from a study of spiders and the ecology of the local lake, to the efficiency and power output of model cars, to the effect of various household chemicals on growth in a herb garden, to studying amino-acid sequences in chicken embryos. He was clearly enormously impressed by the quality of the work produced by each child and concluded that:

- the academic ability of the students varied enormously;
- many of the ideas came from random events in the students' own experience;
- the commitment to the pursuit and conclusion of a project, as evidenced in the displays of enthusiasm and sometimes extraordinary amount of time and trouble involved, was impressive;
- the independence shown in the pursuit of background knowledge and in the arrangement of experimental procedures or design innovations was also very impressive;
- the type of motivation differed from one student to another: for one the drive to build something: for another the urge to find out 'why': for a third to establish a hobby;
- the support of the home environment was very important, providing ideas, resources, encouragement, interest and expectation. The amount of help needed and received from the school or teacher was very small;
- interest and motivation rather than intellect are the key ingredients in pursuing a piece of research or a model to a successful conclusion;
- the level of work that students are capable of and the range of talents they can bring to bear on science are enormous.

A third area of evidence which gives insights into the efficacy of authentic science in schools has arisen from a series of researches seeking to find what influences students in their choice towards continuing their studies in science or engineering. These studies, carried out in England and five other countries, are titled the FASSIPES projects, where 'FASSIPES' stands for Factors Affecting Schools' Success In Producing Engineers and Scientists (Woolnough 1991, 1994c, 1995b and 1997b). One of the significant findings from these researches was that the doing of extended practical projects and the involvement in science and technology competitions were both considered very positive factors in influencing them towards HE courses in science and engineering, for certain groups of students. Those who were subsequently to become scientists responded significantly more positively to such activities than those who would not. The future engineers especially responded most positively to such project work activity in science.

Furthermore, there was a high degree of positive correlation between those schools which were successful in sending a high proportion of their students on to HE to study one of the physical sciences or engineering and those which involved their students in what we might call 'authentic science' (with a Pearson's correlation coefficient of 0.38, significant at the 1 per cent level). In this case 'authentic science' was defined by a group of factors including suspending normal timetables for an extended period for projects, involvement with science clubs and science competitions, and involving local engineers in the work of the science department. Those schools that involved their students in such problem-solving project activity were more successful in producing future engineers and scientists. Such projects seem to have been particularly effective in influencing the career choice of future engineers.

Conclusion

So, through the CREST project, the STS scheme and the FASSIPES researches we have seen that students can become involved with authentic science, and that when they do so they demonstrate the enormous potential they have for doing science. Such science is effective in producing high-quality student work, in developing important personal skills and attitudes, and in motivating students towards science. In doing such science they demonstrate, develop and reinforce the skills and attitudes of initiative, creativity, autonomy, self-reliance, resourcefulness, self-confidence, commitment and analysis. These are exactly the skills and attitudes that employers say they require from school leavers. Furthermore, they are developing an expertise and experience of the area of science which builds up both their personal knowledge and their public knowledge in the area in which they are researching.

Authentic science, as demonstrated by practicising scientists, is rarely a matter of learning the theory, the public knowledge, making it explicit and then consciously applying it to the problem. It is more messy than that, more dependent on the personal, tacit knowledge built up through personal experience, trying out ideas 'which seem appropropriate', and modifying them through iterative evaluation. It utilises commitment, dogged determination and personal creativity until the problem is solved and the goal achieved. School students *can* experience, demonstrate and develop such authentic science if given the opportunity. Learning from personal experience is vital, and though it is 'messy, inconvenient but ultimately profound' (Boud *et al.* 1993), it is necessary to go through such a process in as authentic a way as possible.

I would contend that schools should encourage and provide opportunities for all students to have experience of becoming involved in authentic science through their school science studies. In such a way they will gain motivation towards science, will develop their own personal knowledge of both the phenomena and the procedures of science, will experience authentic science, and will develop the skills and attitudes that employers and future citizens will find useful. Of course, there is the need in schooling to ensure that our students have a mastery of the public, articulatable knowledge of science too. But if we want to introduce them to the way that scientists really work we will need to get them involved with authentic science in problem-solving research projects too, so that they may build up their all-important personal knowledge of science.

Ultimately, it is only as we engage our students' motivation and commitment that any teaching will be really useful (Woolnough 1997c). What matters is not what students know and can do but what they want to do. Once 'switched on' there is no limit to the quality of work, even authentic science work, that students can produce.

References

Adey, P, (1997) 'It all depends on the context, doesn't it? Search for general, educable dragons', *Studies in Science Education* 29: 45–91,

Adey, P., Askoko, H., Black, P. *et al.* (1994) *1994 Revision of the National Curriculum: Implications of Research on Children's Learning of Science, a report to SCAA*, London: King's College.

Albone, E. (1995) *Scientific Research in Schools*, Bristol: Clifton Scientific Trust.

Beatty, J.W. and Woolnough, B.E. (1982) 'Practical work in 11–13 science: the context, type and aims of current practice', *British Educational Research Journal* 8(1): 23–30.

Boud, D., Cohen, R. and Walker, D. (1993) *Using Experience for Learning*, Buckingham: SRHE and Open University Press.

Brown, A.L. and Palinscar, A.S. (1989) 'Guided co-operative learning and individual knowledge acquisition', in L.B. Resnick (ed.) *Knowing Learning and Instruction: Essays in Honor of Robert Glaser*, Hillsdale, NJ: Lawrence Erlbaum Associates, pp. 393–451.

BT (British Telecom) (1993) *Matching Skills, a Question of Supply and Demand*, London: BT.

CBI (Confederation of British Industries) (1995) *A Vision for our Future, a Skills Passport*, London: CBI.

Clarkson, S.G. and Wright, D.K. (1992) 'An appraisal of practical work in science education', *School Science Review*, 74(266): 39–42

Claxton, G. (1991) *Educating the Inquiring Mind*, London: Harvester Wheatsheaf.

Coles, M.C. (1996) 'What does industry want from science education?' paper for 8th IOSTE Symposium, Alberta: Canada.

CRQ (Centre for Research into Quality) (1997) *Graduates' Work: Organisational Change and Students' Attitudes*, London: CRQ.

Davydov, V.V. (1995) 'The influence of L.S. Vygotsky on education theory, research and practice', *Educational Researcher* 24(3): 12–21.

Engineering Industry Training Board (1997) *School Learning and Training*, Watford: EITB.

Hodson, D. (1988) 'Experiments in science and science teaching', *Educational Philosophy and Theory* 20: 253–66.

—— (1992) 'Redefining and reorientating practical work in school science', *School Science Review* 73(264): 65–78.

—— (1996) 'Laboratory work as scientific method: three decades of confusion and distortion', *Journal of Curriculum Studies* 28(2): 115–35.

Hofstein, A. and Rosenfeld, S. (1996) 'Bridging the gap between formal and informal science learning', *Studies in Science Education* 28: 87–112.

Jenkins, E.W. (1996) 'The "nature of science" as a curriculum component', *Journal of Curriculum Studies* 28(2): 137–50.

Kerr, J.F. (1963) *Practical Work in School Science*, Leicester: Leicester University Press.

Lave, J. (1988) *Cognition in Practice: Mind, Mathematics and Culture in Everyday Life*, Cambridge: Cambridge University Press.

Layton, D. (1973) *Science for the People*, London: George Allen and Unwin.

McIntyre, R. and Woolnough, B.E. (1996) *Enriching the Curriculum, Evaluation Report of CREST and GETSET*, Oxford: Oxford University Department of Educational Studies.

Millar, R. (1996) 'In pursuit of authenticity', *Studies in Science Education* 27: 149–65.

Nuffield (1985) *Advanced Level Physics, Revised: Examinations and Investigations*, London: Longman.

OFSTED (1994) *Science and Mathematics in Schools: a Review*, London: HMSO.

Polanyi, M. (1958) *Personal Knowledge*, London: Routledge and Kegan Paul.

RAE (Rotal Academy of Engineering) (1996) *Engineering Higher Education*, London: RAE.

Ravetz, J. (1971) *Scientific Knowledge and its Social Problems*, New York: Oxford University Press.

Roth, W-M. (1995) *Authentic School-Science: Knowing and Learning in Open-Inquiry Science Laboratories*, The Netherlands: Kluwer Academic Publishers.

Smithers, A. and Robinson, P. (1994) *The Impact of Double Science*, London: The Engineering Council.

Sutton, C. (1992) *Words, Science and Learning*, Buckingham: Open University Press.

Thompson, J.J. (ed.) (1975) *Practical Work in Sixth Form Science*, Oxford: Oxford Department of Educational Studies.

Tytler, R. (1992) 'Independent research projects in school science: case studies of autonomous behaviour', *International Journal of Science Education*, 14(4): 393–412.

Woolnough, B.E. (1983) 'Exercises, investigations and experiences', *Physics Education* 18(2): 60–3.

—— (1991) *The Making of Engineers*, Oxford: Oxford Department of Educational Studies.

—— (1994a) *Effective Science Teaching*, Open University Press.

—— (1994b) 'Why students choose physics, or reject it', *Physics Education* 29: 368–74.

—— (1994c) 'Factors affecting students' choice of science and engineering', *International Journal of Science Education* 16(6): 659–76.

—— (1995a) 'Switching students onto science', *British Council Science Education Newsletter,* London.

—— (1995b) 'School effectiveness for different types of potential scientists and engineers', *Research in Science and Technological Education* 13(1): 53–66.

—— (1996) 'Changing pupils' attitudes to careers in science', *Physics Education*: 301–8.

—— (1997a) *Enriching the Curriculum*, Part ii, *Evaluation Report of GETSET*, Oxford: Oxford University Department of Educational Studies.

—— (1997b) 'Factors affecting students' choice of career in science and engineering: parallel studies in Australia, Canada, China, England, Japan and Portugal', *Research in Science and Technological Education* 15(1): 105–21.

—— (1997c) 'Motivating students or teaching pure science?' *School Science Review* 78(285): 67–72.

8

LEARNING ABOUT THE
DIMENSIONS OF SCIENCE
THROUGH AUTHENTIC TASKS

Jenifer V. Helms

Introduction

Science educators argue that students should engage in authentic tasks; that is, students should engage in solving real problems that do not have a predetermined solution (American Association for the Advancement of Science 1989; California Department of Education 1990; National Research Council 1996; Roth 1995). Moreover, students should work collectively on these tasks, ask questions of their own choosing, and negotiate and solve problems in groups (AAAS 1993; NRC 1996; Driver *et al.* 1994; Stahl 1996; Aikenhead 1985, 1994; Kelly *et al.* 1993). Additionally, some science educators recommend there should be some attempt to bridge science with other disciplines, such as maths and social studies (AAAS 1989; Pedretti and Hodson 1995; Hansen and Olson 1995; Rubba 1991). Real-world problems, they claim, demand this approach.

Some who advocate a Science, Technology, Society (STS) approach to the curriculum, in addition to the emphases mentioned above, now call for action-taking on the part of the student, preferably on local scientific or environmental issues. Not all STS curricula include this step, though, and in many cases there is very little that actually supports it. However, some argue that taking action is crucial for the student to have a complete understanding of the nature of science and a sense of the role of science in the construction of a 'vision of sustainability' (Bybee 1993). Embedded in this approach to science education is explicit attention to the *context* and *goals* of science, and the need to construe them more broadly in order to address the impact of science on social life and the relationship of context to the aims of scientific practice (Pedretti and Hodson 1995; Hansen and Olson 1995; Rubba 1991).

Transforming science can begin with science education, and, as Hilary Rose puts it, 'an STS education constructed from the practices of the hand, brain, and the heart offers, conceptually and practically, to deal more gently with the natural and social worlds' (1994: 166). Understanding that the nature of science includes context, and that context is embedded in social, moral and political goals, has become a major aim of some recent STS education (Cross and Price 1992; Solomon 1994; Ramsey 1993; Waks 1992).

Overview of the chapter

In this chapter, I describe a science project done by 15-year-old students, in which science is presented as a practice that involves purposeful doing in context – that is, as an endeavour where goals and setting condition the character and quality of the activity. The data come from a case study of a project that involved a class of students who collected data and reported on a wetlands area in their community that had been created in an effort to restore habitats for endangered species. I focus primarily on the following questions: *How did this experience affect the students' understandings of the nature of science? What do the data tell us about the future of practical work in science education?*

First, I outline a framework – a heuristic – for thinking about the features of scientific work. Second, I describe the research setting and methods used to conduct the case study. Third, I analyse the data using the heuristic, offering samples of students' written and spoken comments that describe their beliefs and experiences. I conclude with a brief discussion and suggestions for the future.

Dimensions of the nature of science: a framework

The activity of science can be described using a simple heuristic:

> Science is an activity in which people employ *lenses* and *methods* to investigate *questions* concerning *natural objects and phenomena* in a particular *context* in the service of some *goal or set of goals*.

As with any organisational framework, there are strengths and weaknesses in thinking about science (and science education) in these terms. Its primary strength is that it captures a more robust description of the practice of science than those currently held by most science educators. One of the limitations of some studies about teachers' and students' understandings of the nature of science is the relatively narrow definition of science that is considered appropriate for teachers to understand. Indeed, much of what are understood to be considered 'nature of science' issues are limited to conceptions of method, argument and logical reasoning. By viewing science through this framework, these issues, while still important, do not eclipse context, goals and the nature of scientific questions. This leads to a second strength of the framework: it keeps all aspects in the foreground and on an even plane – there is no hierarchy structuring the various dimensions. Moreover, this arrangement provides one way to show how all of these aspects are related: one can hardly discuss objectivity without referring to scientific methods of research, scientific questions, context or goals.

Among the limitations of this heuristic framework is the tendency to itemise the practice of science in perhaps artificial ways; separating the elements may result in the loss of some of the richness of the scientific enterprise. Another shortcoming may be its tenuous science-specificity; remove the word 'natural' and it could define any investigative endeavour. Finally, multiple potential meanings exist for each of the dimensions. This feature, though, as I hope to demonstrate in the following pages, could also be considered a strength: for a framework to be useful it needs to be meaningful across a range of situations.

The data from this case study were analysed using this heuristic. In the following paragraphs, I briefly outline *one* way to view each of the dimensions. I will dwell on the 'goals' dimension because of the recent attention the goals of science and science education have received in the literature, and because it emerged as both central and problematic in the students' experiences with the wetlands project.

The lenses of science

The concept of *lens* in science can have multiple meanings. It can refer to the particular perspective a scientist or group of scientists brings to a research problem or question. A lens influences a person's viewpoint; it determines what is considered important, what is considered inessential, and therefore what is worth paying attention to. It also can refer to the overall view science takes on the natural world. In this sense, the lens of science, we are told, is 'objective' in its attempt to determine the nature of things. In other words, discussions about the lens of science might raise issues around the various communities of scientists, bias, values, objectivity and, ultimately, the questions that guide research.

Most characterisations of the nature of science hold objectivity as the hallmark of science. However, objectivity as a lens of science is by no means a clear concept (no pun intended!). Further, when viewed in the light of the other dimensions, the notion of an objective observer or process becomes inextricably linked with context, goals and the nature of scientific questions.

The methods of science

Method has to do with the specific processes a scientist or group of scientists follows to investigate a problem. It involves the employment of certain technologies and tools and procedures for their use. Further, scientists can be creative in developing their tools and procedures to address the problem at hand. They also need to convince others that what they do and how they do it is going to produce valid and reliable results.

As with objectivity, there does not seem to be much consensus on a definition of scientific method, or a sense that such a thing even exists. Harding's (1986) point, that different sciences employ different methods, implies the salience of context; it matters what science one is talking about. Further, Millar's (1994) suggestion that method alone fails to provide us with some explanation of how science is different from other modes of inquiry, and we should instead look at the constructs of science and their purposes, points to the tight connection between the methods of science and the aims or goals methods are designed to serve.

Scientific questions

This dimension seems straightforward. The important aspect here is that the questions asked can vary depending on who is doing the asking, and the context in which they are asked. For example, scholarship in the recent history of primatology has shown that, as more women entered the field, new questions were asked that challenged previous orientations and findings (Haraway 1989; Hrdy 1986). Questions are deemed suitable according to the context, goals established, methods chosen, lenses employed and topics of study. Further, questions don't arise from a vacuum – generally, scientific research stems from or builds upon previous work. Finally, it may be useful to separate questions that are theoretical in nature from those that address primarily experimental issues.

Scientific objects, phenomena and facts

One of the distinguishing characteristics of science is the topic of investigation – scientists are concerned with exploring and theorising about the workings of the natural, physical and, in some cases, human-made world. Some scientists study the way that the world around us works at present, others study events and objects from the past or predict what might happen in the future.

I should note, however, that there exists great debate surrounding the status of *scientific objects and scientific facts*. With the introduction of a social constructivist epistemology, the nature of 'real' objects and facts that scientists use and produce becomes a rather cluttered, as opposed to settled, issue.

The context of science

I use the term 'context' to signify both the internal (or micro) and external (or macro) contexts of science (Cunningham, 1995). The internal context refers to the space, time, resources and conditions of the research: where and when science happens. The laboratory is often invoked as the definitive internal context for scientific practice. External context refers to the socio-cultural, economic, political and historical milieu in which the science occurs. Some argue that the two cannot so easily be separated (Restivo 1994; Harding 1986).

Context can refer to the myriad of situations that condition the work of scientists. These situations can result from the structure of practice in laboratories or the political, economic and other social forces acting from both within and outside the laboratory walls. Context represents, in my view, one of the crucial dimensions of science; it often determines the character of the others.

The goals of science

Most students learn that scientists are only in the business of producing valid and reliable knowledge for informing future scientific and political decision-making. This statement, however, tells only part of the story. Scientists may include social responsibility as a goal for their work, choosing only to investigate questions and problems that have immediate or long-term social benefit. Their goals can also be, in some instances, self-serving. For example, a scientist's goal for a particular research programme may be to procure more funding, get a promotion or become famous. At the end of the day, much scientific work is done in the service of the scientific community first, and society, second.

Linking context and goals

It is hoped that an approach to the science curriculum that takes a broad view on the context and goals of science will result in improved learning of science concepts and skills; a better understanding of the nature of scientific practice; increased student awareness of the interface of science and society; and a greater comprehension of the role of science in students' lives. As Cunningham puts it, by '[d]escribing human relationships, beliefs, and values, sociological insights challenge stereotypes, debunk myths, and erode the status and permanence of science to stress human and societal components and context' (1995: 4). From this standpoint, the nature of science becomes highly contextualised towards more humanistic purposes. At the school science level, engaging students in projects that reflect sociological aspects of the nature of science, and embody an activist orientation to change, becomes a powerful way to realise the link between the goals of science and social context. The research reported in this paper takes the position that a broad view of the context and goals of science is crucial for an authentic understanding of the nature of science, and that projects such as the one reported here have the potential to realise this view.

The research setting

Description of the project

The wetlands restoration project was undertaken in the fall semester of 1995 by a group of 15-year-old students taught by Rachel,[1] a science teacher at a public San Francisco Bay area upper-middle class, primarily Anglo, high school. Under the umbrella of a course called 'Field Outreach', twenty-two students worked for one semester (about sixteen weeks) on a project that investigated the restoration of a wetlands area on San Francisco Bay. The students were part of a voluntary, heterogeneously grouped, ninety-student 'school-within-a-school', referred to as the 'Team'. All ninety students had the same teachers and took all of their classes together. This arrangement started several years ago as an experiment in restructuring. In addition to planning their respective academic subjects collaboratively, each of the Team teachers was responsible for arranging and overseeing one or more outreach experiences.[2] The Team's block scheduling, different from the rest of the school, allowed the students an extended period for their field projects and the teachers some extra time for collaborative planning.

The Field Outreach course was an explicit attempt to infuse community service into the academic programme for this group of students. Grants from Service Learning and other youth service organisations allowed Rachel and the other Team teachers to coordinate with various community organisations to involve students in experiences outside the classroom. These experiences each had a strong element of social service and contained something that would be recognisable as academic content. The students were allowed to choose which project they would participate in, with the exception of those students who were labelled 'honours' in their science class: all of these students were required to do the wetlands project one of the two semesters.[3] The students were all to receive 'general education' credit for this course.[4]

Rachel had worked with students out at the marsh for the previous two years, but the projects her former students undertook were done outside of class time and with very little or no direction. This year, the students were driven to their sites once each week, and attended three additional class periods devoted exclusively to the project. In short, their experience at the wetlands site was a course by itself.

Rachel, and a scientist from the city water control board who managed the wetlands project, Beth, decided that the official purpose for the students was to determine whether or not the restoration project initiated four years previously was affecting the return of wildlife to the area. The data students collected were reported directly to the water quality control board; the city would not have had the resources to collect the data were it not for the students' efforts.

Rachel learned about the restoration project from a local newspaper, which described marsh restoration as 'a relatively new science, having evolved in the past two decades as pressure has declined to fill in the fringes of the bay with condominiums and industrial parks'.[5] She then talked with Beth, who told her of the need for data on the progress of the restoration in terms of the repopulation of the wildlife. The $1.2 million restoration effort involved flooding a 30-acre area with salt water piped in from the San Francisco Bay, and building a freshwater pond and filling it with reclaimed sewage water. The city's primary goal was to encourage the return of two endangered local species: the salt marsh harvest mouse and the California clapper rail. Both of these animals require marsh-specific plants and other organisms to survive. Other species expected to thrive in the new wetlands area include the mosquito fish, the great blue heron, the salt marsh yellow-throat, and the pickleweed plant.[6]

Student activities

Twenty-two students participated in the project in the first semester. Rachel chose six sites in the wetlands area for the students to study. She allowed the students to choose which site they preferred and with whom they wanted to work. The six sites represented the three major habitats in the area: two groups studied the pond, two groups studied the plants and other organisms around the pond, and two groups studied the plants and other organisms in the salt marsh. The students visited their sites every week on Thursday for 2 hours (except holidays) and met in the classroom every Monday, Wednesday and Friday. Tuesdays were teacher planning days.

The students' first task was to mark out a 20 m by 3 m territory that would serve as their study site for the entire semester. After that, they constructed a site profile and estimated percentage coverage of the various plant life. With the exception of the pond group, the students devoted the remainder of the semester to observing and noting any changes in their site and collecting, preserving, recording and identifying samples that represented the dominant plant species in their area. The pond group performed chemical tests on pond-water samples taken from various distances from the water's edge and various depths. Each week, these students measured the pH, salinity, temperature and dissolved oxygen levels of the pond water, and collected water samples to observe under the microscope. Rachel jerry-rigged the equipment used to collect the water, and the chemical tests were performed with equipment and chemicals purchased with a small Service Learning grant.

132

The students were told that their main objective was to help determine the extent to which the marsh was actually being restored. The fact that the students had limited freedom with respect to the overall question proved somewhat problematic, as will be discussed later. The diversity of wildlife and health of the pond were considered the major indicators of successful restoration. In addition, Rachel and Beth wanted the students to have a final product to which the entire class could contribute. They thought that it would be important to create something that was needed by Beth and the scientists she worked with as well as the general public. They decided on a field guide, which would include the major plants and some animals the students chose to study from their sites, along with other general information about the pond and the students' projects. In addition, Rachel arranged for the students to hold a formal meeting at which they would share their data with Beth and other members of the community.

Research methods and data sources

Robert Stake (1995) defines case study as 'the study of the particularity and complexity of a single case, coming to understanding its activity within important circumstances' (p. xi). The mode of inquiry in case study can draw on a number of methods, ranging from naturalistic methods and ethnography to phenomenology and biography. The qualitative researcher 'emphasizes episodes of nuance, the sequentiality of happenings in context, the wholeness of the individual' (p. xii).

My goal was to capture the purposes, intentions and actions of a group of students involved in a project that combined science learning and social service. As a case, it offered insights into the kinds of things students learn about the nature of science from this approach to science instruction. Science educators are beginning to acknowledge the various ways scientific practice can be defined. Consequently, new and varied modes of instruction are being explored. This case provides one example of both the desirable and less desirable results of stretching the definition of science and science instruction.

The questions guiding this study emphasised the students' experiences; much of the data come from formal and informal student interviews, journal writing and observation. Multiple methods of data collection helped me to triangulate my findings. Table 8.1 outlines the major data sources.

All of the data reported in this chapter come from the interviews and student journals.

My role

In 'conventional' research parlance, my role may be considered a permutation of 'participant-observer'. However, I find this description limiting: it

Table 8.1 Data types

Interviews (formal)
- Rachel (4)
- Students (11 x 2)
- Beth (1)

Observations
- In the field (12 visits)
- In the classroom (3 days per week for approx. 16 weeks)
- Final presentation

Student journals
- 5 journal entries

Documents
- Rachel's lesson plans
- student handouts
- readings
- flyers

Analytic memos
- 10 memos, varying length

---

under-describes my involvement, especially with respect to the relationships I developed with both the teacher and the students. I spent over 80 hours with these students throughout the semester, talking with them, teaching them, listening to them and observing them. I had the unique opportunity to play the roles of observer, teacher, mentor, driver (I drove a group of students to their site every week), consultant, advocate, interpreter, and friend. I believe that the different levels at which I interacted with the students and the teacher allowed me to collect a much richer set of data.

This is not to say that each role was emphasised equally at all times. Rather, I had to attend carefully to each situation and determine which role would yield the most interesting and important information. Mostly, I tried to be myself. My primary concern was for the students and Rachel to be comfortable with and accept my involvement. I aimed to provide support and advice for Rachel as the project unfolded. My desire to understand the challenges and puzzlements of teaching this way prompted me to assume a fairly active role in the classroom. As driver, observer, helper and interviewer, I hoped I could get a good grasp of the students' experiences and what they were learning. In the end, I came away with a picture of the project taken from different perspectives that provided an overall view that, I believe, captured the essence of the experience.

Data analysis

As explained previously, I analysed the data based on the heuristic I had created. That is, I coded the interview responses, journal entries and artefacts according to each dimension to get a sense of the overall picture of science that emerged from the students' experiences as well as each student's unique experience with each dimension.

The dimensions of science in wetlands restoration

One of the central features of this project was that it involved service to and within the students' local community. What does this quality reflect about the nature of science? For one, it underscores the central role of the context and goals of science. For another, it lends a sense of *authenticity* to the students' work in the field. In the following sections, I explore the students' experiences in terms of the *lens, methods, context* and *goals* dimensions as I have outlined them.[7] The *context* and *goals* dimensions will be treated at greater length.

Lenses

In the previous section, I described the lens of science as a particular perspective or expectation a scientist brings to his or her problem space. One of the students' responsibilities at their field sites was to take down as many observations of their surroundings as possible as soon as they arrived for each visit. They were not explicitly told the purpose of this activity, but the students seemed to make a direct connection between the act of observing and things scientific. Moreover, the students brought with them certain expectations about what doing science is all about, which were, to varying degrees, borne out in their experiences.

For example, in an interview, when asked to describe the most important things she was learning from the project, one student replied:

> There's a lot of things to science, like there are steps that you have to take, like you go, you explore, there's notes you have to take. You use a lot of notes because you have to refer back to them and stuff. There's a lot of observing, and there's a lot of stuff that you have to do to figure it out. It's basically a lot of work because you have to figure it out for yourself.
>
> (Erica[2])[8]

I asked the students to share with me a typical day in the field. The following is representative of most of the students' responses, particularly with respect to the emphasis on 'seeing':

The first thing we do is we take observations, and the importance of observations every day is to kind of see what is changing, because that is overall what we're trying to see, how the marsh changes. Taking observations for 10 minutes is a good way to do this, seeing if the birds are there or which way the algae has moved, and all kinds of things like that. And then we go and take water samples at all the different sites we selected. We selected them based on a trickle-down thing because right on our site is a current, you can tell by the way the water moves, and we figured it would be good to get it at the beginning of the current, the middle, and the end, just to see kind of see what happened to the water as it came down the pond. So we take the pH, and the pH has been pretty high, actually, which could indicate some amount of pollution that is in the water, but we then also take the salinity from that same water sample. We've also been doing some dissolved oxygen testing to see how much oxygen is in the water, to see if the algae is choking it, and see if it will be suitable to put fish in there.

(Jeremy[1])

This project relied heavily on careful observation and diligent recording of those observations. The students believed that observation is an important and relatively unproblematic scientific process; they believed that the objective lens of science would yield the most reliable information. However, while they did focus on the importance of individual observation, they also noted the consequence of intersubjectivity – the cooperation, coordination and negotiation required to understand the phenomena at hand. This idea will be elaborated in the next section.

Methods

The students referred to aspects of method, such as the significance of collaboration, the diversity of skills required to understand a complex system (namely, the wetlands), the importance of having the flexibility to use methods that best suit their question, and the connection between the methods used and the context of the project.

Many students reflected on the importance of *collaboration* and the crucial role each group member played in the production of knowledge. Some groups were better at collaborating than others, but all types of groups seemed to recognise teamwork as an essential feature of the task. One student, from a particularly dysfunctional group (in terms of staying on task), remarked:

If everybody doesn't do their part in a group, then some people are going to be kind of disgruntled about that, and the other people

136

aren't going to know what's happening. So you all have to do your part and you all have to pay attention to make it work.

(Corry[2])

I asked him if he thought that this kind of cooperation is important in science. He responded:

Oh yeah, I'm sure it is. You kind of have to compromise, too. I'm sure that happens. Cooperation must be an extremely big factor in their success, and uh, I guess you also have people developing different specialties. If you have a big group, you have one person who is good at something and another person who is good at another thing, that kind of thing.

(Corry[2])

This student's allusion to compromise implies an understanding that conflict and disagreements are to be expected in endeavours of this sort. Indeed, many of the students, when I asked them about the most important things they thought they were learning, reported working in a team towards a common goal as one of the most valuable lessons. This student also suggests the rather sophisticated notion of distributed expertise and the value of bringing to bear a diversity of perspectives on a particular problem.

At the same time, some students, especially those who ended up doing most of the work in their group, cited the teamwork aspect of the project to be the least useful (or least liked) part of the project. Here's how another student described her group:

Teamwork was important because when we mapped [our site] out, that took a lot of stuff, because one of us would go out and the other ones would interpret what she kind of yelled back and sometimes it wasn't clear. The other person would write it down, and we'd keep checking on each other to make sure we were in the right area doing the right things. That was one of the really big things we kind of learned.

(Kate[2])

Not only does this student touch on the concept of multiple perspectives, she also refers to the importance of social negotiation to make sure they were 'in the right area doing the right things'.

Some students talked about the inter-group collaboration as a new experience. For example, a couple of students reflected on the production of the field guide, an effort that called for coordination between groups, as an important aspect of their work:

137

> I think it was good to like practise all the researching and putting
> it together into the field guide. I have never done something with
> a whole group of people doing different parts of it. Being able to
> work with other people and manage time and stuff, and be
> responsible for one part [was a good experience].
>
> (Meg[2])

As these comments illustrate, the students recognised that collaborative
work in science can be enhanced when people representing a diversity of
skills and perspectives work together. In their view, scientific methods
entail more than simply following a procedure – they require collaboration
and negotiation on the most effective means to answer the questions or
problems they are trying to address.

Context

Of all the dimensions described thus far, the internal and external context
made the largest impact on the students. They were especially impressed
with their ability actually to 'be' at the wetlands to study it as opposed to
studying from a textbook, film or lecture. Many of the students also felt
strongly about the external context, the community issues that impelled the
city to spend the money to restore the marsh, and the role they played in
helping the community further its goal to beautify the area and provide
habitat for endangered species. The context of the problem they studied was
real, which resulted in many of the students recognising it as a very
different way to learn science.

Being in the field raised a number of issues for the students. For example,
it facilitated a stronger connection to the ideas they were working with, and
they believed it would help them remember the experience better than if
they simply read about it in a textbook.

> I think it's good because it kind of keeps your interest more than
> just same old like notes everyday and lectures and whatever. It
> just keeps you more interested because you actually get to go and
> experience it and you actually get to see it happening, you're not
> just trying to memorise it and going 'this is what happens'.
> You're going to see it so it's easier to know what happens, you
> don't have to memorise it because you've seen it, so you just kind
> of remember.
>
> (Beth[2])

We actually went to the real site and learned about it by doing it
and seeing it, and so I think it was a lot more interesting and
stimulating. We were more excited about actually going to the

marsh than just reading about it, so I think it made it more memorable. Instead of just memorizing facts and then forgetting about it, we kind of remember it for longer.

(Meg[2])

Further, the students felt that the context caused them to care more about the work they were doing, as this comment indicates:

With videos you just kind of see it and write it down, but you don't necessarily understand it, or know what's going on with it. When you do it yourself, it's more close to home and you care more about what's going on. When we're out in the field I feel like it's easier to understand. I learn it better.

(Eve[2])

The field context, coupled with the 'real' question they were attempting to answer, lent a sense of authenticity that the students had not experienced in the classroom setting.

You're going out and you're seeing actual situations. You're doing actual things on an every-day, well actually every-week basis. It gives you a more realistic picture of how science is done.

(Jeremy[2])

The students' experiences in the classroom left them bored and unmotivated. In contrast, the wetlands project offered them a change of venue, a host of new experiences, and an opportunity to apply what they knew to a novel situation. For one student, the wetlands experience presented an opportunity to extend her ways of knowing to make use of a larger variety of senses:

When you're out there you can take in more. Like with a book, you read it, you understand it, that's it. When you're out [at the wetlands], you see it, you hear it, you feel it, you smell it, and it takes you a while sometimes to actually understand it, but that will stick more in your mind than just a simple memorisation thing.

(Kate[2])

In her case, the classroom context limited science to textual representations. The field context, on the other hand, effectively multiplied the possible ways for her to experience science. Another student referred to the authenticity of the project by suggesting that what they were doing was more mature scientific work:

I've never done anything like this. I've always done projects
where a teacher grades them and there's a definite answer to it.
But this is out in the real world and were doing stuff that we
haven't done before, and it's like adult work, not like kids in
school where there's projects and everything. THAT's what was
really interesting.

(Ming[1])

This last comment is particularly informative. The student associated the
work she did in the field with 'adults' and the work typically done in
classrooms with 'kids'. The fact that the questions guiding the project were
open-ended, coupled with the project being in the 'real world' and not in
the classroom (context), impressed this student.

Goals

In traditional instruction, the goals of science are rarely, if ever, discussed.
In the wetlands project, this dimension provided, in many ways, the centre-
piece of their activity. This project embodied four main goals: (1) to respect
the natural world; (2) to serve the local community; (3) to serve the
scientific community; and (4) to take action on science-related social issues.
Most of the students expressed an understanding of the first three goals, but
did not perceive 'action-taking' as important or relevant to science. In other
words, the students could speak eloquently about the need to be aware of
and take care of nature, and while they knew that the project design
involved service to their community and active involvement on their part,
they did not count science-related activism as an important or even worthwhile activity.

More importantly, though, many students concluded that their image
of scientists working alone in a laboratory setting for purposes that have
nothing to do with everyday issues or concerns was probably not accurate. In fact, several students remarked that they were unaware that
scientists can and do work in local communities on local issues, that
the goals of their work can be as simple as saving the habitat of a single
species.

Goal 1   Awareness of and care for the natural world

This project underscored the community-related goals, such that many of
the students, in the end, felt that saving the wetlands was an important part
of an overall vision of ecological sustainability. Their sense of what kind of
projects are worth doing and for what purposes was influenced by this
particular goal. Many students commented in their journals on the importance of saving wetlands areas:

140

If the marsh doesn't get restored, the animals in the Marsh will move to another location; or stay and die because of all the lack of good water and nutrients. The city is trying to keep this place as a natural preserve to save species of animals and plants that would otherwise go extinct. This reflects a bigger worldwide project of keeping the native animals and plants alive.

(Tony[JF2a])

I think that it is very important to restore salt marshes because they are a unique environment which is home to many plants and animals. Without the marsh they would have no home, and they might become endangered or extinct. I think that is the reason why salt marshes should be restored and protected. I think it is overall pretty nice for the community to have the marsh restored, because it provides a beautiful place with lots of wildlife where people can go to walk or bird watch. However, the marsh takes up land that could be used in other ways. I personally think that it is much better to have a marsh than buildings, or whatever would go there, but others may not agree.

(Meg[JF2])

This last student suggests that perhaps not everyone would agree that restoring the area to its original state reflects the best use of the land. Indeed, the reclaimed wetlands area represents a large piece of very valuable real estate. This student detected the difficulty of establishing clear and consensual goals for scientific endeavours. She recognised that even though *she* believed the restoration project was the best way to use the land, others might disagree. Knowing that this debate is possible and that varying beliefs exist in relation to scientists' projects represents an important understanding about the nature of goals in scientific research.

Goal 2 Service to the local community

'Helping', with its multiple meanings, proved very important in the students' overall experience. In general, the students felt that the service aspect of the project, and the connections they made to the community, were well worth their efforts. As noted in the previous section, several students reported that just learning that the marsh existed in their own 'back yard' was enough to pique their interest and motivate them to learn more. Several students reported feeling positive about contributing to a larger effort to do something good for the community:

We're mostly dealing with a whole separate environment that's part of like our whole project, that's really important to like the city and that sort of thing, and it's kind of good to feel like your research will actually help something in the future. I think that's kind of cool.

(Kate[1])

Because it's close to home so you can understand it better and you really feel like it's a thing you should care about.

(Eve[2])

You learn about the environment and actually make a difference while learning about what you're doing.

(Tom[J5])

One student reported that he would be less interested in a project that didn't have a service component. In an interview I asked him if he cared more about this project than other assignments in school. He answered:

Would [the other assignments] be going out in the community? Because that makes a big difference. If you're actually there help-ing, trying to figure something out, it is a lot different than solving it on paper.

(Tom[1])

Similarly, another student responded:

Yeah definitely, because it's something that you've been working on for a long time, and you want to have a good experiment, and it's not like a class assignment. There's no grade, and you just kind of enjoy doing it because it's fun and you get to do things you don't usually get to do, like help your community.

(Ming[1])

The most important aspect of service embedded in this project that the students noted was the realisation that scientists could and often do engage in work outside of a laboratory for the purposes of improving the quality of life in a local community. Strikingly, some students had never before realised that fieldwork such as this was a viable option for a scientific career. Therefore, service to humanity became not only a goal of the project for the students, but also a legitimate goal of science, writ large. Below is a sampling of comments from both interviews and journals:

I think you kind of usually like kind of think of scientists as off in their own world doing something in the laboratory without it really affecting anyone out in the public except if they found an incredible cure for a disease or something. So this [wetlands project] kind of shows that there really are a lot of scientists just doing tons of different things that affect people.

(Meg [2])

I think that the main thing that really hit me was that scientists can really affect communities on a more personal note. I mean all the scientists I know are the stereotypical white lab coats doing like super duper funky lab work that seems like it will never affect me. I never realised that field studies used so much science.

(Tom[JF3])

Before, scientists is [sic] so high tech, and in a laboratory wearing white coats and using all those chemicals and stuff, but it doesn't really have to be that, it's more like just studying something that doesn't really have to have an answer, and you're trying to find an answer to a question.

(Ming[2])

The comments in this and the previous section illustrate the range of understandings the students had of the purposes for engaging in this kind of project. Many of them mention the importance of maintaining a diversity of species, and they each emphasised a different reason for why it matters, ranging from aesthetics to community education. The students experienced science happening in a particular place for a particular purpose. As with the methods dimension, the students gained an understanding of the role of purpose in doing scientific research in ways that traditional instruction would have difficulty capturing.

Goal 3   Service to science

While service to the local community represented an important and very visible goal of science in this project, the students also felt that they were contributing something to the scientific community. This was facilitated by the visible presence of Beth, the city water scientist, and her genuine interest in what the students were doing and finding out.

Since we're writing up this big final report . . . it's going to help scientists figure out how to help the marsh area and keep it in good condition, and keep it in good shape. People are going to want to be there and going to want to see it and study it, what kind of plants should be planted where and what kind of animals should be living where and what kind of food the fish need and what kind of fish should be put in the pond and that kind of stuff. Since we identified some stuff, it will probably be easier for them now.

(Beth[2])

There was also, however, some confusion as to who would be the ultimate beneficiaries of their work. Several students voiced their concerns about the fact that they were the third group of students to contribute to this growing body of information, and they would not be the last. It was difficult for them to visualise their unique contibution.

Goal 4   *Action with science*

It seemed that the wetlands project increased the students' environmental awareness and their appreciation of contributing to the local and scientific community. The teacher was hoping for this. But are awareness and appreciation enough? Did the students feel any greater sense of personal or political efficacy as a result? Unfortunately, it seems that the answer to these questions is mostly no. For example, for their final journal question, we asked the students to write about any lingering questions they had about the project, and how they might go about trying to answer them. While many of them could formulate interesting questions that followed logically from their own research, very few could say how they would investigate them. What is more, those that could, deferred to their teacher or to Beth as sources for the answers – not themselves. While they believed they were reliable spokespersons for the work they had done that semester, this confidence did not seem to extend beyond this project. In this light, there are two ways in which efficacy and confidence came into play: (1) in *doing* science, and (2) in their perceived opportunities (or lack thereof) to act in their community.

Teaching students to take action towards changing or even participating in local science issues has been difficult to realise. Indeed, much of the research on STS curricula admits that this step often gets left undone. Some of the issues connecting *questions* and *context* in the students' minds might also be at work here. That is, the absence of student voice with respect to most aspects of the project could manifest in a resistance to taking action on its behalf. Or, to put it less drastically, their lack of participation in framing and developing the question could cause them to be less interested in acting to solve it. In response to a question about the relevance this project might have for the students' future, many responses echoed this one:

> It doesn't really have a lot to do with my main interests in life. I mean, I don't really want to be a scientist, and I mean I thought it was interesting, just not that important. I mean, I know it is important to other people though. Maybe for other people's future, not particularly for my future, because I don't want a particularly scientific career.
>
> (Beth[2])

In general, the students had difficulty connecting their wetlands experience and issues within the larger community. Moreover, many were unable to make the leap from what they were learning to their own role as producers and users of scientific knowledge. For example, I asked them early on in the study if they thought the project had any relevance for the larger local community. Very few students were able to answer this vaguely worded question. To see if a different medium might help their thinking, I asked a similar question as a journal writing assignment. Students responded:

> I don't think there is any direct relevance, but the things we learn out there maybe are applicable somewhere else in the community.
>
> (Ali[JF2])

> We didn't learn about how the environment affects us at all. I mean if we were to learn, like for example, when you cut down trees, that reduces the oxygen in the air, that affects us, because you need oxygen. But [in the wetlands project] you see little animals dying because of the pH level – you don't know why that would affect you.
>
> (Corry[2])

The 'action' aspect of this project enjoyed a mixed success. There seems to be an important progression of development involved, beginning with awareness, moving through genuine care and the recognition of the value of service, and ending with action, that somehow was truncated in this particular project. Possible reasons for this will be offered in a later section.

The relationship between the contexts and goals of science

The students' experiences with the contexts and goals of science took on different emphases throughout their work in the field and in the classroom. While students are often taught that scientists bring a plethora of prior knowledge and skills to new problems, that collaboration is important, or that scientists have goals that guide their work, rarely do they have the opportunity actually to experience these dimensions of science. These students reported experiencing a different side of science that they had not yet encountered in their education – science became highly collaborative, complex, interactive and diverse. They also saw how scientific knowledge could be used to improve the ecology of their local community. The wetlands project yielded different kinds of understandings of the dimensions of science because of its reliance on group collaboration, its field context, its clear purpose and its community focus.

145

In scientific research, essential connections exist among the underlying purposes of a particular research programme, the context in which it occurs, and the questions that guide it. This is not surprising: we would find it unusual if scientists undertook research that required resources they do not have access to, or for purposes that their questions do not address.

The questions the students investigated in this project were predetermined by the teacher. The major questions guiding their endeavour included: Is the marsh being restored? What is the general health of the pond? How can we find out? What lives in the wetlands? What thrives in the wetlands? With one exception, these are open-ended questions that require long-term investigation. These two particular characteristics highly influenced the students' sense that they were doing authentic work. The students knew that their teacher did not have the answers, and neither did their textbook.

Comments about the open-endedness and long-term nature of the project also speak to the context in which it occurred. The context in this case – an expansive wetlands habitat situated in the local community – provided a unique opportunity for long-term, open-ended, authentic study. One particular aspect of the project that seemed to capture the students' attention was the extent to which the location and nature of the work connected with the goal to serve their community.

The goals of scientists and the context in which science occurs are crucial components that determine how, where and for what reasons science is practised. The relationship between these dimensions is rarely addressed in traditional instruction. While most scientists, when pressed, would say that their research holds some redeeming value for humanity, or some purposeful application that could benefit society, school science rarely connects the two. When teachers link scientific questions and social implications, students do not typically engage directly with the issues. Rather, as much of the research on STS education reveals, students often simply read about or discuss the issues as they relate to a distant world or community.

Discussion and conclusions

Discussion

Given the heuristic I employed to view the science experiences of the students in this case study, I have argued that when the approach to science instruction has at its core purposeful doing, the student experience differs from traditional instruction in potentially important ways. For example, the dimensions of science that I propose – lenses, methods, questions, objects and phenomena, contexts, and goals – take on new, more situational meanings. In particular, the methods of science become a collection of non-linear, task-appropriate investigative strategies devised and performed in a collaborative group. The context of science moved from the laboratory to the field, where science happens in unpredictable ways. The goals of science expanded to include service to society and an ethic of care. Moreover, as the student comments show, the connections between and among the various dimensions of science were not difficult to discern.

One question that remained in the back of my mind throughout this research was this: Could these students have gained these insights about science without the strong ethic of service that defined this project? In other words, what difference did service make? In the end, the students *cared* a great deal about the service aspects of the project. My use of the word 'care' in this context refers both to the students' personal interest and emotional connection to the project, as well as the strong conservationist message that provided the impetus to create it.

As many of the students' written and spoken remarks indicate, this project helped them feel a greater connection to the natural world. Many of them reported that they no longer take for granted that they will always have clean air, water and soil. They felt a greater compassion for the endangered Baylands species and hoped that their efforts would somehow help save the species' lives.

However, there did not seem to be much indication that the students would extend their efforts when the semester was over. In fact, when asked directly about the relevance this project had for their future, some students could not imagine beyond the idea of working in the marsh as a professional scientist. They did not seem to relate the wetlands and their own existence beyond the possibility of some kind of future employment as a wetlands expert. Some students had difficulty linking their work in the wetlands with larger ecological problems or issues, seeing the purpose of the work they were doing, and understanding, to any great degree, the role of science in their own lives and community.

One possible explanation for this is the sense in which the teacher changed the *context* of science without effectively linking this new context to the *goals* implied by it. Perhaps she hoped that changing the context was enough to cause the students to take on new and active roles related to science.

Another possible explanation lies in the design of the project, specifically the teacher-dictated objective that structured the students' activity. Perhaps, since the students did not have a voice in framing the project (that is, in determining the questions that they should or could ask), their understanding of the context of the project was diminished. Likewise, if a student neglected to see the value of restoring wetlands, they might be less interested in the questions that were set before them. These possible situations illustrate how *not* clarifying or explicitly addressing one dimension truncates the richness of the science experience.

Conclusions and future directions

The wetlands project highlighted dimensions of science and aspects of those dimensions that have not traditionally been considered a priority in practical work. In the students' experiences with the wetlands project, the nature of the context in which science occurs, the kinds of goals scientists set for their practices, and the diversity of methods they employ to answer questions they deem interesting and useful, all stood out as central elements of the process of science. Traditional science education – that is, classroom and textbook-based science instruction – might also address these dimensions of science. The difference lies in the 'being there', the open-endedness and long-term nature of the work, and the attentiveness to community needs.

Many might argue that there is nothing new about this claim; educators have always known about the importance of active learning and hands-on participation. They would be right. However they would also be neglecting a pivotal aspect of this kind of experience – namely, its *authenticity*. As project-based instruction becomes more and more part of mainstream education (and I think it will), science educators must attend to the questions that are bound to arise. What kinds of projects should students engage in? For what purpose? What picture of science should projects represent? What should be the nature of the products of students' work? How might science projects integrate with other disciplines?

Based on my experience with the students in the wetlands project, I believe that we should prioritise projects that have the potential to serve both the scientific and local or global community. That is, science educators, curriculum developers, teacher educators and other interested parties ought to consider how to make long-term, authentic (authentic in the sense that needs are met through participation) study of local scientific questions and problems a central focus in science instruction. The wetlands project, with its service learning component, addresses this aspect directly and effectively.

I believe that the goals of science education ought to include transformation of the sciences, and part of that transformation needs to include movement towards more socially just and responsible science. In this light, projects which embody an ethic of care and responsible action become exemplars for schools and teachers wishing to reform their teaching in this way. Table 8.2 contrasts what I am calling 'traditional' instruction with this new vision of science pedagogy that centres on authenticity.

While the two approaches to science teaching may be artificially dichotomised, the contrast serves as a useful place to begin discussion. Attentiveness to authenticity in the sense pictured here brings into view the questions, contexts and goals of science. Lenses, methods, and objects and phenomena emerge, too. Most importantly, authentic projects like the

148

Table 8.2 Dimensions of science transformed

Dimension	Traditional instruction	Transformed instruction
Lenses and methods	Objective application of the step-wise scientific method; performed individually or with a partner	A collection of integrative, task-appropriate investigative strategies devised and performed in a collaborative group
Questions	'Known' answer; asked by experts; require short-term study (40-min. periods)	Unknown answer; not necessarily asked by experts; require long-term study
Natural objects and phenomena	The known facts, theories, and laws of science	Facts and theories constructed by the collective
Context	The school laboratory	Fieldwork in the community
Goals	Learn content and processes of science	Participate in service to community (scientific and local); foster an ethic of care

Baylands project have the potential to focus students on many of the socio-cultural, moral and practical goals of the scientific enterprise. Some people, myself included, believe that among the goals of science should be care for the subjects of study and concern about the consequences of research. Such a perspective suggests we rethink science instruction, and indeed scientific practice itself. It also implies that we consider student action-taking more seriously. However, for students to want to act, they first have to care and understand. To care and understand, they need to have a voice in developing a question, and assistance in making connections among the various dimensions. The wetlands project, even considering its shortcomings, went a long way in building that foundation.

Acknowledgement

This chapter draws on material previously published in the *International Journal of Science Education*, 1998.

Notes

1 All names in this chapter are pseudonyms.
2 The wetlands project represented one of six projects the students could select. Other projects included developing exhibits for a local children's museum, producing a programme for the local cable channel, and team-teaching in a third-grade classroom.
3 'Honours' refers to the accelerated track. Honours students were enrolled in a higher maths course and were, in some cases, given different kinds of assignments than the regular track students. This resulted in a large number of 'honours' students doing the wetlands project. During the semester reported here, there were approximately fifteen honours students and seven non-honours. The element of choice made very little difference in the students' general attitude towards the project. There were honours and non-honours alike who felt positive and negative about different aspects of the project.
4 General education credit is given when the course taken does not easily fit into the standard academic subject areas, such as most electives. Students are allowed a limited number of general education units for graduation. At the present time, Rachel is trying to convince the administrators at her school that the students who worked on the wetlands project should receive science credit for their efforts at best, practical arts at worst. At this time, the outcome is unclear.
5 L. Lapin, (21 August 1990) 'Rebirth of a marsh: Palo Alto project to revive what development has ruined', *San José Mercury News*, pp. C1–2.
6 The pickleweed plant is especially important in that it serves as the main food source for the salt marsh harvest mouse. It needs very salty water to grow.
7 For an expanded discussion of these and the other dimensions, see Helms (1997).
8 Interview sources: numbers refer to whether the excerpt was taken from the first or second interview. A 'J' indicates that that the excerpt is taken from a student's written response in his or her journal.

References

Aikenhead, G. (1985) 'Collective decision-making in the social context of science', *Science Education* 69(4): 453–475.
—— (1994) 'What is STS teaching?' in J. Solomon and G. Aikenhead (eds) *STS Education: International Perspectives on Reform*, New York: Teachers College Press, pp. 47–59.
American Association for the Advancement of Science (1989) *Science for All Americans: a project 2061 Report on Literacy Goals in Science, Mathematics, and Technology*, Washington, DC: AAAS.
—— (1993) *Benchmarks for Science Literacy*, New York: Oxford University Press.
Bybee, R. (1993) *Reforming Science Education: Social Perspectives and Personal Reflections*, New York: Teachers College Press.
California Department of Education (1990) *Science Framework for California Public Schools Kindergarten through Grade Twelve*, Sacramento, CA.
Cross, R. T. and Price, R. F. (1992) *Teaching Science for Social Responsibility*, Sydney: St Louis Press.
Cunningham, C. M. (1995) 'The effect of teachers' sociological understanding of

science on classroom practice and curriculum innovation', unpublished doctoral dissertation, Cornell University.

Driver, R., Asoko, H., Leach, J., Mortimer, D. and Scott, J. (1994) 'Constructing scientific knowledge in the classroom', *Educational Researcher* 23(7): 5–12.

Hansen, K-H. and Olson, J. (1995) 'The moral construction of integrated science and STS: the discipline as a framework for teacher thinking', unpublished manuscript.

Haraway, D. (1989) *Primate Visions*, London: Routledge.

Harding, S. (1986) *The Science Question in Feminism*, Ithaca, NY: Cornell University Press.

Helms, J.V. (1997) 'Science in action, action with science: studying wetlands restoration', paper presented at the annual meeting of the American Educational Research Association, Chicago, IL.

Hrdy, S.B. (1986) 'Empathy, polyandry, and the myth of the coy female', in R. Bleier (ed.) *Feminist Approaches to Science*, New York: Teachers College Press, pp. 119–46.

Kelly, G., Carlsen, W. and Cunningham, C. (1993) 'Science education in sociocultural context: perspectives from the sociology of science', *Science Education* 77: 207–20.

May, W. (1992) 'What are the subjects of STS – *really?*' *Theory into Practice* 31(1): 73–83.

Millar, R. (1994) 'What is "scientific method" and can it be taught?' in R. Levinson (ed.) *Teaching Science*, London: Routledge, pp. 164–77.

National Research Council (1996) *National Science Education Standards*, Washington, DC: National Academy Press.

Pedretti, E. and Hodson, D. (1995) 'From rhetoric to action: implementing STS education through action research', *Journal of Research in Science Teaching* 32(5): 463–85.

Ramsey, F. (1993) 'The science education reform movement: implications for social responsibility', *Science Education* 77(2): 235–58.

Restivo, S. (1994) *Science, Society, and Values: Toward a Sociology of Objectivity*, Bethlehem, PA: Lehigh University Press.

Rose, H. (1994) 'The two-way street: reforming science education and transforming masculine science', in J. Solomon and G. Aikenhead (eds) *STS Education: International Perspectives on Reform*, New York: Teachers College Press, pp. 155–66.

Roth, W-M. (1995) *Authentic School Science: Knowing and Learning in Open-Inquiry Science Laboratories*, Dordrecht: Kluwer Press.

Rubba, P.A. (1991) 'Integrating STS into school science and teacher education: beyond awareness', *Theory into Practice* 30(4): 303–8.

Solomon, J. (1994) 'Conflict between mainstream science and STS in science education', in J. Solomon and G. Aikenhead (eds) *STS Education: International Perspectives on Reform*, New York: Teachers College Press, pp. 3–10.

Stahl, R.J. (ed.) (1996) *Cooperative Learning in Science: a Handbook for Teachers*, Menlo Park, CA: Addison-Wesley.

Stake, R.E. (1995) *The Art of Case Study Research*, Thousand Oaks, CA: Sage Publishers.

Waks, L.J. (1992) 'The responsibility spiral: a curriculum framework for STS education', *Theory into Practice* 31(1): 13–19.

Part IV

LANGUAGE, IMAGES, IDEAS AND PRACTICAL WORK

It has been said several times in the past, with reference to practical work, that children should spend more time on thinking than on doing, 'more time interacting with ideas and less time interacting with apparatus' (Gunstone 1991: 74, in Woolnough (ed.)). Perhaps the most used quote came from Vygotsky, who wrote that 'Children solve practical tasks with their speech as well as their hands' (Vygotsky 1978). In a later section we look at how ICT can free or emancipate learners from some of the drudgery that goes with practical work in order to allow them to move on to higher order skills such as interpreting, explaining and hypothesising. Practical work has become so obsessed with the *collection of data*, at first hand, that it leaves little time for other abilities. This is explored in the later chapters on ICT, but in this section Osborne highlights the potential of unlocking science lessons from the expectation that they should always involve the collection of a learner's own first-hand data.

Osborne starts from the premise that the aims of science education have swung over time from the need for an education *for* science (for example, training for a scientific career) towards the need for an education *in and about* science. He makes certain criticisms of existing practical work in science which link well with other discussions in this book: learning 'to do' science at school is very different from learning scientific skills in the real world (different instruments, different skills); experiencing the process of scientific enquiry in science education may be important, but again how does this model the huge variation which exists across the range of real sciences (cf. Leach's chapter). Osborne's key message is that practical work has a role in science education (in illustrating macroscopic phenomena), but the key element is the concepts or spectacles through which we see phenomena. With the excessive emphasis on pupils collecting their own data in the past, the abilities to present, interpret, discuss and evaluate data have been neglected. His suggestion is that the time devoted to traditional practical work should be reduced, leaving time for students to read about and understand the discourse of science in a critical way. With this new emphasis, the science curriculum can focus on the big ideas of science (Osborne's 'overarching themes') and include a focus on the contemporary, controversial, science-based issues of current society. In this way, students will learn far more about the nature of science, its methods, its limitations and its strengths than they would through attempting to mimic scientific activity in a school lab.

Osborne's argument for a new focus and emphasis on the language and discourse of science is taken up by Sutton in his chapter. Sutton's work on language in science is well known, and this chapter relates his creative thinking in this area to the issue of practical work. He distinguishes 'science in the making' from 'ready-made science' and clearly most school learning is about the latter. Scientific language becomes less tentative as we move towards ready-made science, which has 'insider conversations' using insider language. The history of science shows that 'doing science' involves a lot more than 'doing experiments' (see earlier discussion of the term 'experiment') – scientific activity involves talking, meeting, discussing, reading and thinking (and, as we see later in the book, using ICT to communicate). Sutton's key argument is that *effective* practical work requires a combination of practical experiences together with conversation, discourse or mental acts that is, a combination of the physical and the mental – 'hands-on plus minds-on'. Sutton illustrates how this major shift might occur, and argues that it will require a huge change in initial and in-service professional development for teachers – a point taken up at the end of Solomon's chapter.

Solomon's chapter explains clearly and succinctly her view of the importance of 'imaging' or 'envisionment' in practical work. She, like other authors in the book, is a strong advocate of the importance of practical work (indeed, most people will remember the rhyme in her 1980 book on teaching and learning in the laboratory: 'Science teaching should take place in a laboratory, about that at least there is no controversy'). Here she talks about the interplay between doing, observing and thinking. All are deemed to be essential elements of practical work, a common theme throughout this book. But the difficulty involves creating the link between internal ideas or images, and doing and observing. She uses several fascinating examples from her own teaching to show how the teacher's envisionment of a problem or phenomenon (such as shadow formation) can be vastly different from that of the learners'. Her discussion relates closely to Sutton's view (and Millar's earlier remarks) on the importance in science of 'seeing things as. . . .' and the value of metaphor, although she points out the limitations of certain teaching metaphors such as the water model of electric current. Solomon's message is that doing and envisioning are both equally important, as is the idea of play and getting a feel for things.

References

Solomon, J. (1980) *Teaching Children in the Laboratory*, London: Croom Helm.
Vygotsky, L. (1978) *Thought and Language*, Cambridge, MA: MIT Press.
Woolnough, B. (ed.) (1991) *Practical Science*, Milton Keynes: Open University Press.

9

SCIENCE EDUCATION WITHOUT A LABORATORY?

Jonathan Osborne

This chapter seeks to argue that the centrality of the laboratory in science education leads to an overemphasis on practical work. A critical examination of the arguments for practical work shows that it only has a strictly limited role to play in learning science and that much of it is of little educational value. Instead, students would benefit from more opportunities to engage with the language and discourse of science through reading, writing and discussion. Such work would help them to interpret and understand the meaning of the science, its beauty and its value – an understanding of which existing science curricula singularly fail to achieve. Examples of possible techniques are used to illustrate the argument.

In the post-war era science education has remained fundamentally an education *for* science rather than an education *in* science (Ziman 1968). For science education still serves the preparation of an elite, where low-level or entry-level courses are seen as a preparation for the next rung on the ladder which, in itself, serves the rung above. Those who choose to step off, or even worse, those who fall off are simply regarded as the inevitable casualties to be expended in the process of producing the few who will enter the institution of science. Furthermore, the introduction of GCSEs and the National Curriculum have not changed this pattern (Millar 1996). However, at the *fin de siècle*, the current demands of a science education *for all*, and the need for a better public understanding of science coupled with the changing nature of the public's perception of science and technology, require that science education addresses itself to the development of a new set of competencies. It is my contention that these are not well served by an overemphasis on practical work, and that during this century, the centrality of the laboratory to the teaching of science has become like the addicts' relationship to their drug – an unquestioned dependency which needs to be re-examined and weakened, if not broken altogether.

Essentially in the latter third of the twentieth century, the image of science and technology as a source of solutions to technical and scientific problems and of 'man's' domination of nature has changed. As well as being the conqueror of disease and the producer of a life-enhancing material technology, science and technology have also become *the producer* of an increasing number of risks and threats to our lives, livelihoods and civilisation. Consequently, the public's attitude has changed from a blind faith in the 'white hot heat of the technological revolution' of the 1960s to one of ambivalence or distrust. Now that the food we eat or the air we breathe is considered problematic, the handling of risk and insecurity becomes a basic cultural qualification, and the cultivation of the abilities demanded for handling and assessing risk become an essential mission for science education, otherwise 'people expect the unsaid, add in the side effects and expect the worst' (Beck 1992).

In this context, where the public faith in science and scientific advice has been severely dented, science education needs to emphasise *not only* how to 'do' science and learn scientific knowledge, but rather to explore how to 'read' and understand the *discourse* of science in a 'critical', 'educated' way (Sutton, Chapter 10). Such a need places an emphasis on learning *about* science in order to understand what science *is* – a cultural product. Information in science needs to be approached in much the same way as texts are approached in literary studies, not simply in a search of their manifest content (or 'plot'), but in an attempt to understand how scientific knowledge is produced, negotiated and transformed – that is, to recognise not only the strengths and achievements of science but also its *limitations*. Confronted with an ever-expanding body of knowledge, where even scientists are scientifically illiterate outside their own field (Greene 1997), it is essential to develop 'pedagogies which focus on the development of student's ability to 'retrieve', 'to think', 'to assess', 'to react', 'to understand', and 'to digest' such information, as well as to know and recall specific pieces of 'universal' knowledge' (Gilbert 1997). Only such skills will enable the future citizen to manage and assess the diversity of risks that constantly assail them and cope more effectively with the uncertainty they generate (Hood and Jones 1996).

Given the finite time available for teaching science, such a transformation of school science can only be achieved by a reduction of content, with a concomitant diminishment in the time devoted to practical work. In too many classrooms, practical work is the consequence of a kind of Faustian contract, entered into by teachers and pupils because it is the essential *sine qua non* – the cardinal defining characteristic of school science. However, it is a pact which has a cost – which is the lack of time that can be devoted to the development of activities that require reading about science; activities that develop the skills of interpreting and analysing scientific evidence; and activities that use discussion, argumentation and writing about science. All of these, I would contend, are central to developing an understanding of the nature of science and the skills of synthesis and critical evaluation, fundamental for participation in a society where science increasingly impinges on our society and daily lives. School science can no longer preserve the hermetic seal offered by the laboratory door that excludes all consideration of such issues. For the real world seeps in and demands attention for which current pedagogic practice is ill prepared.

The trouble with practical work

Essentially, as Hodson has argued, both in this volume – see Chapter 6 – and previously (1990), there are three justifications for the learning of science: the need to *learn* science – that is, to learn the core concepts, theories and models developed by science to explain the world; the need to *learn to do* science – that is, the processes by which scientists gain new knowledge; and the need to *learn about* science – to understand its epistemological base, the cultural achievement that such knowledge represents, and its implications for our society. The relative weighting of these components and the role of practical work rest on a set of assumptions, often tacit, that bear further examination.

One argument for the value of practical work is that it is illustrative. To have seen the complexity of the organs of a rat, to have observed Brownian motion, or the vigour of the reaction of magnesium with oxygen is to give an essential meaning to phenomena that mere words cannot convey. However, many of these phenomena can be observed *as well*, if not better, by demonstration, where students' attention can be drawn to the salient features which provide the key evidence for the picture which the teacher constructs. For instance, unprepared observation of wave phenomena in ripple tanks rarely results in observation of reflection, refraction, interference or diffraction, but instead, of other associated but irrelevant events. Even then, the chances of the student constructing the conventional textbook representation of these phenomena are as likely as a new tourist in London of producing a useful map of the Underground after one visit (Driver 1983). In short, there is rarely any justification for all children to engage in class practical for the purpose of phenemonological observation when demonstrations are a much more efficient and effective means of illustrating not only the phenomena but also the scientific description of events.

As Lakin and Wellington (1991) have argued, there *is* at least a motivational justification for practical work, which arises from the excitement and engagement with the concrete manipulation of the world – an essential precursor to the construction of many of the macroscopic entities of science. It was Harré (1986) who pointed to the fact that sense, that is our cognitive representations of the world, and reference, our active exploration of the material world, are the fundamental basis on which we construct our mental models of the world. For him, both are irrevocably intertwined – that is, 'sense determines the possibility of reference . . . while reference, when achieved, brings about the refinement of sense'. Hence, the young child needs to experience a range of phenomena (acts of reference) that illustrate and give meaning to words such as 'hard', 'strong', 'brittle'; to distinguish between mixing and chemical combination; to construct an electric circuit and explore the variety of effects produced by electricity; and to a range of other material phenomena. This argument is the major rationale for practical-based work which provides a repertoire of phenemonological experiences essential to the construction of a scientific understanding.

However, beyond this basic repertoire of sensorimotor experiences, the objects of science are essentially iconic – accessible to our senses only through the use of instrumentation, and consequently are the products of human representation. For example, in developing an understanding of the human body, apart from simple observations of gaseous exchange and the beating of the heart, the child's understanding is constructed through the use of models of organs and their manipulation, or from videos of dissected animals. Arguments for their function and purpose are presented which are dependent on a knowledge and experience of basic bodily functions – that is, reproduction, excretion and temperature control – but essentially, students are *persuaded* of the scientific representation by a set of carefully prepared arguments and focused illustrations in which practical work *per se* has little role to play. For instance, what is the evidence that the function of the heart is to circulate blood (the modern view since Harvey's work in 1688) as opposed to being an organ which manufactures blood and dispenses it radially throughout the body? No school practical investigation can justify our modern understanding. Similarly, the need to establish a basic vocabulary of constructs, such as 'speed', 'atom', 'cell', 'molecule', 'wave', 'radiation', 'gene', and so on – which must be understood to engage with the standardised discourse of science, is dependent on a set of basic experiences – of moving objects, the divisibility of matter, the observation of waves on water and the similarities between parents and their offspring, and more. The representation of such concepts is also dependent on the use of metaphor and simile – the heart is like a pump, an electromagnetic wave is analogous to a water wave, the genetic code is similar to the coded instruction on a computer disc – that is, on language and intralinguistic meaning creation rather than on a set of experiences offered by the limited apparatus and facilities of the school laboratory, from which the chances of the concept successfully emerging are about as low as that of winning the lottery.

Moreover, within schools, the lack of any instrumentation – that is microscopes, telescopes, spectrometers, vacuum chambers or the facility to dissect living organisms – which illustrate phenomena first hand, makes science teachers dependent on a set of texts for the development of the modern scientific account of the world, and *not* practical work. As I have argued previously (Osborne 1996b), this requires a recognition that as science educators, we are first and foremost communicators of science who must organise our lessons/lectures to facilitate the analysis and comprehension of text. It is my contention that recognition that learning science is so, and that an understanding of science has to be constructed from a focus on its epistemic basis, often through the interpretation and reconstruction of texts, be they written or visual, would lead to a fundamentally different emphasis in the pedagogy of science education. Instead of focusing on the manipulation of a plethora of standard apparatus and the gathering of experimental data, science education needs to shift its focus to the language of science, the means by which it constructs its knowledge and the interpretation of the data that science gathers.

Learning to do science

The rebuttal to the previous arguments may well be that these arguments have missed the point – that the essential function of practical work is to develop a repertoire of manipulative skills with basic scientific apparatus and students' investigative skills (Woolnough and Allsop 1986). However, since when did any industry or institution ever use the kind of instrumentation to be found in the school science laboratory? Digital thermometers are now *de rigueur* – as are gas chromotography, DNA testing, pollution monitoring, microbiological techniques and others, which bear as much relation to the skills developed by school science as riding a bicycle does to driving a car. As Bryan Chapman elegantly asserted as long ago as 1984:

> No physics experiment today or indeed industrial applications of physics relies on someone reading mercury-in-the-glass thermometers or using a U tube manometer. Readings are taken via sensors and data logged and processed by microprocessors. *All other techniques are archaic and give a false picture of physics and its industrial applications.*
>
> (Chapman 1984: 261; author's original emphasis)

Furthermore, implicit in the skills-based argument is an assumption that such skills will be useful in the child's future career. Yet as Chapman (1991) has also argued, the evidence from present and future employment trends that there is a widespread demand for skilled technical staff is circumspect and open to challenge. Even the government's own figures (Department for Education and Employment 1996) project that such staff will form only 15 per cent of the workforce by the year 2006. For the majority then, there is little justification for the time devoted to the development of outdated and unwanted skills on utilitarian grounds.

A more sophisticated argument for the value of practical work is that an understanding of science and its nature can only be developed by allowing students to experience the process of scientific enquiry (Woolnough and Allsop 1986). Only an exposure to genuine investigation of real, as opposed to artificial, problems will provide the opportunity for children to understand the nature of the epistemic foundations of science and its legitimate claims for human knowledge. However, which processes should children be shown? For, not only is there no universal method employed by scientists (Laudan *et al.* 1986), but also the range of procedures is immense. As Stephen Norris (1997) points out, 'merely considering the mathematical tools that are available for data analysis immediately puts the study of method beyond what is learnable in one lifetime'. In short, the methods used by the evolutionary biologist are as distinct from those of a theoretical physicist as chalk and cheese. The particular focus of the English and Welsh National Curriculum on a model of experimental and investigative science that emphasises the identification and control of variables has severely constrained science teachers to a limited subset of investigations, predominantly in the physical sciences (Donnelly *et al.* 1996). Moreover, the inflexible assessment requirements, conducted in a highly competitive ethos between schools, has meant that many of these have been reduced to a set of formulaic, procedural steps which are followed rigidly.

The *singular* dominance of experimental procedures – that is, the collection of experimental data and its interpretation – has, in my view, been at the expense of an exploration of the *variety* of techniques and approaches deployed by scientists. For instance, substantive scientific evidence for the effects of smoking, u-v exposure, and ionising radiations is based on epidemiological evidence in which naturally changing variables are monitored and correlations are later sought (Bencze 1996). This approach is a powerful technique which introduces important notions of probability and statistical measures of whether effects are random or causal. Yet, any mention of such approaches, let alone treatment, does not even come within shouting distance of the curriculum. Similarly, the role of theory, thought experiments, the process of peer review, the determination of reliability, the assessment of validity – all of which are central to the scientific enterprise and the *doing of science* are rarely considered. This is not to argue against offering students the opportunity to do any practical science as part of their education, but against the *overemphasis* on one limited aspect of science and its misrepresentation of the range of methods deployed by scientists. It is like offering the nineteenth-century novel as the sole paradigm of what it means to write great literature. Ultimately, too, it is also a form of 'bad faith', for knowingly to present science, not *as it is*, but *as it was*, is to mislead and misrepresent the nature of the scientific enterprise and its cultural, personal and societal consequences.

The argument for devoting considerable time to the activity of students conducting their own investigations is further undermined on two counts. First, practical work in schools is used to show how, confronted with a problem or desire to know more about the natural world, scientists use instrumentation to collect data which they then analyse, interpret and evaluate. The most easily comprehensible aspect of the experimental approach is the collection of data – that is, identifying the salient variables and selecting and using instruments which enable quantification of the relevant parameter. However, the more complex and demanding task is choosing an appropriate means of presenting the data, using standard tools such as spreadsheets to present the data in graphical form and then assessing its reliability, validity and evaluating the implications. But the evidence from research undertaken at King's College London (Watson 1997) suggests that it is these *latter* stages of investigations that are given a restricted consideration. Watson's findings show that whole investigations follow a pattern of introductory discussion, conducted as a whole class activity, which then serves the function of developing a focus on the chosen phenomena. This stage is followed by a phase of planning and the doing of the experiment. Then the exigencies of time are such that the ensuing phase of writing up, interpreting and presenting the findings are often conducted at home, and the final phase of evaluation is generally *omitted altogether*. Now if the major warrant for devoting so much time to such practical tasks is to familiarise children with the epistemic basis of scientific knowledge, then a basic aim of such experimental work should be to develop the critical and analytical faculties necessary to interpret data and assess its reliability and validity. Yet if the evaluation and interpretation of experimental findings remain undiscussed, it is hard to see how such skills will emerge *ex nihil*, and even harder to justify the extensive time devoted to such activity.

Familiarising students with a wide range of experimental procedures and apparatus only has any value if there is a reasonable expectation that the student will continue to a career in science, and then, only if the techniques and instrumentation are commensurate with those used beyond school. Since this second assumption is also untenable, the only justification for the value of practical work is to develop a familiarity and understanding of the basic epistemology of science which enables more effective judgements to be made of claims of scientific knowledge. Yet the emphasis on experiment and experimental procedures, and the lack of focus on interpretation and evaluation, would suggest that, rather than an education in science which attempts to develop the knowledge and critical skills to judge contemporary scientific issues in an informed manner, the current curriculum is still essentially conceptualised and delivered as a preparation and *training* for a scientific career. Such an emphasis is singularly inappropriate for the development of a scientifically literate citizenhood for the twenty-first century. Essentially, it is like arguing that the way to appreciate great poetry, its relevance and its meaning is by writing poetry (Ogborn 1994).

Furthermore, as Donnelly *et al.* (1996) point out, the lack of sophistication of pupils' knowledge of content and experimental procedures commonly results in the following situation when pupils conduct investigations:

> The pupil's investigational methodology and the predictions they make might be, independently, either scientifically acceptable or they might not. If one or either of the investigational methodology or the prediction were unacceptable, the outcomes of pupil's investigations and their predictions would be inconsistent (assuming pupils were able to achieve and interpret outcomes, which is not always the case). How were pupils to identify which (scientific theory or experimental methods) was unacceptable? If both predictions and methodology were inadequate the situation was, if anything, yet more difficult. At its worst, inadequate experimental findings could correspond with, and support, pupil's inadequate predictions. The room for misunderstanding and confusion in all of this was substantial, and often realised. We more than once saw pupils 'confirming' the fact that yeast worked better at 100°C than at room temperature, on the basis of the foam produced.
>
> (1996: 177)

Donnelly *et al.* conclude that 'only when the methodology and the scientific reasoning were acceptable was there likely to be any consistency between prediction and outcome and a contribution to pupils' learning'. More recent research by Isobel Robertson (1997), who looked at the performance of 300 14–16-year-old pupils on investigative tasks, found that these children had difficulties in identifying key evidence and problems in wording a hypothesis. They found that the task often resulted in an overload of working memory; that there was a tendency to compartmentalise evidence and a failure to see significant relations. And they were inclined to suggest additional variables to 'explain away' contrary evidence. In evaluating her findings, she calculated that only 15 per cent of the pupils were capable of representing and manipulating two continuous variables. All of this would suggest that, valuable as the opportunity to conduct whole investigations may be, few children have the skills or competencies to benefit educationally from the experience.

In short, the current overemphasis on investigational work in the existing science National Curriculum for England and Wales contributes little to an effective science education, failing to assist the learning of science whilst overemphasising experimental techniques at the expense of developing the critical faculties necessary to evaluate the epistemic claims of contemporary science.

Reconceptualising science education

It is my belief that unpicking the Gordian knot that ties science education to its practical base requires, first and foremost, a reconceptualisation of the aims and purpose of science education. Such a position arises from considering the needs of the majority – those who will *not continue* with science – rather than the needs of the minority who will. For both groups, at present, there is little reason to justify why the achievement of an essentially linguistic understanding should require eleven years of formal education and prevent a consideration of at least some of the major 'stories' of science which would enable children to see the trees for the wood. Confronted with an ever-burgeoning canon of scientific knowledge, there are always demands for the curriculum to accrete more material, generally accompanied by concomitant reluctance in individuals to relinquish their own favoured aspects of the curriculum. However, in focusing on the detail promoted by an atomistic conception of scientific knowledge, which is embodied in the English and Welsh National Curriculum, we have lost sight of the major stories that science has to tell. To borrow an architectural metaphor, it is impossible to see the whole building while focusing on the presence or absence of individual bricks (and at the same time rigorously testing for their presence or absence). Yet, without such a repositioning, a change of focus, it is impossible to see whether you are looking at St Paul's Cathedral or a pile of bricks, and for that matter what it is that makes St Paul's one the world's great churches or why Darwin's theory of natural selection is one of the most significant pieces of knowledge developed by modern science. Is it any wonder, then, that most pupils emerge from their formal science education with the feeling that the knowledge they acquired had as much value as a pile of bricks and that the task of constructing any edifice of note was simply too daunting – the preserve of the boffins of the scientific elite?

For instance, children *do need* to develop a holistic picture of the major themes of science – to know how the particle model of matter has been achieved, its justification and the understanding of materials and how they behave that it has led to. Similarly, a basic understanding of the modern cosmological picture and our place in the Universe; a conception of the major parts of the body, their function and interrelationship; an understanding of genetics, the mechanisms of inheritance and the basic picture provided by evolutionary biology – all of these are a minimal intellectual toolkit necessary to participate in our modern culture. But just as one does not need a knowledge of bricks, plumbing or engineering to appreciate the elegance and beauty of Cathedral at Chartres, focusing on the overarching themes of science would allow the excision of all content which is not essential in order to view its significance, beauty and meaning.

Currently, what we offer schoolchildren is predominantly a one-dimensional science. For the dominance of the technocratic imperative which sees education as an economic utility, a commodity to be marketed, places emphasis not on the development of critical thinking but on the mastery of a given body of knowledge. Assessment and evaluation become a key feature of monitoring the system to determine its efficiency, and the result is an education that focuses on that which is easily assessed – 'what we know'. Yet science has additional dimensions, which are essential if children are to begin to see the whole edifice and understand its significance. Briefly, these are:

- The need for students to understand not only 'what we know' but 'how we know'. That is the epistemological basis for scientific beliefs.
- The need for students to appreciate that scientists may differ in their interpretation, and why.
- The need to provide experience of collecting and developing arguments about *contemporary* science-based issues.

The first of these requires the development of an understanding of the general shape that a justified scientific belief would have to take. Broadly speaking, that is a process which consists of identifying a problem, using relevant theoretical knowledge to select appropriate variables, assembling experimental apparatus, collecting and recording data, analysing and presenting the findings, and arguing for the interpretation offered. Its particular focus should be *not* on the collection of data, but on the *claims* that are made and the *warrants* that are used as justification.

What follows, then, are some examples of activities that science education needs to seek to emphasise that are currently so critically absent.

Example 1

On what grounds are the following knowledge claims justified?

Matter is made up of atoms.
Day and night are caused by an Earth which spins.
The Earth is at least one thousand million years old.
Human characteristics are transmitted from one generation to the next by molecules called genes consisting of DNA.
Plants take in carbon dioxide to make food.
Astrology is not a science.
We live at the bottom of a 'sea of air'.
Burning is not a process in which matter is broken up into small pieces of ash but a process in which matter combines to make new substances.

A simple, but engaging task is to hand out cards, each containing a singular statement such as the ones above, to small groups of pupils, and ask them, first, to discuss whether they agree or disagree with the statement, and second, what evidence enables them to justify their belief. More importantly, if the evidence is not to hand, or based on knowledge derived from texts – how would they attempt to test the truth of such assertions? For, as I have argued previously (Osborne 1996a), if one of the aspirations of science education is to develop critical thinkers able to understand and examine the myriad claims made on a scientific or pseudo-scientific basis, surely it is important to focus not just on 'what we know' but on the justification of belief – that is, the epistemology of science.

Example 2

Second, science education requires exposure to a greater variety of data sets, the methods of their representation, and the procedural basis on which such data can be considered evidence for justified knowledge. Simple data sets can either be collected – for instance, is there a relation between hair colour and eye colour? Is there a relation between lung capacity and the speed of running 100 m? Or alternatively, they can, and often should, be provided so that precious educational time is not wasted on the mechanical and essentially routine collection of data. Rather, the presentation of data sets for analysis offers a valuable opportunity to use information technology to represent graphically continuous variables and to consider the nature of the relationship. Rather than the careful selection of the few experiments that offer simple linear relationships between variables, such as the current through, and voltage across a conductor, the relationships in such data sets are rarely self-evident. Beyond the simple visual analysis of whether there is any pattern or not, there is the need to introduce basic statistical techniques of a simple exploratory and confirmatory nature. Thus science education should offer the opportunity to plot histograms and scatterplots; to discuss the likely nature of the relationship revealed; and, at a more sophisticated level, to introduce the notion of regression coefficients and statistical probability. The latter do not require the method of their derivation for, rather as it is not necessary to know how a car engine works in order to drive a car, neither is it necessary to know how to calculate a regression coefficient in order to understand its meaning.

Table 9.1 gives an example of the kind of data set that science education should consider.

Confronted with such a set of data, there are immediate questions such as 'What is the pattern of variation?' 'Which foods have the most/least carbohydrate?' 'What is the median value?' 'What is the typical range of variation?' One simple method is to collect such information from food wrappers and hang the food wrappers on a string along the classroom

Table 9.1 Carbohydrate content of foods

Food	Portion size (g)	Carbohydrate content (g)
All-Bran	30	19
Barley, whole	100	69
Brown bread	60	27
Chickpeas	200	44
Cornflakes	30	27
Corn-on-the-cob	200	46
Crisps	50	25
Custard	100	27
Fish fingers	100	17
Jelly	100	0
Kedgeree	200	20
Lentils	200	34
Macaroni	200	50
Noodles	200	48
Oatmeal porridge	200	16
Pancake	30	11
Pizza	150	38
Potato, baked	150	20
Potato, chips	150	45
Potato, boiled	150	30
Quiche	150	30
Rice	100	86
Sausage roll	50	18
Shepherd's pie	200	20
Sponge pudding	150	63

wall. The length of the string is used to scale 0–100 g, and this provides a quick visual picture of the range of variation in the carbohydrate content of different foods. A more sophisticated method of approach is to draw a histogram (Figure 9.1) – a relatively laborious task simplified by information technology.

But although such a diagram shows the pattern of distribution, it does not show the median value easily. Such information is revealed by a box and whisker plot (Figure 9.2).

Only such a plot clearly reveals that the majority of the foods listed have a carbohydrate content of 25 g or less and that the spread of values range from 20 g (the lower quartile median) to 45 g (the upper quartile median). This example is offered simply to make the essential point: that the use of such techniques for data analysis, presentation and interpretation should be part of the standard fare of science education. For it is an understanding of the basic methods of representing data in science that is a rudimentary element in the development of the skills required to analyse critically the many data sets that may be encountered in adult life.

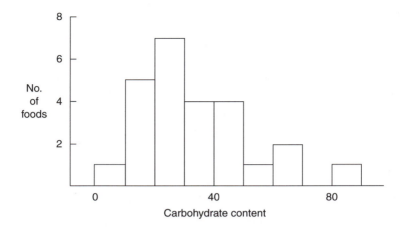

Figure 9.1 Histogram of carbohydrate content of food

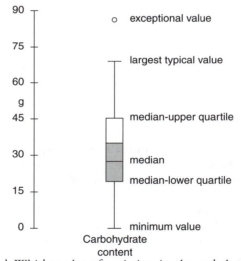

Figure 9.2 Box and Whisker plot of variation in the carbohydrate content of food

Example 3

Recently, ever since the unexpected popularity of Stephen Hawking's book *A Brief History of Time* (1988), science has benefited from a large number of scientists and non-scientists who have attempted to communicate their ideas and their significance of them to the general public. Many of these books, notably those of Stephen Jay Gould (e.g. Gould 1992), have succeeded in producing clear and lucid prose that convey the excitement of

168

science and contemporary scientific ideas. At one level, these texts can be read simply for the scientific story that they tell. They are examples of good imaginative and creative writing that can be used as a focus for discussion of the science. Imagine, then, reading the following extract from Primo Levi's marvellous book *The Periodic Table*. Here Levi asks us to imagine the journey of a carbon atom which has just been released as a carbon dioxide molecule from a lime kiln in 1840:

It was caught by the wind, flung down on the earth, lifted ten kilometres high. It was breathed in by a falcon, descending into its precipitous lungs, but did not penetrate its rich blood and was expelled. It dissolved three times in the water of the sea, once in the water of a cascading torrent, and again was expelled. It travelled with the wind for eight years: now high, now low, on the sea and among the clouds, over forests, deserts, and limitless expanses of ice; then it stumbled into capture and the organic adventure.

The atom we are speaking of, accompanied by its two satellites which maintained it in a gaseous state, was therefore borne by the wind along a row of vines in the year 1848. It had the good fortune to brush against a leaf, penetrate it, and be nailed there by a ray of the sun. If my language here becomes imprecise and allusive, it is not only because of my ignorance: this decisive event, this instantaneous work – of the carbon dioxide, the light, and the vegetal greenery – has not yet been described in definitive terms, and perhaps it will not be for a long time to come, so different is it from the other 'organic' chemistry which is the cumbersome, slow, and ponderous work of man: and yet this refined, minute, and quick-witted chemistry was 'invented' two or three billion years ago by our silent sisters, the plants, which do not experiment and do not discuss, and whose temperature is identical to that of the environment in which they live.

Our atom of carbon enters the leaf, colliding with other innumerable (but here useless) molecules of nitrogen and oxygen. It adheres to a large and complicated molecule that activates it, and simultaneously receives the decisive message from the sky, in the flashing form of a packet of solar light: in an instant, like an insect caught by a spider, it is separated from its oxygen, combined with hydrogen and (one thinks) phosphorus, and finally inserted in a chain, whether long or short does not matter, but it is the chain of life.

. . . But there is more and worse, to our shame and that of our art. Carbon dioxide, that is, the aerial form of the carbon of which we have up till now spoken: this gas which constitutes the raw material of life, the permanent store upon which all that grows draws, and the ultimate destiny of all flesh, is not one of the principal components of air but rather a ridiculous remnant, an 'impurity', thirty times less abundant than argon, which nobody even notices. The air contains 0.03 percent; if Italy was air, the only Italians fit to build life would be, for example, the fifteen thousand inhabitants of Milazzo in the province of Messina.

This wonderful, poetic piece of writing contains so much science that can be explored:

- Why is the carbon dioxide not absorbed by the falcon?
- What happens when carbon dioxide dissolves in water?
- What are the two satellites of the atom that Levi is referring to in the second paragraph?
- What does Levi mean when he says the atom is 'nailed' in the leaf?
- Why is it so surprising that this reaction takes place at normal temperature and pressures?
- Why does Levi describe this as the 'chain of life'?
- Why does Levi think it so amazing that photosynthesis happens at all?
- Levi describes the molecules of nitrogen and oxygen as being useless here. What other situations are there where they might be useful?

It seems to me that such an approach has much to offer. First, it introduces the personal and subjective voice, offering a distinct contrast to the dry, detached objectivity of traditional texts. The latter endows scientific knowledge with the status of being 'exact' and 'true' but separates the science from its culture (and hence the culture from science), which contributes to its apparent lack of meaning to most schoolchildren. Second, at another level, in this approach, the emphasis is distinctly *not* on how to 'do' science, but rather on how to 'read' and understand the *discourse* of science in the contexts which are typical of the media accounts they will meet in their adult lives. Using such texts focuses on the interpretation of meaning and requires the talk and discussion which is a feature of the English language classrooms. It is a skill which is essential for the future citizen and offers one small step to distancing science teaching from its central dependency on the laboratory.

Another contemporary piece, by Richard Dawkins (1976), paints a graphic and vivid picture of genetic inheritance, demonstrating that, even within science, there are phenomena for which there are multiple interpretations.

It is raining DNA outside. On the bank of the Oxford canal at the bottom of my garden is a large willow tree, and it is pumping downy seeds into the air. There is no consistent air movement, and the seeds are drifting outwards in all directions from the tree. Up and down the canal, as far as my binoculars can reach, the water is white with floating cottony flecks, and we can be sure that they have carpeted the ground to much the same radius in other directions too. The cotton wool is mostly made of cellulose, and it dwarfs the tiny capsule that contains the DNA, the genetic information. The DNA content must be a small proportion of the total, so why did I say that it was raining DNA rather than cellulose? The answer is that it is the DNA that matters. The cellulose fluff, although more bulky, is just a parachute, to be discarded. The whole performance, cotton wool, catkins, tree and all, is in aid of one thing and one thing only, the spreading of DNA around the countryside.

Why is this picture controversial? Because it implies that the organism exists solely to transmit its DNA – put simply, the chicken is the egg's means of reproducing itself. The classical position limits the role of genes to the acquisition of the physiological characteristics of the organism. One might ask, which of these interpretations is more appropriate or even correct? But from a pedagogic point of view that would be to miss the essential point – which is to expose that there exist differing views of similar data and that interpretations are often the product of the available social and cultural context in which the scientists are situated. As Clive Sutton (1996) has shown, descriptions and explanations often 'depend on language imported from some other area of use in an attempt to figure out what is going on; they depend, that is, on metaphor'. For instance, many of our current models, particularly those associated with the brain, draw heavily on ideas associated with computers. Inevitably, such socially constructed representations are open to critical evaluation, challenge and reconstruction.

Conclusion

The examples above have been offered as possibilities of a different vision of what science education might be – that is, a science education which seeks to break the Gordian knot that ties it to the context of the laboratory. The argument here has sought to question the notion that *learning* science itself is best approached by *doing* science in a laboratory. Such an emphasis on direct experience is strongly associated with the conception that scientific knowledge is lying around out there to be discovered by the curious. This unfortunate legacy of the Nuffield innovations of the 1960s has now become so strongly imbued in the culture of science teaching that it is central to the science teacher's self-identity (Jenkins 1997). Yet so many of the ideas of science, from the explanation of day and night in terms of a spinning Earth to the theory of evolution, are neither self-evident nor easily 'discovered'. Rather, the 'strange' stories that science tells have to be introduced and explored – to be mulled over, reconsidered and personally reconstructed so that understanding their meaning can begin. An *education* in science, rather than a *training* in science, would see practical work and the 'doing' of science as only one element of the process of learning science, and a minor element at that.

Yet attempts to change the practice and culture of science teaching, what Bourdieu and Passeron (1977) so elegantly describes as the 'habitus' – that set of implicit values and ideological commitments that permeate the discourse of any group – have often fallen on stony ground. Perhaps then, it is time to consider the inconceivable – that the laboratory is only an adjunct and not a necessity. That the learning of science is not dependent on a practical offering for every lesson and that there is much that can be done in a normal classroom with no more facilities than would commonly be found in an English classroom. For concept maps, small group work, discussion of instances, DART activities, writing about science, researching relevant material, using material from newspapers, role plays, the examples used above and many other strategies have no need of a laboratory. Only such radical surgery will force a re-examination of the cultural sclerosis that predominates in the teaching of science where the adherence to the laboratory blocks progression in our pedagogy. Perhaps then it is time to think the unthinkable. For is it only a physical untying of the knot that binds science education to the laboratory that will ultimately force a reconsideration of the role and value of practical work?

References

Beck, U. (1992) *Risk Society: Towards a new Modernity*, London: Sage.

Bencze, J.L. (1996) Correlational studies in school science: breaking the science-experiment-certainty connection', *School Science Review* 78(282), 95–101.

Bourdieu, P., & Passeron, J.C. (1977) *Reproduction in Education, Society and Culture* (trans. R. Nice), London: Sage.

Chapman, B. (1984) 'Core physics revisited', *Physics Education*, 19: 261–2.

—— (1991) 'The overselling of science education', *School Science Review*, 72(260): 47–63.

Dawkins, R. (1976). *The Selfish Gene*, Oxford: Oxford University Press.

Department for Education and Employment (1996) *Labour Market and Skill Trends*, Department for Education and Employment.

Donnelly, J., Buchan, A., Jenkins, E., Laws, P. and Welford, G. (1996) *Investigations by Order: Policy, Curriculum and Science Teachers' Work under the Education Reform Act*, Nafferton: Studies in Science Education.

Driver, R. (1983) *The Pupil as Scientist?* Milton Keynes: Open University Press.

Gilbert, J. (1997) 'Thinking 'Otherwise': re-thinking the problems of girls and science education in the post-modern era, unpublished PhD, University of Waikato.

Gould, S.J. (1992) *Bully for Brontosaurus: Further Reflections in Natural History*, London: Penguin.

Greene, M.T. (1997) 'What cannot be said in science', *Nature*, 388: 619–20.

Harré, R. (1986) *Varieties of Realism: a Rationale for the Natural Sciences*, Oxford: Basil Blackwell.

Hawking, S.W. (1988). *A Brief History of Time: from the Big Bang to Black Holes*, London: Bantam.

Hodson, D. (1990) 'A critical look at practical work in school science', *School Science Review* 70(256): 33–40.

Hood, C. and Jones, D. (eds.) (1996) *Accident and Design: Contemporary Debates on Risk Management*, London: University College London Press.

Jenkins, E. (1997) 'Change and continuity in secondary science teaching', paper presented at the First European Science Education Research Association Conference. Available from the author: School of Education, Leeds University, Leeds LS2 9JT.

Lakin, S. and Wellington, J. (1991) 'Teaching the nature of science', *Education in Science* 144, 16–17.

Laudan, L., Donovan, A., Laudan, R., Barker, P., Brown, H., Leplin, J., Thagard, P. and Wykstra, S. (1986) 'Scientific change: philosophical models and historical research', *Synthèse* 69(141–223).

Millar, R. (1996) 'Towards a science curriculum for public understanding', *School Science Review* 77(280): 7–18.

Norris, S. (1997) 'Intellectual independence for nonscientists and other content-transcendent goals of science education', *Science Education* 81(2): 239–58.

Ogborn, J. (1994) 'Theoretical and empirical investigations of the nature of scientific and commonsense knowledge', unpublished PhD, King's College London.

Osborne, J.F. (1996a) 'Beyond constructivism', *Science Education* 80(1): 53–82.

—— (1996b) 'Untying the Gordian knot: diminishing the role of practical work', *Physics Education* 31(5): 271–8.

Robertson, I. (1997) *'Key Evidence in testing hypotheses'*, paper presented at the First European Science Education Research Association Conference. Available from the author: Faculty of Education, University of Strathclyde, Scotland.

Sutton, C. (1996) 'The Scientific model as a form of speech', in G. Welford, J. Osborne and P. Scott (eds) *Research in Science Education in Europe*, London: Falmer Press, pp. 143–52.

Watson, R. (1997) 'Kinds of investigations', paper presented at the First European Science Education Research Association Conference. Available from the author: King's College London, Waterloo Road, London SE1 8WA.

Woolnough, B. and Allsop, T. (1986). *Practical Work in Science*, Cambridge: Cambridge University Press.

Ziman, J. (1968). *Public Knowledge: the Social Dimension of Science*, Cambridge: Cambridge University Press.

10

SCIENCE AS CONVERSATION
Come and see my air pump!

Clive Sutton

Meaningful practical work, whether by scientists or by children, is always embedded in a conversation – a discussion of ideas that makes it necessary to check those ideas against experience. I argue that we should focus the attention of learners on this conversation and help them to *hear* it and to understand how people have come to talk that way. By recognising science as conversation they can gain a fuller understanding of how scientists work and also increase their own sense of involvement with scientific ideas.

Two kinds of conversation for scientists

Notice the difference between *'science in the making'* and *'ready made science'* as described by Bruno Latour[1]. The first involves debate and discussion about matters which are uncertain, with a lot of speculative talk about possibilities and how to design an experimental test or what to search for as crucial observations. It is full of argument over how to interpret evidence and what can be taken as acceptable evidence. It is driven by a desire for insight into 'what might be going on' – that is, some mental model of how things work. Practical activity is embedded in animated talk about all those things, and because no one definitely possesses 'the' right answer yet, there is an equality of status amongst the talkers.

For a recent example of science in the making consider the debates about the alleged iridium-rich layer at the cretaceous–tertiary boundary of the geological record. Does it really exist? In all parts of the world or only some? Is the evidence unequivocal? Is it reasonable, anyway, to interpret such a layer as debris from a large meteor impact just because some meteors contain iron and iridium? What do we find around known sites of impact? Where else and for what else would it be worth searching? Is it going too far to link a supposed impact with disastrous climate change and the death of the dinosaurs? What other evidence is relevant? What other theories are there for the 'death of the dinosaurs' and how long did it really take? And so on and so on.[2]

Ready made science, on the other hand, is the established knowledge in textbooks which has lost its former uncertainty and is no longer a matter of debate. Expressions like 'It might be' have long ago been replaced by 'It is'. Dinosaurs are now part of ready made science, along with 'jurassic period', 'cretaceous period', 'mesozoic era' and suchlike. We have it in the books that 'chalk *is* a sedimentary rock' – an apparently simple fact. It was once intensely controversial as to whether *any* rocks were really hardened sediments from old sea floors and so on, but the debate is now closed and many people encountering this knowledge are unaware of the arduous process whereby the scientific community came to accept it. The term 'sedimentary rock' sounds nowadays like a 'natural fact' which scientists 'discovered' rather than a concept they hammered out by fierce argument.

Learners in school are exposed to a lot of ready made science and are liable to get a distorted view in which the subject seems to be about certainties, about facts read off directly from 'the book of nature'. They may indeed experience it as a mass of given information rather than as an on-going discussion, unless the teacher can re-animate the doubt of the past and show how today's taken-for-granted knowledge was constructed. What was the conversation like when topics now settled were explored for the first time? How did new ideas arise? Why did the problem matter? What arguments did people put forward? What evidence did they use?[3]

Ready made science is a different kind of conversation, from which the uncertainty and the open-ended quality have largely gone. It has become the accepted conversation amongst 'insiders' who are now familiar with a certain way of thinking. It expresses their consensus of understanding about what things are well known and important in their particular area of study. It also becomes surer and more closed as time goes on, so a stranger cannot join in immediately, for he or she has first to work out what these people are 'on about', with their 'sedimentation' and 'deposition rates' or whatever. Each branch of science is, in effect, a little area of special discourse like that – the kind of conversation you will be able to have once you gain the appropriate insights and the expressions that go with them. For rock studies the necessary expressions include 'erosion' and 'deposition', and the mental image to go with these terms is one of a sequence or cycle that links the processes. For wave studies you have to take on terms like 'propagation', 'vibration' and 'frequency', linked by an image which teachers try to make visible in ripple tanks.

It is quite characteristic of ready made science to include many new nouns which capture the objects of study that people think about in that branch of science. Noun-heavy, ready made science then appears to be *a conversation about things* rather than about people's ideas. It has become a depersonalised account of how things 'just are', in which it is difficult to find any identifiable voices of the human beings who created these systems of talk and thought.

Note also the large disparity of status between the insiders who already possess the accepted system and newcomers who do not. That is what can make exchanges between teacher and pupils in lessons very false if they try to discuss 'what is going on' when the teacher really has in mind the official story. However right it is to value children's ideas and to encourage them to articulate those ideas, the invitation to do so when the insiders' story is also on offer creates a lot of problems. The learners know that the teacher already has the best or 'right' answer!

Are there better ways for learners to gain access to insider conversations? It might be better if they took only a listening role for a time, and spoke up later in a context that is less asymmetric in power. Certainly I think it will mean planning lessons in a different way – not around the practical work as such, but around the idea of a group of insiders or 'discourse community' whose language we want to learn.

This is *not a small change*, and to explore what it entails I propose to examine what 'appreciating the discourse' or 'getting in on the conversation' meant in times gone by, and then to return to what it could mean in tomorrow's science lessons.

1660: come and see my air pump

New apparatus that does interesting things often provides the practical focus of attention around which scientific conversations can develop, and this was markedly true of Robert Boyle's experience in the 1650s and 1660s. We can think of him as one of the founders of such conversations, taking a lead in the Royal Society and becoming a principal architect of its ways of working. He was also one of the first people to possess a really impressive demonstration kit. His innocent invitation to 'Come and see my air pump' would have been tempting to his contemporaries for more than one reason. Some of them would just be curious to see this new and expensive device – based on Continental designs, paid for by a wealthy man, and reputedly capable of showing up strange phenomena with pigs' bladders and silent bells. Any teacher knows however that curiosity and novelty can soon wear off, so for those who stayed there must have been something much more appealing. It lay in the character of the conversation, and the intellectual and emotional satisfactions of a new approach to knowledge.

In effect, those who persisted in going to see the pump, or who seriously attended to reports of its use, were opting in to membership of a new commmunity, joining in with people who hoped to build up a store of 'natural knowledge' that would be more reliable than the doctrines

Figure 10.1 Boyle's first air pump of brass, oiled leather and wood, with its glass
globe into which various items could be placed. As drawn in *New
Experiments Physico-Mechanical, touching the spring of the air* (1660)

promulgated everywhere around them. This hope for firmer knowledge
affected many parts of Europe but was acute in England after years of civil
strife, when religious and political enthusiasms had proved extremely
socially divisive. It was unclear how society would hold together at all.
Royalist or Parliamentarian, Romist or Puritan, Millenarian, Baptist, Ran-
ter or Quaker, Socialist Leveller or Land-owning Squire . . . in whom or
what could we trust? What would restrain people from killing each other
through their beliefs in their different systems? What authority could
people accept?

At such a time, 'Come and see my air pump' probably offered a safer kind
of activity than direct involvement in religious and political controversy,

and moreover it promised a new kind of authority outside mere human opinion – the authority of nature, ascertained by putting ideas to the test of experiment. For those who went to see new devices such as the pump or the microscope, there was the growing hope of incontrovertible new knowledge rather than constantly arguing schools of thought.

Of course there would still be argument and discussion, but on the basis of agreement about what members of the group would know to be indisputable. In modern terms a *new community of discourse* was growing up in which people talked to each other in certain ways, and accepted certain kinds of argument. Its members had a *characteristic epistemological stance* about what could be counted as trustworthy and reliable knowledge. They regarded themselves as concentrating on what they could see as definite rather than getting into 'speculative' matters. Steven Shapin and Simon Schaffer[4] have analysed how these pioneers managed to share ideas without letting controversy get out of hand, and they distinguish three aspects which all helped to minimise discord:

1   a new *material* way of working – using kit such as the pump or the microscope and thus being able to say, 'This is not just my opinion, you know; see what the apparatus says'.
2   a new *literary* system, in which claims from an experimental event were written down in a way that was convincing for people not actually present. This was the beginning of the 'matter-of-fact'-ish scientific report, or, as it was called at the time, 'a philosophical account'.
3   a new *social* arrangement (how the investigators should treat each other in their meetings; for example, in the courteous 'receiving' of a member's paper).

This analysis by Shapin and Schaffer is valuable for teachers because it shows that there is a great deal more to 'doing science' than just 'doing experiments'. Science involves talking to others and writing for others, attending conferences, discussing, reading, thinking, re-thinking (and also getting funds!). These are are all part of a scientist's life. If citizens are to have a better understanding of how scientists work, we shall need to teach them more about the whole range of such activities and escape from over a century of tradition that has focused too strongly on benchwork on the one hand and ready-made textbook facts on the other.

Members of the new community in Boyle's day increasingly came to believe that 'experimental facts' could be separated from 'speculations', and that 'plain descriptions' could be made (as opposed to 'persuasive interpretations with evidence'). They used this distinction in developing their new ways of communicating, and as time went on some of their successors also spoke more and more about *fact* on the one hand and *theory* on the other.

Such distinctions have been very important in science, but this particular one is less than fully secure and it has had some unfortunate consequences for the public understanding of science right down to the present time, when schoolchildren think of scientists as just going out and 'finding' new facts. As I suggested at the beginning of this chapter, they fail to appreciate all the argument and discussion that is involved. Many teenagers think that arguments in science, if they occur at all, can be settled simply by getting 'better results' and do not understand the need for re-thinking one's mental models[5], which sometimes changes the status of what is acceptable as fact.

Today, a better distinction to make is that between *claims* and *evidence*, and one thing to take from the memory of Robert Boyle is that when learners handle the kit we provide it is not just a matter of seeing but also of discourse. We let them see and feel something, but also *we invite them, if they can, to join the discourse community* of science, attending to certain kinds of argument, tuning in to what is meant by evidence in science, and talking in a way that uses such evidence.

So much for the epistemological aspect of the conversations, but there was an even more important attraction in the pump and pump-talk when it was offered by Boyle, and that was a new ontological stance in relation to air. He had a new vision of air as a material stuff that might be partially removed from a certain space (whether completely, he was careful not to say). Of all the things one might attend to about air, he chose to focus on its *springiness* – its squashiness, its stretchability, its 'elasticity' – and his language in discussing it became laced with words and phrases like 'rarefaction', 'exuction', 'fluid', 'weight of the atmosphere', which would not have occurred so readily in the speech of people who did not have his imagery. His mental picture of air was linked on a larger scale with Toricelli's new image of human beings crawling about on the bottom of an 'ocean' of the stuff, and so talk about baroscopes and barometers came into the same scheme of thought and powerful system of discourse, which I abbreviate as 'pump-talk'. To understand what Boyle was 'on about' a person had to enter into this new mental world and make sense of pump-talk until their own mind's eye was gradually linked with that way of talking. In other words, they took on not only the detail of the pump and a general scientific discourse using evidence but also a particular *discourse about air*. This is what made the sessions so intellectually illuminating, or, as they put it in those days, so 'luciferous in philosophy'.[6]

Turning to our situation in schools, the equipment and particulars of what happens should very rarely be the sole centre of attention. No air pump of the past or present will reveal to the uninitiated the mental world to which it is related unless that world is talked into existence by the teacher. The teacher must work deliberately on the mind's eye of the learner and introduce the language of the topic in relation to the imagery, in effect *showing the learner the discourse about air.*

In a recent analysis of the art of explaining, Jon Ogborn and Gunther Kress and their colleagues suggest introducing the 'entities' which matter from a scientific point of view as principal characters or *protagonists* in the scientific story of what we think is going on.[7] For a modern account of air that could mean taking the learners in imagination upwards to the vast ocean of air above us as the major 'player' affecting what happens on the bench, and also downwards to our picture of molecules in motion — for which the behaviour of the balloon on the bench is supportive evidence. The learners need the big picture, the overall story. Ontologically we have to create the cast of that story; epistemologically we have to persuade the learners that what happens on the bench is reasonable evidence. Seeing the apparatus and physically feeling the effects can both contribute to this process of persuasion, but they cannot do so without the discourse.

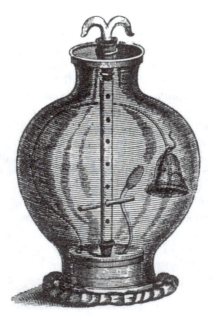

Figure 10.2 Turn the stopper to release the clapper . . . but why? . . . and what was he on about in all that talk about 'the propagation of sounds' rather than just 'what we heard'? A further illustration from Boyle's *New Experiments Physico-Mechanical* (1660)

To read more about how the discourse of science creates new abstract nouns like propagation which then become objects of study in their own right, see chapter 1 of Halliday and Martin's book *'Writing science'*

1800 onwards: 'Conversations' at the Royal Institution

In the 1800s it became very popular to go to lecture demonstrations at which people were exposed both to the general discourse of science, with its emphasis on tangible evidence, and to the new and specific mini-discourses, such as charge and current talk for electricity, or atom and element talk for chemistry. At the Royal Institution in London people were enthralled by Humphry Davy and later by Michael Faraday and later still by John Tyndall. They set a very high standard for such presentations, and many schoolteachers, drawn in to the new ways of talking about 'electrolysis' or about 'energy', have been inspired by their methods. All of them tried to carry the audience imaginatively into the new worlds of scientific thought, so that *seeing* the actual demonstrations, *hearing* the way of talking, and *seeing with the mind's eye* would all be interconnected.

Tyndall was especially accomplished in practical work. For example, he would focus unseen radiant heat to ignite a cigar at the focal point, mould ice by pressure into almost any shape, display large line spectra of the

Figure 10.3 John Tyndall lecturing at the Royal Institution, as represented in the *Illustrated London News* of 1870. As is the case with some school pupils, the artist seems interested in the excitement of the occasion, and the spectacle it offers, rather more than in the continuity of the story for whose reasonableness the demonstrations provide evidence.

chemical elements, and even produce 'singing flames' which responded to notes from his own voice, but while these things were often spectacular, they were not just spectacles. They were part of a discussion about the constitution of matter which would explain what was happening, and he was very much aware of the importance of the imaginative understanding within which the practical experience starts to make sense[8]. His contemporary, James Clerk Maxwell, picked up this emphasis on the imagination and has left us a most interesting portrayal of Tyndall in action, written in verse. Perhaps we think of Maxwell as immersed in theoretical physics, but these lines show him to have been also a keen observer of people and commentator on educational philosophy. He knew Tyndall to be in awe of the power of ice in the glaciers and fascinated by its consolidation and movement, so he chose the rhythm of Tennyson's poem 'The Brook' ('I come from haunts of coot and hern . . .') for this teasing and slightly mocking appreciation:

A Tyndallic ode[9]

I come from fields of fractured ice,
Whose wounds are cured by squeezing,
Melting they cool, but in a trice,
Get warm again by freezing.
Here in the frosty air, the sprays
With fern-like hoar frost bristle,
There, liquid stars their watery rays
Shoot through the solid crystal.

Notes

Discussing the latent heat of fusion was a key part of any presentation of what we now call the kinetic theory of matter. To demonstrate the re-gelation of ice would have been a part of that discussion.

I come from empyrean fires –
From microscopic spaces,
Where molecules with fierce desires,
Shiver in hot embraces.
The atoms clash, the spectra flash,
Projected on the screen,
The double D, magnesian b,
And Thallium's living green.

Tyndall had been a pupil of Bunsen at Marburg in Germany at the end of the 1840s. It was Bunsen with Kirchhoff who later developed a way of analysing the spectra of flames to show the characteristic spectral lines of elements. The audience would see the spectra, but also hear Tyndall's evocation of the clash of atoms in motion.

This crystal tube the electric ray
Shows optically clean,
No dust or haze within, but stay!
All has not yet been seen.
What gleams are these of heavenly blue?
What air-drawn form appearing?
What mystic fish, that, ghostlike, through
The empty space is steering?

The 'Tyndall effect' of light scattering is one of the things for which he is most remembered, along with the excitement of discussing why the sky is blue.

I light this sympathetic flame,
My faintest wish that answers.
I sing, it sweetly sings the same,
It dances with the dancers.
I shout, I whistle, clap my hands,
And stamp upon the platform,
The flame responds to my commands,
In this form and in that form.

Here is the practical showmanship of an accomplished demonstrator . . . before he moves on to consider explanations.

Here let me pause. – These transient facts,
These fugitive impressions,
Must be transformed by mental acts
To permanent possessions.
Then summon up your grasp of mind,
Your fancy scientific,
Till sights and sounds with thought combined
Become of truth prolific.

The educational philosophy:
Tyndall's audience would have gained much more than 'fugitive impressions'.

Do we act on this today, allowing pupils space for such things to be 'transformed by mental acts'?

Go to, prepare your mental bricks,
Fetch them from every quarter,
Firm on the sand your basement fix,
With best sensation mortar.
The top shall rise to heaven on high. . . .

Here Maxwell is thinking about how observations connect with speculations, and he makes a biblical allusion. Our scientific 'houses', which we rightly try to base on observable sensations, are nevertheless to some extent built on sand.

James Clerk Maxwell

Notice how, in verse 5, Maxwell was saying (as Tyndall himself would say): Take care – take care of your imagination, for that is where the real learning happens. Even if the practical work is done to the perfection achieved on the bench of the Royal Institution, its meaning will be lost unless it is 'transformed by mental acts'. In today's language, it's the minds-on work that matters.

So here with Tyndall as with Boyle, the demonstrations on the bench provided a focus, but it was the quality of the talk and the speaker's personal involvement in making sense of things which helped the listeners to do their own mental work. To appreciate his science of ice, for example (first verse) they had to go with him in imagination to the level of water molecules in the ice crystals, to share his vision of what might be going on there, and then upwards to the level of the Alpine range – the 'great condenser of Europe' as he called it, which for thousands of years had been capturing and precipitating atmospheric water to make the glaciers. He was able, in words, to take his audience on both these journeys, and as he debated with himself and quoted other scientists, members of the audience were able to listen in on this conversation of ideas.

Tentativeness and humanity

When scientists are still saying, 'It might be that . . . ' or 'It probably works like this . . . ' or 'Let's suppose . . . ', the individual investment of thought is very clear and is signalled partly by the tentativeness of expression. Such tentativeness is more engaging than outright assertion, and I read it not as vagueness but as an invitation to think with them. It helps me to see science as an adventure of ideas. Of course there are times when all of us prefer to be *told* what *is* the case, but I think that when it comes to keeping a stranger involved, science in the making is at an advantage as compared with ready made science, because of its tentativeness. In my experience, when working with teenagers, a combination of the definite and the tentative is necessary but I see it as part of a science teacher's job to help them to understand both.

All scientific language, however, becomes less tentative as time goes on. It loses its as-if-ness[10] and turns into a straight description of how people have come to believe things 'really are'. For people whose philosophy of science is that all scientific knowledge remains provisional, the phrase 'really are' may be only a shorthand for 'the best model we have at the moment', but for others it means 'nature's truth'.

Tentativeness is maintained much longer when scientists are dealing with things unseen, and we can see this in the title of Tyndall's most famous series of lectures, which were first given in 1862 and first printed in 1863. On the title page that year we find the heading: 'Heat *considered as* a mode of motion'. He discussed the ways in which people had tried to account for the phenomena associated with heat. Either there could be an invisible fluid that flows from hotter to cooler places, or all heating effects could be the outcome of molecular motion. Lavoisier and many others had claimed the former, and it was still an adequate idea to account for simple heat transfer, but much more evidence now inclined the scientific community to think of heat in 'dynamical' terms. Nevertheless his science is cautious on such matters – hence 'considered as' in the title. In later editions he dropped the 'considered as' and left the more assertive title: 'Heat a Mode of Motion'. He and others had concluded that atoms and molecules must be real, at a time when many still regarded them as just convenient hypothetical constructs. As for the supposed 'luminiferous aether', however, needed for propagation within an undulatory theory of light, he would only say that it was *as if* such an aether were disturbed.

As the conversion of tentative ideas to accepted facts runs its course, there is a danger that teaching science will degenerate into passing on established information assertively, transmitting facts rather than exploring ideas. The subject might well lose some of its appeal when that happens, so many science teachers have felt that this literalisation of knowledge should be resisted. They don't want pupils in a 'take it or leave it' situation in relation to what the teacher says ('Atoms are like this, I'm telling you, write it down') because that cuts them off from active discussion, and fails to engage their imagination. One such teacher in the middle decades of this century was Frank Halliwell, who became Organiser for the Nuffield O Level Chemistry Project.

In Chapter 3, Edgar Jenkins points out that one of the unfortunate outcomes of the Nuffield period was a consolidation of naïve (now *antique*) views about scientific method, but some of the leading individuals had thought deeply about the nature of science, and Halliwell made much of the importance of tentative ideas. He had been influenced by Hans Vaihinger's

HEAT

CONSIDERED AS

A MODE OF MOTION:

BEING

A COURSE OF TWELVE LECTURES

DELIVERED AT

THE ROYAL INSTITUTION OF GREAT BRITAIN

IN THE SEASON OF 1862.

BY

JOHN TYNDALL, F.R.S. &c.

PROFESSOR OF NATURAL PHILOSOPHY IN THE ROYAL INSTITUTION.

WITH ILLUSTRATIONS.

LONDON:

LONGMAN, GREEN, LONGMAN, ROBERTS, & GREEN.

1863.

The right of translation is reserved.

Figure 10.4 Title page of *Heat Considered as a Mode of Motion*, first edition (1863). Note that in later editions the phrase 'considered as' was left out

book *The Philosophy of As If*, and would constantly use phrases such as 'Think of it like this . . .', 'It is as if the molecules were clinging to each other . . .' or 'It is as if the effort exerted here were stored up here . . .'. He was another master of the art of demonstration-with-discussion and I remember him talking about science as an alternation 'between the black-board and the bench'. 'See this . . .' (at the bench). 'Now what we think might be going on here is . . .' (at the board) '. . . and if so we would expect . . . So try this . . .' (at the bench). Only teachers who understand *how we know* as well as *what we know* can put back the tentativeness in this way.

Tentativeness in a wider context: the limits of science

Today we need ways of dealing not only with the balance of doubt and certainty in scientific theorising but also with over-certainty and a set of exaggerated, unrealistic expectations about what science can offer. Can it answer all our questions? Can it solve all our problems? What about the awareness from the environmental movement that solving one problem often generates others? Conversations in classrooms today cannot and should not avoid those problems.

What about the ill-considered idea that the only real knowledge is scientific and science will eventually tell us everything we need to know about human life – from our origins in a Big Bang to why we smile at each other? Such arrogant claims are strongly anti-educational, but they are easily picked up when the tentativeness of science is drowned out by its definiteness. They probably have effects on teenagers' sense of identity which we cannot respond to if the lessons remain strictly technical and we talk about the facts of genes and generation but not about the big questions of life (casting them as someone else's job under 'moral and spiritual education'?). I return to Maxwell and Tyndall to show that their thoughts were not confined to technical matters. Tyndall let his quest for understanding take him into the big questions not only of 'atomism' (are atoms real?) but also of 'materialism' (can life and human consciousness be accounted for as an evolutionary outcome of physical processes?). That latter problem is still with us today, even if insufficiently discussed in school. In his presidential address to the British Association in Belfast in 1874, he explored how far he could push the 'materialist' approach to understanding life, and was widely criticised for doing so. Maxwell had been president the previous year and had observed the growth of interest in these matters year by year, with the rise of palaeontology and the first speculations about a possible 'molecular evolution' before that of dinosaurs, mammoths and apes. Musing on this, he wrote another poem with a semi-ironic summary of Tyndall's words, ending as follows about the human condition and the effects of scientific understanding upon it. His words surely illustrate an aspect of conversations about science which we need to take into account in school. Below is Maxwell's ironic rendering of Tyndall's account of the new vistas in human history (1874):

> We honour our fathers and mothers, grandfathers and grandmothers too,
> But how shall we honour the vistas of ancestors *now* in our view?
>
> First, then, let us honour the atom, so lively, so wise, and so small;
> The atomists next let us praise, Epicurus, Lucretius and all;
> Let us damn with faint praise Bishop Butler, in whom many atoms combined
> To form that remarkable structure which it pleased him to call – his mind.
>
> Last, praise we the noble body [i.e. the British Association] to which, for the time, we belong,
> Ere yet the swift whirl of the atoms has hurried us, ruthless, along,
>
> The British Association – like Leviathan worshipped by Hobbes,
> The incarnation of wisdom, built up by our witless nobs,
> Which will carry on endless discussions, when I, and probably you,
> Have melted in infinite azure – in English, till all is blue.

Perhaps this was just a Scottish Calvinist raising his eyebrows at his colleague from Ireland and London, but it was also an expression of the limitations of science. My impression is that Tyndall from the agnostic wing and Maxwell as a conventional churchman *both* sensed a limit to human reason over questions of ultimate origins, in a way which does not seem to have bothered some present-day contributors to the debate. A few years ago in the United Kingdom we had it in the National Curriculum (Attainment Target 17) to alert pupils to the powers and limits of science. That section was then axed just when sections of the public were beginning to resent some scientists' claims to omniscience. In future it may be our task to find better ways of teaching science as an adventure of ideas rather than a revelation of irrefutable truths, and this will include taking into account the emotional significance of scientific knowledge for teenagers, connecting the within-science conversation with others that are personally important to them.

Classroom talk tomorrow

I have used the word 'conversation' in a rather special way, to stand for the discourse that binds a scientific community together. It consists of certain ways of talking, tentatively at first with personal suggestions and claims, and later, more definitely, with a voiceless impersonal universality, but always with a constant reference to tangible evidence. It involves the development of new mental worlds peopled by abstract 'things' on which the talk centres. In my analysis, to 'understand science' means to appreciate such discourse, and so now I must return to the question of what kinds of classroom activity can best help the learners to do so.

Unstructured and informal classroom talk around a circuit board or other piece of equipment is *not* a version of the 'conversation' I have described. If the kit is on the pupils' bench, their only access to the scientists' way of talking about the topic is in a worksheet or in an earlier or subsequent briefing by the teacher; that is, there is too little influence by the teacher. Around the teacher's bench, on the other hand, there is too much. Even when the teacher is hoping to replicate the scientists' consideration of possibilities and discussion of evidence, what commonly happens is that the pupils are 'led by the nose' to the one 'right' interpretation.[11] In all lessons there is a danger that too much of the talk will be done by the teacher, but pupils do need some clear, *uninterrupted* examples of how the particular branch of science is talked. They also need time and freedom to do their own mental work, to summon up their 'grasp of mind' and take possession of what they have seen and heard.

How can this be done? And where would practical work fit? It seems to me that lessons should have *as their object of study* short samples of how the relevant bit of science is talked, with the practical work in a supportive, not a leading, role. The task for the pupils would then be to arrive at their own expression of 'what these people are on about', and to turn that in as the outcome of the lesson, in a spoken report or a written one. There could be a cyclical repetition of a sequence as follows:

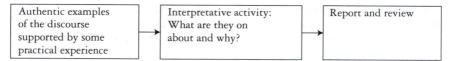

| Authentic examples of the discourse supported by some practical experience | → | Interpretative activity: What are they on about and why? | → | Report and review |

Pupils' written reports could be in a variety of formats, including posters of key points, which give a fairly easy option for beginners and can form the basis of coaching in more carefully argued communication. Contrasts between 'what they seem to be on about' and 'how I thought of it myself' could be encouraged at the report stage, and teachers would respond as now to these personal investments in learning. Practical work could form a part of the initial presentation ('Here's some of the evidence which makes people talk like this') and it could also be a resource in the room to help the pupils to get a feel for the phenomena as interpreted in the discourse ('Hold these magnets and push them together; this is what we mean by the force increasing as you get closer in the field'). Practical work gives a physical feel for the relevant phenomena, as argued by Jonathan Osborne in Chapter 9 of this book, but it only makes sense within the discourse.

One of the main resources for this approach would be the genuine voices of scientists in thought or persuasive argument, as opposed to a textbook account of the eventual outcomes. Often those voices will have to be re-created by the teacher, but sometimes they could be brought to the classroom directly in the form of *original* writing. As I said earlier, this is not a small change, and it is unlikely to come about without A BIG INVEST-MENT IN IN-SERVICE STUDY FOR TEACHERS, about the history of ideas and how to handle such work in the classroom. Coursebooks with a different feel to them are also likely to be needed if science lessons are thought of less in terms of informing learners about 'what is the case' and more in terms of helping them to appreciate circuit talk, electrolysis talk, electromagnetic wave talk, and so on. The time and effort spent on experiments must be kept subsidiary to the exploration of images and the story that binds a topic together. If we can make the 'cast' of that story into the focal point of lessons we have a better chance of communicating what scientists really achieve.

Relevant material can be on paper, on film, or in uninterrupted talk by the teacher, but it must be provided with the expectation of interpretative activity by the pupils. Expectations about what happens in a science lesson at present tend towards an assumption that the practical work is the object of attention so that we are trying to see 'what happens'. I must deny that utterly, and ask that instead we attend to 'what Michael Faraday and his successors *thought* was happening', or 'what people have said and thought about heat', and the equivalent in other topics, but always with the question '. . . and with what evidence?'.

Lastly, it seems to me that we might get a greater emphasis on thinking and re-expressing ideas, rather than being told information, by using some material which is in language styles totally outside the Spartan limits of factual description. For example, readers may be surprised at Maxwell's poems, yet get a glimpse of the man and his thought. At present, if such material is used at all it tends to be as light relief from 'the main business of the lesson', but if we really want to understand science we must know what makes scientists tick, and hear their authentic voices. Maxwell's poems may not be great poems, but they do indicate his thought and feeling. Thus, I would say, they are a suitable resource for the classroom – better in some ways than a ray box or a ripple tank – but certainly an important supplement to those things. There are limits to talking about things. Classroom talk can deepen when it is about people and their ideas and why they have those ideas.

Notes

1 'Ready made' and 'in the making' are terms from Bruno Latour's book *Science in Action*.

2 Debate about dinosaur extinction: E.O. Wilson in *The Diversity of Life*, Harvard University Press (1992) comments that in the decade after the initial paper by Luis Alvarez and others in 1979 there were over 2,000 further articles, and innumerable conferences, discussing the idea. This is a long way from the simple idea that scientists try out something in an experiment and 'report what happens'.

3 In the jargon of the British National Curriculum this is 'Sc0' – understanding how creative thought and evidence come together in the development of ideas and how these ideas have changed through time. It is about the process of scientific argument in the broadest possible sense, not just the 'Sc1' version of 'process' where the focus is on experiments. One way to improve school science would be simply to include more examples of science in the making – present-day examples and case studies from history.

4 Three systems used in securing firm knowledge: see chapter 2 of Shapin and Schaffer (1985). For a further development of such study, see also Steven Shapin (1994) *A Social History of Truth*.

5 Teenagers' limited conceptions of what scientists do: see Driver *et al.* (1996).

6 For more about how the selection of a new metaphor forms the basis of scientific model building and also the basis of new insight for a learner, see Sutton (1993): 'Figuring out a scientific understanding'.

7 Introducing the cast of the scientific story: see Ogborn *et al.* (1996: 9).

8 Tyndall's understanding of the imagination in science was explored in lectures to the British Association, printed as a booklet called *Use and Limit of the Imagination in Science*, London: Longmans Green and Co. (1870).

9 'A Tyndallic Ode' appears on page 412 of the 1884 edition of Campbell and Garnett's *Life of James Clerk Maxwell*. It is not dated there, but is printed amongst other verses which were written in 1874. The poem about Tyndall's address to the British Association in Belfast is in the same volume.

10 Loss of as-if-ness: see Sutton (1996).

11 *Pupils 'led by the nose'*: see Lemke (1990) and, much earlier, Barnes *et al.* (1971) on the prevalence of the pseudo-open question in science lessons.

Bibliography

Barnes, D., Britton, J. and Rosen, H. (1971) *Language, the Learner and the School*, Harmondsworth: Penguin.

Campbell, L. and Garnett, W. (1882, 1884) *The Life of James Clerk Maxwell*, London: Macmillan.

Driver, R., Millar, R., Leach, J. and Scott, P. (1996) *Young People's Images of Science*, Milton Keynes: Open University Press.

Halliday, M.A.K. and Martin, J.R. (1993) *Writing Science, Literacy and Discursive Power*, London: Falmer Press.

Latour, B. (1987) *Science in Action*, Cambridge, MA: Harvard University Press.

Lemke, J. (1990) *Talking Science*, Norwood, NJ: Ablex Corporation.

Ogborn, J., Kress, G., Martins, I. and McGillicuddy, K. (1996) *Explaining Science in the Classroom*, Milton Keynes: Open University Press.

Shapin, S. and Schaffer, S. (1985) *Leviathan and the Air Pump: Hobbes, Boyle and the Experimental Life*, Princeton, NJ: Princeton University Press.

Sutton, C.R. (1992) *Words, Science and Learning*, Buckingham: Open University Press.

—— (1993) 'Figuring out a scientific understanding', *Journal of Research in Science Teaching* 30(10): 1215–27.

—— (1996) 'Beliefs about science and beliefs about language', *International Journal of Science Education* 18(1): 1–18.

—— (1997) 'The scientific model as a form of speech', in G Welford, J. Osborne and P. Scott (eds) *Research in Science Education in Europe*, London: Falmer Press.

Vaihinger, Hans, *The Philosophy of As If: a System of the Theoretical, Practical and Religious Fictions of Mankind* (trans. (1935) C.K. Ogden) London: Kegan, Paul, Trench and Trubner.

11

'IMAGING' OR 'ENVISIONMENT' IN PRACTICAL WORK

Developing the link between action, thought and image

Joan Solomon

Probably we would all agree that the pupils' practical work in a laboratory should not be confined to just following a recipe, either written or spoken. But how much further would we agree? We have a shopping list of wants for practical work which sound eminently sensible but, when taken in pairs, are uncomfortably demanding. We want the pupils to be active, and yet to think deeply while they are being active; we want to be creative and free from too many constraints, and yet we want their practical work to contribute to their learning of the concepts of science, which are certainly not unconstrained. The basic problem illustrated by those pairs of wants is the interplay between doing, observing and thinking. One alone will not do – we need all three. That is the point of the present chapter, in which it will be argued that behind the deliberate actions undertaken in a laboratory there is, and should be, a whole picture gallery of internal ideas of a kind which makes them able to combine action and observation with past experience and further knowing.

Play and exploration

One way to approach the nature of the central guiding image is to look for a situation in which practical activity is *not* guided by imaging: 'just playing about with the apparatus' is one of these. A visit to some of the interactive science centres may offer examples of this sort of mindless play, although that is certainly not all that is going on. An important distinction must be made here between *playing about* without any plan, and *purposeful play* such as the mock fights in which children and cubs indulge, or a child trying out a new toy. Play can have at least two important functions to fulfil: (1) getting a feel for the equipment and the associated bodily movement; and (2) acquiring a plan or intention for an exploration. Unless these two motives are in operation the play remains unguided and unmeaningful. We commonly use the word 'playful' for activity without any plan, and when Ziman (1984) commented that *scientific experiment is never playful*, it seems clear that it was this lack of intention he was using to distinguish between play and scientific experiment.

In school science clubs, if they are very loosely run, it is quite common to find children begging to use the same apparatus again and again (see Solomon 1980) and then putting it to use without any change in what they do for several weeks. There is a meaning in this kind of activity which is just rehearsing the same actions with the same outcomes; they are a special kind of internalisation.

Robin Hodgkin drew a thought-provoking diagram to illustrate this in his book *Playing and Exploring* (1985).

The left-hand loop is the one Hodgkin calls *practice*. Only the right-hand loop goes out into new territory and may be called *exploring* in a sense which a scientist or teacher would recognise. Practice is important and provides that familiarity with the object or tool on which all good, thoughtful, practical work depends. Those enthusiasts who write about hands-on

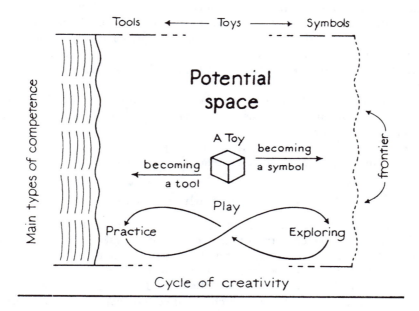

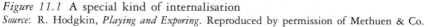

Figure 11.1 A special kind of internalisation
Source: R. Hodgkin, *Playing and Exploring*. Reproduced by permission of Methuen & Co.

science, like Richard Gregory, call the object an 'explore-with' or even a 'plore'. This is their way of emphasising that the object is going to be central to a non-playful activity which we might call exploration. Later in this chapter it will be claimed that the actions observed during play with the object become part of its image or envisionment.

In Helen Brooke's perceptive account of young children in an Inter-active Science Centre (Brooke 1994) much the same points are made, examined and illustrated. The children she observed often began rather aimlessly; they may even have admitted to not knowing, or even caring, about what would happen. She described how they laughed when a car they had constructed out of cardboard flew backwards out of the wind-tunnel instead of forwards! The adults thought that they should have tried to make the car go down into the wind, but the children had not adopted this intention. No one seemed disappointed because no one was concerned with the outcome. The whole activity had not yet 'made sense'; it was playful and had no purpose.

Nevertheless actions performed during this kind of play, even when it has no clear intention, do seem to have a function. There was a classic experiment performed many years ago by Bruner *et al.* (1974) which is still too little known by science educators. In this there were three groups of children, two of whom were given training sessions with the stacking sticks either to teach them how to join them together, or to demonstrate how the extension mechanism worked, while the third group was simply allowed to play with the materials without any instructions. Finally, when all the groups tried to use the sticks to reach out and get some prized object by fastening them together, it was the 'play' group which succeeded first! Now that there was a purpose it seemed that the play had provided something of value.

We might assume from that experiment that familiarity with the use of objects somehow makes their use in new and extended situations easier to imagine. About how it does so, or about the new perception of the object which is built up by playing with it, this experiment has nothing to tell, but we can piece together some evidence from other sources.

Making sense without words

'Playing about' does sometimes change into exploration of its own accord, and this rather wonderful transition is described several times in Brooke's work (1994), where it is easy enough to see that a purpose has been acquired. Is this also the start of imaging? Polanyi (1958) certainly thought so. For him the familiarity with tools of any kind, or new body movement, resulted in a kind of *body image* which he called *'in-dwelling tacit knowledge'*. The driver with tacit knowledge of the shape of her car, for example, hunches up her shoulders when driving between two concrete posts which might scrape the paint work, showing just how strongly the outline image of the car's chassis is in-dwelling in her body.

Polanyi (1958) gives an example of the growth of an image which is a little closer to the kind of 'envisioning' we have to help our pupils acquire so that they can carry out meaningful practical work. When he was a medical student Polanyi was shown his first X-ray photograph during a lecture. He reports how at first neither the words of the lecturer nor the dark and light patches on the X-ray photograph made any sense to him. When sense did come to him it arrived as a whole. The meaning created by words interpreted the photograph, and the images retrieved from the photograph made sense of the words. The point to note here is that neither the one nor the other is primary, and that neither of them alone correspond to full internal envisionment. Pictures, or remembered images, and words both need to be linked into a trace in our understanding and imagining in order to make sense. This is important in practical work.

Activity and images

The genetic epistemology of Jean Piaget is going through a trough of neglect at the present time but no one can write of thought and activity without paying due regard to his work. It was one of his greatest achievements to disconnect thought from mere inner contemplation, where it had been for all previous centuries since the time of the ancient Greeks, who held mechanical work in such contempt. For Piaget the function of thought was the reconstruction of action. Even in the famous conservation of volume experiments, for which so many jugs of orange juice have been poured out from one beaker into another, the objective of the test was always to learn about the kind of thinking which involves *the envisioning of action*. The child has to operate in her mind with reversed pouring, emptying back of the juice into the first jug, as well as the idealised nature of volume which supersedes and builds on the action of pouring.

Volume is certainly not the only scientific concept which contains, and is constructed from, a whole series of possible actions. Until we arrive at the far borders of modern physics almost all concepts are similar in this respect. It is possible to see a floating object as just that. Then it is just a simple percept. The instructed student will see it balanced between the pull of gravity and the upthrust of the water not only because the scientific instruction is remembered, but because possible actions are now included in what is seen. The act of pushing it down and the feeling of its attempt to bounce back up are incorporated into its mental image, thus making the simple percept at least half-way to becoming a concept.

it is not enough to perceive the solid [object] clearly, or even to record this percept in the form of a drawing . . . the [symbolic]

image is a pictorial anticipation of an action not yet performed.
. . . Thus what the image furnishes, to a far greater degree than
perception, is a schema of action. That is why the image is more
mobile and sometimes richer in content than perception.'

(Piaget 1956: 294)

The youngest baby begins by exploring the world in terms of action, as do
animals. Piaget famously called this the sensori-motor phase of development. In this age of neo-Piagetian criticism we are not so ready to take on
board the invariant sequence of development stages that he postulated, but
we neglect the next great step forward in human thinking into operational
ideas at our peril. Jerôme Bruner appreciated this aspect of Piaget's work
better than most. He wrote of children's emergence from the earlier simple
world of sensori-motor action and simple percepts as 'a great achievement.
Images develop an autonomous status, they become great summarisers of
action' (Bruner 1966: 13).

Robin Hodgkin took these ideas forward so that the image of the object,
complete with all the actions that could be performed with it, was somehow
reproduced inside our brains. The brain as camera, having a one-to-one
correspondence with what is being thought of in the outside world, may be
too simplistic a copy of thought, percept and action. However, there are
plenty of anecdotes from the work of inventors, who have operated with
these images so skilfully in their minds that we may have to accept this
correspondence as a first approximation, at least in the field of learning
through doing.

when we visualise a pattern – a coiled rope, say – something
representational of space must be happening in the deep strata of
our brains, and furthermore we can *do* something with such an
image if we wish.

(Hodgkin 1985)

Images for learning

Making sense in the laboratory is difficult. Percepts are never enough, and
just carrying out the teacher's instructions is of little conceptual use.
Actions need to change what is seen into an image which contains the
capacity for further action; then this envisionment can become so deeply
ingrained that it goes some way towards explaining why things behave the
way they do. This means that the floating object is *balanced* between sinking
and rising, an ammeter needle is recording *flowing* current, and the pairs of
complementary muscles in the wing of a bird are packed with the *potential
movements* of flight.

I still remember quite vividly my own bewilderment when, as a young, unreconstructed, empiricist physics teacher, I was accosted by a pupil who demanded to know what her experimental result meant. 'I can see what happened', she said, 'but you haven't explained it to us.' Seeing, I gradually came to understand, is no more making a meaningful image than is copying down a sentence. In this chapter we are using the more clumsy word 'envisionment' (which may also have a misleading link with seeing) as being an 'image' packed with past action to get an understanding of what is happening. Can children envision heat radiation, or the flow of liquid through the turgid cells of a flower stem, while they are carrying out their science investigations? It is argued here that for real learning – knowledge-building – they must do this. Without such envisionment no experiments and no diagrams will make sense of the practical work. It will, sadly, remain just 'playing about', albeit without the fun that accompanies this kind of activity in an exuberant hands-on centre.

It follows that there is a close connection between envisionment or image, in the sense in which we are using these words, and basic scientific concepts in the topic area being taught. Different topics require different images and different levels of envisionment. Some of these are so simple that they may be acquired with only the minimum of teaching imput, while others need a teaching *tour de force* as well as personal action. In the following section I will use four different topic images, or envisionments, to illustrate their effects on pupils' learning through practical work.

The first of these will be the envisionment of shadow. It is a good place to start because we can immediately disabuse ourselves of the idea that a shadow is itself an envisionment. Once, when I was beginning to teach a class of 13–14-year-olds about light I asked them to draw the shadow of a pin-man at midday and in the evening. Of course the point of this was to see if the pupils could use the newly taught idea of light travelling in straight lines related to shadows. I also had the hope that their drawings would confirm that they could use straight lines for the determining the lengths of the shadows. It turned out, as we can see below, that some could and some could not.

I was amazed! I turned to the pupil who had drawn the second diagram and commented that it 'looked more like a dead body than a shadow'. She was not so much offended as surprised; clearly it looked quite all right to her. That was how she envisioned shadow. Then, to confirm that these drawings also contained the cognitive component of an envisionment, I asked all the class to write down what they thought a shadow was. Once again it was possible to divide the answers into two kinds. On one side I put all those answers where the pupils wrote about the light being 'blocked out', or 'not getting through' – the ones that included action. On the other side I put those answers which just said that a shadow was a 'shape', an 'image' or a 'reflection'. (The sophisticated reader should try to ignore the incorrectness of the last of these. 'Reflection' was clearly only used in the

Figure 11.2 An envisionment of shadow

sense of repeating the shape of the original.) Now came the interesting part. Almost all of those who had drawn a disconnected shadow had simply written about shapes, while most of those who had drawn the shadow connected to the feet of the pin-man, and also of approximately the right size compared with the orientation of the light, had given the action type of definition about light 'not getting through'. A simple calculation showed that the writing matched exceedingly well with the drawings with a coefficient of association of better than 0.76.

From this we may infer that shadows were not just remembered (or misremembered) as visual images or simple percepts. They were complete envisionments of how a shadow is formed as well as seen. It is not difficult to see that practical work which set out to measure the length of a shadow

198

under different light conditions would become no more than meaningless drill for those without an envisionment connecting the direction of the light, and the position of the obstacle, to the size of the shadow.

The second example is instructive because it showed the teacher (once again it was me!) that her instruction had been internalised but had produced *an incorrect envisionment*. In the example a golfer had hit a ball which bounced several times, lower and lower, until it rolled across the green and came to rest in the bottom of the hole. The picture was drawn for the pupils and they were asked to say what had happened to the energy that the ball had possessed when it first left the golfer's club. Several able pupils, although not the majority, wrote that the energy was all stored up in the ball at the bottom of the hole. Rather facetiously I asked if the ball was in danger of exploding! More surprised than hurt they answered accusingly that this was what (they thought) I had said when I taught them that energy was 'neither created or destroyed'. They concluded that the energy had no alternative but to stay where it was – in the ball. My words had formed their envisionment of the problem, and had deceived them. Now if any practical work had followed up that problem, without correction of their understanding of the conservation of energy, a rise in temperature of the ball would have simply confirmed their erroneous envisionment.

My third example is a notoriously difficult practical observation, and concerns looking at smoke particles when learning about Brownian motion. The interesting feature of this exercise is that it could be based so strongly on an only partially correct envisionment that, as in the case of shadows, it interferes strongly with observation. The students are usually introduced to the idea that the particles of air are in perpetual motion colliding with each other and the walls of the container. No doubt the teacher also explains that what they are going to see is not air particles but those of smoke, but this part of the preparatory information is often not so well absorbed. Once the microscope is focused on the smoke particles a considerable number of students report that they can see particles colliding with each other, instead of just jigging about under the bombardment of high-speed and unseen air particles. Why do they report seeing what we know they cannot possibly see, in the perceptual sense of this word? The answer has to be that the envisionment, made from knowledge incorrectly received, is superimposed on top of the retinal perceptual image either at the moment of seeing, or in recollection. In effect, that means that the whole of this potentially valuable observation has been of no value whatsoever to the student. It cannot be used either to support the kinetic theory of gases or for further understanding, such as Brownian motion in water, or at different temperatures.

For my fourth example I shall use a slightly different and more positive situation where the teacher tries to present an envisionment of electric current by the use of a mechanical model. It is often assumed that every child knows that current 'flows'. Some simple questionnaire studies carried out with colleagues (Black *et al.* 1987) showed that this was not the case. Some pupils only know that plugs or appliances must not be touched because they are 'electric' or 'live'. So the teacher's first task is to get across the idea of current movement. The pupils will never see the current move; even the swing of the ammeter needle cannot carry this conviction. So generations of teachers have come to the conclusion that some kind of analogy is required and usually they tell a story of water in pipes (Black and Solomon 1987). Many explorations of metaphor have shown that students' understanding of water flow is not good enough to make this a useful teaching ploy, and neither is traffic flow along our only intermittently crowded roads. Neither of these dominant teaching metaphors avoids the impression that current starts at one end of the circuit, first fills up empty pipes, and then continues on its trip at a slower or faster pace. Thus current is envisioned in a way which can make no sense of the observation that the same current is flowing at all points round a simple circuit. Often the pressure of the untaught internal image supersedes the percept we would have expected from simple observation (as we have seen above in examples two and three) so that pupils even read the instrument from the side in order to make its reading coincide more comfortably with what they envision must be happening. The following is a model which the children themselves put into action by twisting a cotton reel, to acquire a better envisionment of electric current to match the experiments about to be done with wires and batteries.

From this sort of evidence I conclude that students need not only to carry out practical work, but also to incorporate the previous manipulations of the laboratory objects, and of stories about them, into what they do.

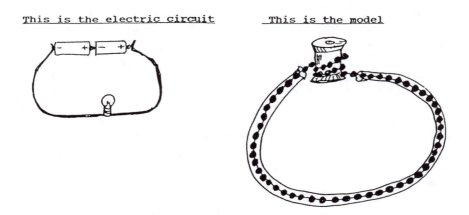

Figure 11.3 An envisionment of electric current

Conclusions

Practical work has few friends in the philosophy of *general* education, except where rather low-level vocational training is involved. Maybe this too has its roots in the old classical tradition of education. However, I think it is more likely to be the outcome of a way of thinking about learning which is firmly embedded in the transmission model of education. Paul Hirst (1974), for example, held the traditional liberal educator's view of the paramount, even exclusive, importance of the 'cultivation of the mind', and he set out four general mental abilities which all true education should support:

- to think effectively,
- to communicate effectively,
- to make relevant judgements, and
- to discriminate effectively.

We look in vain within this list for 'learning through action' or 'knowing as transforming'. For Hirst, thinking effectively, making relevant judgements and discriminating are all non-problematic; they are abstracted cerebral acts with no connection with particular situations. None includes the envisionment of past actions in a particular context, or the possibilities of those to come. For him the criteria of true education transcend the context of the subject being taught, while it is easy to see from examples that envisionment is always specific to the context in which something happens. Thus technology and practical work do *not* find a place in Hirst's seven forms of knowledge. Instead, he wrote about a 'practical field of knowledge' which applies quite generally to all his forms of knowledge, but merely as hands-on application of principles learnt elsewhere and being applied again. Laborious and careful titrations of volumetric solutions, and verifying Archimedes' principle with a bucket and cylinder, can be found within this rather soul-destroying category.

The argument of this chapter is that images of potential action, and the action of doing experiments mutually benefit each other. No pencil-and-paper alternative (such as Osborne 1997) can possibly substitute for that. Sometimes the teacher can see the synthesis of action and image at work; more often they hear it in the comments that pupils call across to each other – 'pour the water on further out from the pivot'; or 'Stand back! It's going to accelerate like mad'. More often the effect is internal, building up the envisionment of these valuable action-packed concepts on which the understanding of science depends.

Although this chapter has been in praise of practical work and of the indwelling knowledge it can use and substantiate, it may not itself sound practical from the teacher's point of view. That is because teachers, like the pupils they teach, have already acquired situational knowledge. In their case it is knowledge about the action of teaching which is also in-dwelling (see Ogborn *et al.* 1996). So the most important part of communication with teachers is laying out what this envisionment is all about; then they will find their own ways of getting some of it across. Of course you cannot force children to imagine, but you can help them to start. No one who has understood this chapter will send pupils off to do practical work without first talking in an imaginative and inspiring way. Some will tell stories about what electrons or cells might be like. Some will give a startling demonstration, and then talk their way out of it. Some will show a concrete model and let their students crank the handle until they begin to imagine what electron flow or transpiration might be like. Only then are the students ready to carry out investigations, using and building upon envisionments that can add meaning to action in the laboratory.

To know an object is to act upon it and transform it.

Piaget (1956)

References

Black, D. and Solomon, J. (1987) 'The use of analogy in the teaching of electricity', *School Science Review* 69(247): 249–54.

Black, P., Solomon, J. and Stuart, H. (1987) 'The pupil's view of electricity revisited: Social develoment or cognitive growth?' *International Journal of Science Education* 9: 13–22.

Brooke, H. (1994) 'Playing and learning in an interactive science centre: a study of primary school children', unpublished diploma thesis, Oxford University Department of Educational Studies.

Bruner, J. (1966) *Towards a Theory of Instruction*, Cambridge, MA: Harvard University Press.

Bruner, J., Sylva, K. and Genoa, P. (1974) 'The role of play in the problem-solving of children aged 3–5 years old', in J. Bruner, A. Jolly and K. Sylva (eds) *Play – its Role in Development and Evolution*, Harmondsworth: Penguin.

Gregory, R. (1986) *Hands-on Science: an introduction to the Bristol Exploratory*. London: Duckworth.

Hirst, P.A. (1974) *Knowledge and the Curriculum*, London: Routledge and Kegan Paul.

Hodgkin, R. (1985) *Playing and Exploring*, London: Methuen.

Ogborn, J., Kress, G., Martins, I. and McGillicuddy, K. (1996) *Explaining Science in the Classroom*, Buckingham: Open University Press.

Osborne, J. (1997) 'Practical alternatives', *School Science Review* 78(285): 61–7.

Piaget, J. (1956 trans.) *The Child's Conception of Space*, London: Routledge and Kegan Paul.

Polanyi, M. (1958) *Personal Knowledge*, London: Routledge and Kegan Paul.

Solomon, J. (1980) *Teaching Children in the Laboratory,* London: Croom Helm.

Ziman, J. ((1984) *An Introduction to Science Studies*, Cambridge: Cambridge University Press.

Part V

FURTHER IDEAS ON THE FUTURE OF PRACTICAL WORK

In many ways previous chapters in this book have already put forward practical, specific ideas for new strategies and teaching approaches in practical work. The aim of this section is to offer further ideas and approaches. All are based on recent research carried out by the authors. This section could have contained numerous possibilities but space only permits five short chapters. The book had to stop somewhere although I know at least ten other authors who could have written valuable chapters for this final section. Each chapter is different, although three focus on the use of ICT as a way of enhancing science education.

Beginning with the most general, Masters and Nott explain the importance of implicit personal knowledge in practical science, and describe how it differs from the explicit knowledge which is so often asked for when pupils are required to give accounts of investigations or other practical activities. Implicit knowledge is almost impossible to formulate in words and hence is rarely part of assessment. Yet, as Masters and Nott show, it is a remarkably resilient and effective component of the skills and processes of science, and indeed of other skill-based activities such as writing, speaking, tennis or golf. Their argument is that implicit knowledge needs to be recognised and developed. They outline ways of achieving this in science education and argue (somewhat unfashionably) for the importance of *training* in skills development and a closer, more intense focus on a narrower range of processes in science education.

Howe and Smith offer an equally focused chapter in which they concentrate on a specific approach to practical work, which involves hypothesis planning and testing. They report on their own classroom-based research into approaches of this kind, which is both detailed and honest. One of the broader questions they pose, which links well with earlier chapters, is whether practical work can develop both experimental or procedural skills *and* conceptual growth. They analyse and discuss different types of collaborative group work which can be used in investigational science and show their advantages and drawbacks. Once again, they argue for the importance of structured debate and discussion when pupils are carrying out practical tasks. For classroom teachers, they put forward a clear structure which can be followed in hypothesis-led work. This sequence, which can be guided either by a teacher or using a computer, is one of the practical outcomes of their research.

Barton's chapter, again based on his own recent research, illustrates how the use of ICT, in particular data-logging, can change the focus of practical work in science. Barton describes how using computers to collect and present data in school labs can emancipate learners, allowing them time to interpret and discuss their results. He talks of the higher-order skills which can be enhanced as a result of data-logging in science education. As well as the changes in, and value added to, learning, Barton points out that we also need to examine the role of the teacher in future practical work. If less time is spent on collecting data – by manually recording readings, and processing it (for example, by drawing graphs on graph paper) – how should time be best exploited and what part should the teacher play? This again points to a need for careful, sensitive professional development of teachers to accomplish what Barton calls a 'pedagogical shift'.

From the perspective of multimedia, Baggott's chapter considers the same general issues of emancipation, use of lesson time, and the question of what counts as authentic (that is, valuable, educational) and not-authentic (drudgery; of no educational value) labour in practical work. Is it justifiable to use a mercury-in-glass thermometer in a classroom if the school has temperature probes which can be connected to a data-logger? Should pupils use microscopes to observe small things and phenomena when they can see similar images on a multimedia system? This is the issue which Baggott explores, again drawing upon her own recent research. She argues that simulations are an important tool in the work of real scientists; as she puts it, 'an important way of representing knowledge'. Her chapter, based on evaluations with pupils in secondary schools, highlights the potential of multimedia in science activity in 'freeing' pupils to exercise higher-level skills, in promoting active learning, and in providing ethical ways of investigating life and living processes. Like Barton, she talks of the 'pedagogical shift' which will be required if we are to make full use of ICT in practical science activities.

Finally, Wardle discusses the lessons learnt from the successful Schools On-Line project for science, based at Sheffield Hallam University. Scarcely a day passes without some mention of the Internet on radio, television or in the papers. Wardle shows how controlled and well-structured use of the Internet can enhance practical science work in schools. It can be not only a source of information but also a vehicle for sharing and comparing data, a support for pupils' investigations, a resource for on-line simulations, and a source of data from other people's practical work which can be used in lessons. Wardle describes the idea of 'the pupil as researcher', a concept and an initiative which has been the focus for a major project in practical work (the Pupil Researcher Initiative or PRI, also based at Sheffield Hallam University).

12

IMPLICIT KNOWLEDGE AND SCIENCE PRACTICAL WORK IN SCHOOLS

Richard Masters and Mick Nott

In this chapter we explain some of the research findings about children's abilities with practical work and investigations. We draw on psychological literature about implicit knowledge. We argue that if these models of knowledge are accepted as applicable to practical work in school science, then we may be trying to assess children in inappropriate ways. From the same premises we also argue that proficiency in practical work requires teaching with as few rules as possible and that these rules should be clear and preferably use images and pictures, not just written text. Concomitant with this is the argument that children may be better off trying to master fewer skills but taking longer over each one because mastery will only come with frequent, continuous practice and this may entail training.

Introduction

In school lessons learners are asked to demonstrate their knowledge overtly. Teachers ask pupils and students to articulate through discussion and text what they know, how they know it and, more and more, to tell us how they learned it. Learners are asked to be explicit about knowledge. For example, when we test them we ask them not only to recall what they know but also to justify what they know. 'Show your working' is the exhortation, as the working allows the teacher to follow the pupils' thinking about a problem. Much teaching is composed of explicit and often complex chains of rules and reasoning. The assessment of students frequently requires them to articulate their knowledge of these chains and reasons.

This can be seen in school science in both content and process. When a child sits a paper-and-pencil test they have not only to recall but also to show understanding by explaining and writing the rationales and rules behind their answers. Pupils are also assessed for their performance in practical investigations or parts of investigations. When undertaking an investigation in school science a pupil will have not only to carry out the investigation but also to explain their thinking behind the investigation. Education in science requires students to 'show why they know what they know'.

Children, skills and investigations

Research has shown that when they are doing practical investigations children are worse at overtly explaining, by talk or writing, what they have done or why they have done it (APU 1988a, 1988b) than they are at actually planning and doing it. Their performance of the investigation is better than their account of the investigation. Research also indicates that when children are using apparatus and measuring instruments then, 'performance of these tasks is less well known than the theory of how to carry them out' (APU 1988b: 49). In other words, children can articulate what they should be able to do if they were doing the task correctly but can't actually do the task. The research goes on to note that when particular manipulations or operations are repeated, then children's performance will tend to improve. So there is a paradox. Children find it hard to articulate tasks they can be seen to be performing satisfactorily and tasks they can articulate satisfactorily they can't do very well. In some cases they can do techniques and procedures well and not be able to explain them, and at other times they can say what they are supposed to be doing better than they can actually do it. The APU looked at whether failure to complete invesigations or complete practical tasks was to do with children's inability to follow written instructions, and came to the conclusion that the cause of pupils failing to complete a stage in an experiment has more to do with a lack of manipulative skills, irrelevant observations, or failure to recall appropriate techniques than with the ability to follow instructions, (1988b: 51). Children do not seem to be able to demonstrate competence in key skills which allow the successful accomplishment of a practical or investigation.

Later work has focused on the procedural and conceptual knowledge in science that children would need to conduct an investigation successfully. The PACKS (Procedural and Conceptual Knowledge in Science) project looked at children's conduct of investigations, particularly the way in which they gathered empirical data, and then manipulated and interpreted the data so that they became evidence (or not!). In one example (Duggan *et al.* 1996), three girls conducted an investigation where they had to examine how the force needed to drag a brick up a plank depended on the height of the plank.

The girls took only three readings using equal intervals but these readings were spread over a limited range. Katie recorded the results in a table:

Height (cm)	Pull (N)
27	7.5
45	10
60	10

They did not repeat any readings and *their results also suggest that accuracy in measuring the force may have been questionable.*

(Duggan *et al.* 1996: 153 – our emphasis)

The pupils appeared to lack the ability to conduct the investigation with appropriate procedures – for example, selecting an appropriate range, repeating results. However – and this is not alluded to in the rest of the chapter by Duggan *et al.* – they also appear to be incompetent at reading and recording and/or using the forcemeter, as the last two readings of pull for different heights are recorded as identical. The chapter goes on to discuss how the children found it difficult to interpret and predict from the data they got. It seems that the children were unable to conduct a valid or reliable investigation not only because they did not know procedures but also because they did not have the required skills of observation or manipulation.

In another report on the PACKS project (Duggan and Gott 1996), it is claimed that much of school practical work has become a ritual. The researchers were observing and recording pupils drawing a graph of their results. The teachers and researchers saw the purpose of the investigation as the determination of relationships between the variables. For the children, the purpose of the investigation became the drawing and completion of the graph, not the use of the graph in interpreting the data for some kind of prediction, pattern, meaning or understanding,

> the surface features of practical science such as the drawing of graphs may have been overemphasised to the extent that pupils lose sight of the meaning of the investigation and the significance of the evidence and the interpretation.
>
> (Duggan and Gott 1996: 29).

In summary, the evidence from educational research seems to be paradoxical. On the one hand, children can do investigations better than they can describe them; on the other, children can talk about specific techniques and skills better than they can do them. Children's competence at using apparatus and observing are often at a level which invalidates their recorded results. The demands of the separate tasks in an investigation or practical can be such that children lose track of what the purpose of the whole exercise is. The original overt purpose of all this practical science education is for children to be able to execute skills competently, conduct investigations smoothly, and overtly explain the processes and tactics followed. It is debatable whether this latter requirement is desirable or even possible.

Implicit knowledge

There are many things we can recall, recognise or accomplish without explanation. By experience we can recognise misspellings without explaining the spelling rules, or poor grammar without being able to explain the rules of grammar. We can ride a bike without being able to explain how to keep balance. We can recognise something as belonging to a particular class without being able to state the criteria which categorise it in that class; we just know it 'belongs'. This kind of knowledge is implicit or, in psychological terms, 'procedural knowledge'; that is, knowledge learned by going through the procedures or process. It can be acquired unconsciously, as in the bike-riding example, or it can be acquired consciously and then forgotten over time, as is the case for most of us who recognise poor grammar. If we think long and hard, we may recall the rules that tell us it is poor grammar but more often than not they are long forgotten. This process by which knowledge is initially explicit and then later non-verbalisable and implicit has been described as the transition from declarative knowledge to procedural knowledge.

It impacts on everything we do and each way in which we behave. Take, for example, riding a bike. No amount of mechanics theory will enable you to ride a bike. Instruction from another person is of some but limited value when actually learning to ride. Ultimately one has to feel what it is to ride a bike, and no amount of explanation can pass on that knowledge to another person. Knowing how to ride a bike is implicit or procedural; knowing how to explain the way a bike works is explicit or declarative.

Polanyi (1958), writing about personal knowledge and his experience as a research scientist, talked of tacit knowledge. Tacit knowledge is knowledge which cannot be articulated. Polanyi argued that tacit knowledge was an intrinsic and important part of the doing of science. Scientists doing research often display tacit knowledge – they know what feels right when doing a certain technique or investigation but are unable to explain clearly why or how they do it that way. Some people in laboratories are often said to have 'golden hands'. Tacit knowledge is a form of implicit knowledge.

Types of and evidence for implicit knowledge

The learning of implicit knowledge has been generally explored using three main experimental models: control of complex systems, sequence learning and artificial grammar learning. According to Berry and Dienes (1993) these models correspond in that 'a person typically learns about the structure of a fairly complex stimulus environment, without necessarily intending to do so, and in such a way that the resulting knowledge is difficult to express' (p. 2). We will concentrate on the first two, as they are most relevant to practical work.

In the control of complex systems, people can learn to organise complex sets of variables without being able to say how they do so. For example, Broadbent and Aston (1978) asked management teams to manipulate a hypothetical model of the British economy and found that these teams became better with practice, yet their knowledge of the governing principles of the model, as shown in multiple choice examinations, remained unchanged. Using other complex computer-systems tasks or simulations such as a sugar production task (Berry and Broadbent 1984) and a city transport system task (Broadbent *et al.* 1986), it has consistently been shown that subjects will improve in their ability to control the systems without exhibiting an increase in their ability to answer verbal questions about them. In most cases those people who are better at controlling such systems are significantly worse at answering questions about them. Additionally, there is evidence that changes in performance do not parallel changes in verbalisable knowledge. Stanley *et al* (1989), for example, showed that although performance on the sugar production task improved with practice this did not mean that people became better at explaining the task to others. Stanley *et al.* concluded that people can become skilled in tasks 'long before they gain verbalizable knowledge about them'.

An alternative paradigm used to explore implicit knowledge and learning can be explored with sequence learning. An example of sequence learning is the serial reaction time task developed by Nissen and Bullemer (1987), in which people were required to indicate, as rapidly as possible, which of four lights appeared horizontally on a visual display unit. These lights were presented either randomly or in a repeating ten-sequence pattern. Reaction times improved considerably when subjects practised on the repeating pattern but not when they practised on the random presentation. When the task was unexpectedly switched from patterned to random presentation, reaction times immediately increased. People were able to respond more quickly to the repeating pattern than the random presentation because they anticipated which light would appear. Although normal subjects were aware of the patterned sequence and were even able to describe chunks of it, amnesic subjects had no awareness of the sequencing yet exhibited the same pattern of behaviour; responding more quickly to the repeating pattern than the random pattern of lights. These examples are pertinent to practical skills because they indicate that people may be able to perform according to a regular pattern without being able to explain what the pattern is or why they are performing in that way.

We hypothesise that the findings above may be applicable to practical and experimental processes and manipulations in science. People can do them much better than they can describe how and why they do them. The ability to do something is not necessarily related to the person's ability to describe it. People can detect and act on underlying patterns of behaviour even though they may be unaware that they are doing so. If knowledge can be implicit, then this may be an explanation for why children's performance at investigations can be better than their ability to write a report on the plan, the experiment and the evaluation. All this resonates with the findings of the APU.

The persistence of implicit knowledge and learning

In the two examples presented above it is apparent that learning has taken place in a manner beyond the ability of the learner to explicate in the way that traditional schooling demands. One of the striking characteristics of such implicit knowledge is that it appears to be more durable than explicit knowledge.

For example, in word completion tasks where people had learnt the words maybe months earlier (Tulving *et al.* 1982), it was found that priming effects on word completion tasks persisted over time, while recognition memory did not.[1] It has also been found (Allen and Reber 1980) that the ability to distinguish between grammatical and non-grammatical sequences on an artificial grammar learning task (lasting some 10 to 15 minutes) remained accurate to a level of 68 per cent some 2 years after learning the grammar, despite the fact that subjects could not explain what the rules of the artificial grammar were on which they had based their decisions. In terms of practical skills, the most compelling support for the durability of implicit knowledge has been forthcoming from work with an amnesic patient in the late 1960s. Following extensive brain surgery the patient, H.M., was found to be profoundly amnesic. Despite this, HM was able to acquire normal motor and sensorimotor skills (Corkin 1968) and mirror tracing and tactile maze learning (Milner *et al.* 1968). Starr and Phillips (1970) provide evidence of similar findings in other amnesic patients. The conclusion generally drawn from such findings in the literature is that unconscious, implicit processes tend to survive neurological and psychological trauma better than conscious, explicit processes.

Another characteristic of implicit knowledge is that it is resistant to skill failure under pressure. Masters (1992) noted that experts who fail under pressure will often report that they are too aware of what they are doing, they have too much explicit knowledge. He argued that on such occasions the many rules that the performer has accumulated in becoming an expert will be 'reinvested' in the skill, disrupting its automaticity. In these instances it appears that the expert attempts to recall, explicitly, the rules for performance and then follow these rules. Masters argued that if the movement can be learned implicitly, without any explicit knowledge or rules of performance, then on occasions on which the performer comes under pressure this interference will not be possible.

Novices were asked to acquire the skill of golf putting either explicitly (with knowledge of how to putt) or implicitly (without knowledge of how to putt). In the explicit condition they were simply instructed, through coaching manuals, in the techniques and rules of golf putting. In the implicit condition they received no instructions and were required to carry out a highly demanding random letter generation task throughout all practice sessions. Efficient movement patterns developed despite the fact that the learners in this secondary task condition were unable to comprehend any conscious knowledge or rules about what they were doing. More importantly, when both groups were placed under stress by the introduction of an audience who evaluated their performance the explicit learners showed a decline in their performance, whereas the implicit learners showed no decline and in fact in many cases appeared to improve. This finding has been replicated by Hardy *et al.* (1996).

The case for implicit learning will surely resonate with the experiences of many readers. There are implications for the teaching and learning of science in schools. Knowing things implicitly explains why it is sometimes best to go with your first response in a multiple choice test, why some people seem to have 'golden hands' when doing practical work, and why a teacher should not always be irritated when they ask a student, 'Can you explain why you did that?' and the pupil replies, 'Don't know, miss'. In the implicit learning literature this is known as a phenomenal sense of intuition (Berry and Dienes 1993). However, school knowledge is explicit knowledge in both the way that teachers and texts explain it to the learner and the way that the learner is asked to reproduce it in order to demonstrate their understanding. If much of the skill knowledge taught is explicit, then as the pressure increases on the student to demonstrate this knowledge their skills performance, according to Masters (1992) and Hardy *et al.* (1996), will decrease. Problems will arise, for example, when a learner must simultaneously follow set rules for using apparatus and yet keep in mind the conceptual demands of the practical – in other words, juggle what they have to do with what they wish to achieve. Clearly, if the learner is busy trying to recollect the rules they have been taught for competent manipulation of the apparatus, they will be less able to focus on the purpose of the whole activity. This fits with the evidence from the PACKS project (Duggan and Gott 1996) mentioned previously which suggests that pupils lose sight of the meaning and significance of their investigations as a result of the current overemphasis on surface features of practical science.

Implicit knowledge is also context bound. It is learnt in a particular situation with a particular system or piece of apparatus. Readers may be able to empathise with this if they think about their experience of changing from 'command-driven' to 'icon-driven' software. Similarly, scientists have effectively to relearn how to do something when a new technique or piece of apparatus becomes available. They may well be able to describe how the apparatus should work but getting it to work requires a different form of knowing. Collins (1985) provides an example of an expert physicist trying to get a particular type of laser to work. Even though the physicist had clear explicit knowledge of lasers in general and the particular laser and its functioning, he could not get it to work with this knowledge but had to resort to trial and error.

Children at school may well be like Collins' example of the physicist who could say what he was supposed to be able to do and yet be unable to do it. This could be an explanation of the APU evidence that children could say what they were supposed to be doing (namely, demonstrate explicit knowledge), and yet be unable to do it (that is, not have the implicit knowledge).

Implications for teaching and learning practical work

The implications for teaching and learning science investigations and practical work are clear. If we want children to be successful with practical investigations, be competent and confident with practical work and have robust, skill-type knowledge, then it may be better for them to learn the knowledge implicitly. This is not as straightforward as one might think. Scientific apparatus conforms to certain rational conventions (for example, the direction to move a microscope barrel or twist a burette tap) and there are dangers (such as, using acids or certain electrical apparatus). As teachers we would not be responsible if we let children take risks with themselves or the apparatus, but there are ways in which learning can be made less explicit without compromising the need for consistency and safety.

Scientific apparatus requires rules for its safe, accurate and sensitive use. These rules are explicit or declarative knowledge. However, explicit knowledge through practice and habituation can become safe and accurate with no or hardly any conscious reflection or processing at all. An example is typing (Eysenck 1994). When people are trained to touch-type then at first they have to concentrate to put their fingers in the right place in relation to knowledge of the layout of the QWERTY keyboard. When the touch-typing is automatic then the knowledge is implicit, and a question about the layout of the keyboard may require the typist to use their fingers to help them imagine the location of a position of a letter on the keyboard. Another example is driving (Gagné, 1985). Driving a car with manual gears requires a set of rules and skills which have to be brought together into a smooth routine. At first neither skill (such as, shifting from gear to gear) nor rule (like depress clutch before moving gearstick) is implicit. However, we become proficient at bringing the rules and skills into one routine or procedure to the point where we talk, listen to the radio, concentrate on other things and even arrive at our destination not having recollected some of the journey.

With relation to practical work in school science, Millar (1996) talks of practical techniques, inquiry tactics and general cognitive processes. He goes on to argue that practical techniques (for instance, using a millimetre scale) and inquiry tactics (such as repeating readings) probably need to be taught. White (1996) in the same volume argues that if children are to learn to be proficient at skills then they have to practise them as well be told them. The implications are that children need to be explicitly taught *and then* they need to practise so that techniques and tactics become implicitly known.

Practice takes time, and therefore it may be that the demands on children are too much. They only ever have explicit knowledge of tactics and techniques, and the proficiency which comes with implicitly knowing the practical skills and procedures is, perhaps, unattainable. If this is so then the science curriculum may need redesigning by decreasing the range of techniques required, thus allowing more time with any particular technique, explicit teaching of Millar's inquiry tactics and frequent opportunities to use them with investigative practical work. In schools we teach children by expecting them to remember and act upon large and complex chunks of rules and steps. If we ask children to recall this knowledge infrequently then we probably expect too much of them in terms of retaining practical knowledge and skills. If children handle microscopes once or twice a school year in one or two lessons then we may have to accept that basically each encounter is going to be a 'fresh' encounter, and that it is unreasonable for us to expect them to retain the explicit knowledge of using a microscope from one occasion to the next. If children are to be able to demonstrate competence and confidence with apparatus then we ought to let them work on fewer tasks for longer, in order that they become habituated to using the apparatus and its procedures.

Training and coaching

Scientific techniques do require rules for their execution and for safety; for example, handling of corrosive liquids, reading a measuring cylinder. It may be irresponsible and undesirable to allow children to learn scientific skills and procedures implicitly by trial and error. If there are practical skills we do want children to have as automatic behaviours, then we may have to be much more careful in terms of the children's first experiences with them. The first experience with any new technique can be the most influential, particularly if an unconventional technique produces successful results! If this happens then it is very difficult to persuade the learner to unlearn the unconventional technique. If we want children to use apparatus in certain ways, then we may have to *train* them with as few rules or explanations as possible as to why they are doing it that way. For example, using a bunsen burner is a practical skill that we expect children to reproduce constantly and automatically. Therefore we suggest that the first experience should be a thorough training in how to use it – not what it is and why it works. That can come later when using it is automatic.

If the number of rules and steps can be reduced, then learning will have more of the characteristics of implicit knowledge than explicit knowledge. An effective method of bridging the gap between implicit learning and explicit knowledge is 'coaching by analogy'. The aim is to get the performer (often a novice) to perform the to-be-learnt skill using one general, analogical rule which in fact encompasses many of the technical rules necessary for successful execution of the skill. The learner follows the simple analogy and inadvertently employs these rules. For example, a top-spun forehand in tennis can be taught by employing the right-handed triangle as an analogy. The learner is asked to describe a right-handed triangle with their tennis racquet and to bring it squarely up the hypotenuse. Figure 12.1 illustrates this. Once they have accomplished this with reasonable accuracy and consistency (most people manage it immediately), the learner is told that every time they hit the ball to concentrate on nothing other than bringing the racquet squarely up the hypotenuse. The physical implication of making such a movement with the racquet is to impart top-spin to the tennis ball.

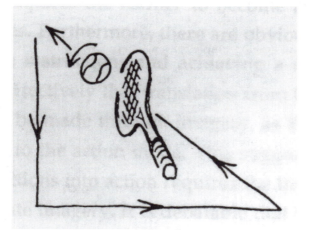

Figure 12.1 An illustration of the 'Analogical Forehand' method employed to teach a top-spun forehand in tennis implicitly

Disguised in the analogy are explicit rules often taught to beginners. For example, brush up from beneath the ball, complete the swing with the racquet above the ball, keep the wrist firm. The excerpt presented below gives an example of the traditional way in which the top-spun forehand is taught:

> take the racket head back parallel with the ground. In this shot, as all others, the wrist has to be locked rigid, absolutely firm, or the end product will be messy. Then move your left leg in front of you, at an angle of 45 degrees, to a comfortable position. The body should be at 90 degrees to the net and sideways on. Keeping the racket at the same level at which it was taken back, move it forwards and intend to meet the ball in front of the left toe. Don't tuck the elbow right in and don't have your arm straight out. The elbow should be slightly bent and once more remember to keep the wrist locked. The more rhythm the better but this will come in time. To finish the forehand, the racket should continue over your left shoulder in the direction in which you have hit the ball.
>
> (Cox 1975: 39)

Clearly, this method requires the learner to become aware of a far greater number of explicit rules. Furthermore, there are obvious drawbacks in terms of comprehending the instructions and achieving a desired result. In fact, Annett (1988) argues effectively that translation from the verbal mode to the action mode can only be made through imagery, as the verbal system does not have direct access to the action mode. This suggests that to translate verbal instructions successfully into action requires the instructions to stimulate formation of appropriate imagery. It is debatable that traditional methods of instruction such as those above succeed in this. If this finding is applied to school science education, then it means that science teachers need to develop simple rules which involve simple, effective images for children to memorise so that practice can concentrate on execution of the action and not recollection of the rule.

Summary and conclusion

Our argument has been based on acceptance of the explicit and implicit models of knowledge as explanatory of research findings for children's attainment and performance in practical work. These models of knowledge suggest that some of the things we expect of children − such as explaining how to do an investigation − are not an appropriate test of their ability to do it and are inappropriate because they test the wrong form of knowledge. Implicit knowledge is contextually bound, and if you want to know if a child can do an investigation then you may have to watch them do it − not ask them to write about it. Writing requires explicit knowledge which needs to be explicitly taught. If a learner is to understand the tactics and processes of an investigation then they will need to be taught these, but probably with reference to investigations they have done so that they can relate their implicit knowledge to the teacher's explicit knowledge.

If we want children to be proficient with skills so that they can concentrate on procedures, processes and purposes, then these models of knowledge suggest that children need to know at least the skills or techniques implicitly and perhaps the inquiry tactics. The implication for the science curriculum is that the range of skills demanded must be reduced so that learners can have the time necessary to become automatic with them. Children will need to be explicitly taught and then allowed to practise – this is a form of training. Science teachers and curriculum developers will need to develop simple, effective rules which use imagery to help the learning. If we want children to be proficient with tactics then children will need to do investigative work frequently.

We believe that our suggestions are radical in that we raise the spectre of training which is often interpreted pejoratively. 'Training' has become a dirty word in some circles. However, this craft aspect of doing science is important in science research (Ravetz 1996), and if school science is to reflect science in the making then we believe the curriculum should acknowledge that in the way we ask children to do practicals. It is also radical because we believe that frequent investigative work would challenge current practice both in the amount of investigations and the nature of investigations, which themselves may be becoming rituals of: one lesson, plan an investigation; next lesson, do the investigation; last lesson, evaluate the investigation. Science in the making is not done in time slots of 70 minutes and the apparatus is not all cleared away at the end of one lesson and put back out again at the start of the next lessons. It could be that the present structure and organisation of schools, the school day and the logistics of departmental resources will not allow children to become proficient at practical work or to become a scientist in the making.

Acknowledgement

Thanks to Robin Millar for his comments on a draft of this chapter.

Note

1 The word completion paradigm presents subjects with a fragment of a word (e.g., -ar-va – for aardvark) and asks them to complete it with the first word they think of. Priming occurs when such fragments are completed with words presented previously in a separate list – sometimes months earlier. The perceptual identification paradigm presents subjects with a transient exposure to a word, and priming is shown when the subject is more rapid at identifying words presented previously.

References

Allers, R. and Reber, A.S. (1980) 'Very long-term memory for trait knowledge', *Cognition* 8: 175–85.

Annett, J. (1988) 'Imagery and skill acquisition', in M. Denis, J. Engelkamp and J. Richardson (eds) *Cognitive Neuropsychological Approaches to Mental Imagery*, Dordrecht: Martinus Nijhoff.

Assessment of Performance Unit (APU) (1988a) *Science at Age 11: a Review of APU Findings 1980–1984*, London; HMSO.

—— (1988b) *Science at Age 15: a Review of APU Findings 1980–1984*, London: HMSO.

Berry, D.C. and Broadbent, D.E. (1984) 'On the relationship between task performance and associated verbalisable knowledge', *Quarterly Journal of Experimental Psychology* 36: 209–31.

Berry, D.C. and Dienes, Z. (1993) *Implicit Learning: Theoretical and Empirical Issues*, Hillsdale, NJ: Lawrence Erlbaum.

Broadbent, D.E. and Aston, B. (1978) 'Human control of a simulated economic system, *Ergonomics* 21: 1035–43.

Broadbent, D.E., Fitzgerald, P. and Broadbent, M.H.P. (1986) 'Implicit and explicit knowledge in the control of complex systems', *British Journal of Psychology* 77: 33–50.

Collins, H. (1985) *Changing Order: Replication and Induction in Scientific Practice*, London: Sage.

Corkin, S. (1968) 'Acquisition of motor skill after bilateral medial temporal lobe excision', *Neuropsychologia* 6: 225–65.

Cox, M. (1975) *Lawn Tennis: How to Become a Champion*, London: William Luscombe.

Duggan, S. and Gott, R. (1996) 'Scientific evidence: the new emphasis in the practical science curriculum in England and Wales', *The Journal of Curriculum Studies* 7(1):17–33.

Duggan, S., Gott, R., Lubben, F. and Millar, R. (1996) 'Evidence in science education', in M. Hughes (ed.) *Teaching and Learning in Changing Times*, Oxford: Blackwell.

Eysenck, M. (ed.) (1994) *The Blackwell Dictionary of Psychology*, Oxford: Blackwell.

Gagné, E. (1985) *The Cognitive Psychology of School Learning*, Cambridge, MA: Little, Brown.

Hardy, L., Mullen, R. and Jones, G. (1996) 'Knowledge and conscious control of motor actions under stress', *British Journal of Psychology* 87: 621–36.

Masters, R.S.W. (1992) 'Knowledge, knerves and know-how: The role of explicit versus implicit knowledge in the breakdown of a complex motor skill under pressure', *British Journal of Psychology* 83: 343–58.

Millar, R. (1996) 'A means to an end: the role of processes in school science education', in B. Woolnough (ed.) *Practical Science*, Buckingham: Open University Press, pp. 43–52.

Milner, B., Corkin, S. and Teuber, H.L. (1968) 'Further analysis of the hippocampal amnesic syndrome: 14 year follow-up study of HM', *Neuropsychologia* 6: 215–34.

Nissen, M.J. and Bullemer, P. (1987) 'Attentional requirements of learning: evidence from performance measures', *Cognitive Psychology* 19: 1–32.

Polanyi, M. (1958) *Personal Knowledge*, London: Routledge.

Ravetz, J. (1996) *Scientific Knowledge and its Social Problems*, London: Transaction.

Stanley, W.B., Matthews, R.C., Buss, R.R. and Kotler-Cope, S. (1989) 'Insight without awareness: on the interaction of verbalization, instruction and practice in a simulated process control task', *Quarterly Journal of Experimental Psychology* 41A: 553–78.

Starr, A. and Phillips, L. (1970) 'Verbal and motor memory in the amnesic syndrome', *Neuropsychologia,* 8: 75–88.

Tulving, E., Schacter, D.L. and Stark, H.A. (1982) 'Priming effects in word-fragment completion are independent of recognition memory', *Journal of Experimental Psychology: Learning, Memory and Cognition* 8: 336–42.

White, R. (1996) 'Episodes, and the purpose and conduct of practical work', in B. Woolnough (ed.) *Practical Science*, Buckingham: Open University Press, pp. 78–86.

13

EXPERIMENTATION AND CONCEPTUAL UNDERSTANDING IN SCHOOL SCIENCE

Can hypothesis testing play a role?

Christine Howe and Pamela Smith

Although experimentation has always played a central role within school science, ideas have changed as to how it should be taught. A favoured approach at present is to locate experimentation in a broader hypothesis testing context, such that key techniques are mastered while being applied in the exploration and furtherance of conceptual content. Recognising the popularity of the approach, the chapter investigates its viability in practice. Research is outlined which shows that experimentation can be successfully taught in the context of hypothesising. However, success here does not guarantee a positive (or indeed neutral) impact upon conceptual understanding. On the contrary, additional, far from obvious steps have to be taken to ensure that the teaching of experimentation serves rather than undermines the background concepts. The chapter ends by explaining in detail what the steps involve, and showing that, despite their non-obviousness, they do mesh with authentic science activity.

Introduction

Although practical work in science can mean many different things, experimentation has remained at its core for some considerable period of time. Thus, it is not surprising to find experimentation emphasised in recent curricular initiatives, notably the *National Curriculum for England and Wales* (Department for Education 1995) and the *Environmental Studies 5–14 Programme for Scotland* (Scottish Office Education Department 1993). However, within these initiatives, there has been a subtle shift in ideas about how experimentation should be taught. In particular, there has been a move to contextualise experimentation within the promotion of conceptual understanding. Thus, in the *National Curriculum*, it is stated that 'contexts derived from life processes and living things, materials and their properties and physical processes should be used to teach pupils about experimental and investigative methods' (1995: 3, 8, 15 and 26). In similar vein, the *5–14 Programme* advises that 'the development of knowledge and understanding . . . will come from the pupils' participation in a wide range of learning activities, including some in which the pupils will also develop skills and attitudes' (1993: 4), with experimentation explicitly included in the concept of skills.

In its own right, contextualisation within conceptual advancement is open to several interpretations, and there is in fact a degree of vagueness within both the *National Curriculum* and the *5–14 Programme* as to what is intended. However, one possible reading would lead to experimentation becoming part and parcel of a broader hypothesis testing approach, with pupils formulating conceptual knowledge into researchable ideas, designing experiments to test whether the ideas are correct (being supported in this process), and evaluating the ideas in the light of the evidence. Thus in the context of studying heating and cooling, pupils might focus on the propositions that *Metal things heat up more quickly than plastic* or that *Thick things cool down more slowly than thin;* they might be engaged in controlled investigations of the impact of material and/or thickness; and they might be asked to relate their results back to the initial propositions. Certainly, activities of this kind have been advocated in the literature, and they would, on the face of it, seem to have advantages. At the very least, they would bring the science learning process into line with professional science activity (Wellington 1988), and would bear therefore on another *National Curriculum* aim, that pupils should learn about the nature of science. Nevertheless, they would also create an exceedingly complex learning environment. Quite apart from the multiplicity of steps and sub-steps involved in formulation, design and evaluation, there is the fact that two aims, experimental skill and conceptual understanding, would be addressed simultaneously. As a result, there appears to be a distinct possibility of creating confusion, and by virtue of this of achieving less than could be managed by keeping matters separate.

Hypothesis testing therefore has both appeal and potential danger, and recognising this the present chapter attempts a detailed analysis of what might be achieved in practice. The chapter starts by considering the teaching of experimentation within a hypothesis-testing context. The message is reasonably encouraging: the research indicates sustainable growth in experimental skills after teaching which is integrated with hypothesis-testing activities. The chapter then turns to the implications for conceptual understanding, considering the extent to which conditions conducive to growth can be achieved when the teaching of experimentation is in progress. It cautions against placing too much emphasis on what superficially might appear promising signs, using background theory and evidence to highlight deeper tensions. Nevertheless, while the tensions must be recognised, the problems which they cause may not be insuperable and the chapter ends by proposing a way forward. Thus, the overall answer to the question posed in the chapter's title will be that hypothesis testing can serve both experimentation and conceptual understanding, but only if certain additional conditions are also fulfilled.

Guided participation, contingent control and experimental skill

Experimentation is not simply a skill; it is also a series of skilled activities. It involves planning which variables to explore, manipulating apparatus in accordance with plans, registering results as they occur and comparing results across test cycles. When integrated with hypothesis testing, there is also a need to formulate predictions in accordance with hypotheses and to draw conclusions in the light of results. Seeing experimentation in terms of skilled activity, it seems necessary to refer to work in the neo-Vygotskian tradition when considering how it might best be supported. After all, this work not only treats skilled activity as a core construct but has also generated a substantial body of evidence. Particularly significant perhaps is research concerned with 'guided participation', which, as Rogoff (1990) states, shows progress to depend upon 'building bridges from children's present understanding and skills to reach new understanding and skills, and arranging and structuring children's participation in activities with dynamic shifts over development in children's responsibilities' (p. 8). The implication for experimentation is that pupils should be set investigatory tasks, and receive feedback and guidance as they attempt these tasks for themselves. As performance improves (with feedback becoming increasingly positive), guidance should be reduced until acceptable performance occurs unaided.

Nevertheless, while the notion of guided participation may provide a framework, there are numerous possibilities within it for further elaboration. Looking to the literature for tighter specification, Wood's (1989) theory of 'contingent control' appears to offer some promise. This theory stipulates the levels of directiveness to follow when offering guidance and details principles for moving from level to level. As regards the levels, an example of relatively low-level guidance would be indicating that a problem has occurred. An example of relatively high-level guidance would be explaining the precise nature of the problem and suggesting an alternative approach. Wood proposed that guidance should progress upwards one level at a time until success is achieved, and then downwards one level at a time so that unaided success is approximated gradually. The evidence used to support the theory comes mainly from research where mothers guided their pre-school children through problem-solving tasks. However, Wood saw no reason in principle why the approach should not be extended to older age groups and classroom contexts.

Accepting then that contingent control may be the best strategy for supporting experimentation in science, the question is what happens when experimentation and therefore contingent control is embedded within hypothesis testing. This question prompted a programme of research conducted at Strathclyde University by the first author and Andy Tolmie. The research involved developing and evaluating computer software which was capable of directing pupils through cycles of hypothesis testing and of providing contingent control for experimental activity. The use of computers rather than, say, classroom teachers was not seen as essential. Nevertheless, it was deemed to have an important practical advantage. As noted by Crook (1994), contingent control implies individually tailored feedback more or less immediately after actions occur, and this might be difficult for classroom teachers to organise. Although it is unrealistic to imagine a situation where every pupil has their own computer and therefore truly individual feedback (Jackson *et al.* 1986; McAteer and Demissie 1991), it should be possible to arrange matters so that machines are accessed by (at worst) small groups. Thus, by utilising computers, the Strathclyde research was following a strategy for providing a good approximation to contingent control which could readily be extended to genuine classroom contexts.

The software that was produced required the generation of ideas regarding causal variables, and the design of experiments to test the ideas out. Decisions regarding design features and eventual conclusions had to be registered onscreen, and inappropriate decisions triggered prompts which varied in directiveness. Two levels of directiveness were incorporated, the first indicating a problem (and its broad character) and requesting reconsideration, and the second giving details of what the problem involved. The software was developed in two forms, one relating to *water pressure* and the other to *shadows*. In both forms, it was constructed to be used alongside physical equipment. For pressure, the equipment consisted of plastic bottles with plugged holes in their sides, a holder in which the bottles could stand, and a rectangular tray positioned with the holder against one of its short sides. The tray was divided into sections for measuring the distance travelled by a jet of water from a bottle placed in the holder when one of its plugs was removed. The equipment could be set up to investigate the impact on distance travelled of: (1) hole height; (2) bottle width; (3) bottle shape; (4) water frothiness (that is, whether or not air was being pumped through it); and (5) water colour. For shadows, the equipment consisted of a screen with a track at right angles to it, along which a wooden triangle and a lamp could be moved to different positions. The triangle could be selected from a set which varied in size and colour. There was a switch associated

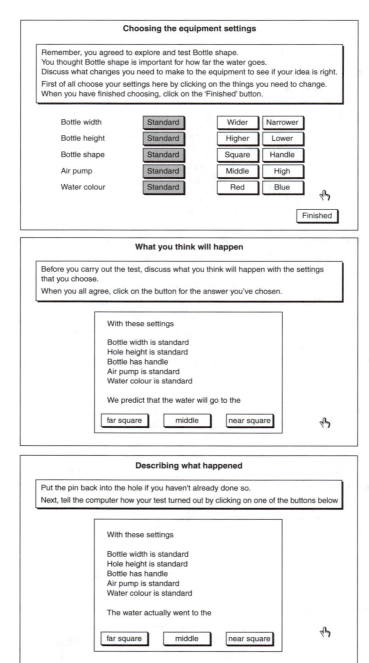

Choosing the equipment settings

Remember, you agreed to explore and test Bottle shape.
You thought Bottle shape is important for how far the water goes.
Discuss what changes you need to make to the equipment to see if your idea is right.

First of all choose your settings here by clicking on the things you need to change.
When you have finished choosing, click on the 'Finished' button.

Bottle width	Standard	Wider	Narrower
Bottle height	Standard	Higher	Lower
Bottle shape	Standard	Square	Handle
Air pump	Standard	Middle	High
Water colour	Standard	Red	Blue

Finished

What you think will happen

Before you carry out the test, discuss what you think will happen with the settings that you choose.

When you all agree, click on the button for the answer you've chosen.

With these settings

Bottle width is standard
Hole height is standard
Bottle has handle
Air pump is standard
Water colour is standard

We predict that the water will go to the

far square   middle   near square

Describing what happened

Put the pin back into the hole if you haven't already done so.
Next, tell the computer how your test turned out by clicking on one of the buttons below

With these settings

Bottle width is standard
Hole height is standard
Bottle has handle
Air pump is standard
Water colour is standard

The water actually went to the

far square   middle   near square

continued . . .

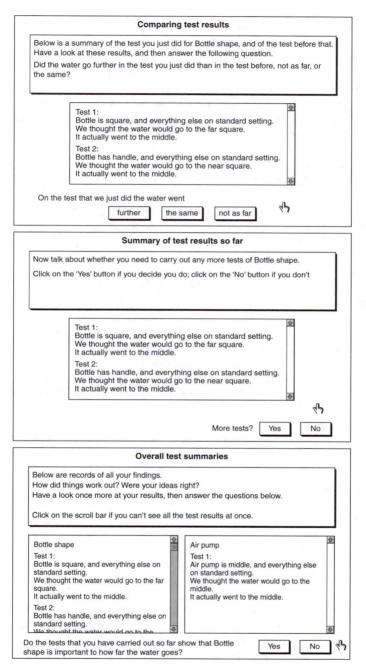

Comparing test results

Below is a summary of the test you just did for Bottle shape, and of the test before that. Have a look at these results, and then answer the following question.

Did the water go further in the test you just did than in the test before, not as far, or the same?

Test 1:
Bottle is square, and everything else on standard setting.
We thought the water would go to the far square.
It actually went to the middle.

Test 2:
Bottle has handle, and everything else on standard setting.
We thought the water would go to the near square.
It actually went to the middle.

On the test that we just did the water went

| further | the same | not as far |

Summary of test results so far

Now talk about whether you need to carry out any more tests of Bottle shape.

Click on the 'Yes' button if you decide you do; click on the 'No' button if you don't

Test 1:
Bottle is square, and everything else on standard setting.
We thought the water would go to the far square.
It actually went to the middle.

Test 2:
Bottle has handle, and everything else on standard setting.
We thought the water would go to the near square.
It actually went to the middle.

More tests? | Yes | No |

Overall test summaries

Below are records of all your findings.
How did things work out? Were your ideas right?
Have a look once more at your results, then answer the questions below.

Click on the scroll bar if you can't see all the test results at once.

Bottle shape

Test 1:
Bottle is square, and everything else on standard setting.
We thought the water would go to the far square.
It actually went to the middle.

Test 2:
Bottle has handle, and everything else on standard setting.
We thought the water would go to the

Air pump

Test 1:
Air pump is middle, and everything else on standard setting.
We thought the water would go to the middle.
It actually went to the middle.

Do the tests that you have carried out so far show that Bottle shape is important to how far the water goes? | Yes | No |

Fig. 13.1 Key steps in the contingent control software

225

with the lamp which allowed its brightness to be varied. The equipment allowed investigation of whether the size of shadow projected onto the screen would be affected by: (1) triangle size; (2) triangle position; (3) triangle colour; (4) lamp position; and (5) lamp brightness.

The software was designed so that, after seeing the equipment in operation, pupils were directed to decide whether or not each variable exerted an influence upon outcome, and plan which variables they needed to change to test their ideas about one of the variables (other variables to be taken up later). Then, as Figure 13.1 shows, they were asked to: (1) decide on the actual manipulation of the equipment; (2) predict the outcome of that manipulation; (3) observe and record the actual outcome; (4) compare the outcome with any previous tests; (5) decide whether further manipulations were needed; and (6) when testing was deemed complete draw a final conclusion. At each stage, activity was monitored by requesting decisions to be recorded onscreen, thereby allowing information to be first saved as an index of performance and second deployed in the guidance of prompting. Prompting occurred after departures from what might be regarded as the hypothesis-testing ideal; for example, invalid testing when manipulating (failure to manipulate only the variable under investigation whilst holding all others constant) or inappropriate conclusions (erroneous statements about the relevance or otherwise of the variable under investigation). As noted already, two levels of prompt were used, and these are illustrated in Figure 13.2. The second-level was introduced only if the first level did not eliminate the errors. If second-level prompting had no impact, the errors were accepted and the activity proceeded to the next stage. Correct decisions were met with positive feedback.

The impact of the software has been evaluated in two studies (Tolmie and Howe 1994; Howe and Tolmie 1998), one study utilising the pressure version and the other the shadows. Both studies involved around 100 pupils aged 9 to 14, and both began with individual 'pre-test' interviews to ascertain beliefs about which variables were relevant to outcome and which were not, and how relevance or irrelevance could be determined empirically. Questions were asked (with reference to the equipment) which bore upon planning, manipulation, prediction, observation, comparison and conclusion as defined above, with opportunities being provided for interim and overall conclusions. Subsequent to the pre-tests, the pupils were assigned to small groups (three to five pupils per group for pressure and four per group for shadows) to work with the software. The group size was felt to reflect the probable arrangement in routine classrooms. Roughly half of the pupils worked with 'supported' software as described above, and for purposes of comparison the other half worked with an alternative 'unsupported' version which lacked the prompts. Three to five weeks after the software sessions, all group participants were post-tested, along the lines of the pre-test.

Comparisons were made between the pupils who worked with the

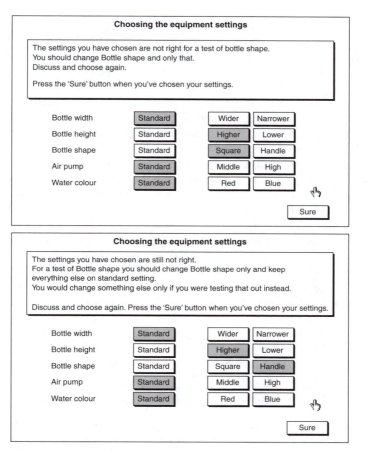

Fig. 13.2 First- and second-level prompts

supported as opposed to unsupported software over both computer-based activity and pre- to post-test change. Computer-based activity was evaluated with reference to eight indices recovered from the software records: (1) the time spent on task in minutes; (2) the number of moves made in terms of onscreen responses; (3) the time spent deciding the manipulations to be carried out for the various tests; (4) the number of moves made whilst deciding manipulations; (5) the total number of tests carried out; (6) the number of valid tests conducted; (7) the number of accurate reports of outcome; and (8) the number of appropriate overall conclusions drawn. There were no differences between the supported and the unsupported groups on five of the indices with both forms of software. However with the pressure software, the supported groups made significantly more moves than the unsupported and conducted significantly more valid tests. They also drew more appropriate conclusions than the unsupported groups, although here the difference only approached statistical significance. With the shadows software, the supported groups conducted significantly more valid tests than the unsupported and drew significantly more appropriate conclusions. This time however there were no differences over the number of moves. Because the differences in valid testing occurred despite no differences in the overall number of tests, they must have reflected a genuinely improved performance in the supported groups, and not a heightened level of general activity.

Pre- to post-test change was assessed from scores assigned to the pupils' responses to the interview questions. Relating pre- to post-test change to computer-based activity, it transpired that for the pupils who worked with the supported software there were strong positive correlations between change scores and the number of valid tests. This was the case for both the pressure and the shadows software, and it suggests an enduring impact of the supported software. Given that the supported pupils conducted more computer-guided valid tests than the unsupported pupils, it has to be treated as a promising result. Nevertheless, the picture is clouded somewhat by the fact that the unsupported pupils also progressed, albeit not in direct response to the software (since for these pupils pre- to post-test change was unrelated to computer-based activity) nor, as far as could be judged, to the accompanying interaction and dialogue.

Pupil collaboration and conceptual growth

Taken as a whole, the results are encouraging rather than discouraging for contingent control in the teaching of experimentation, and hence also for the Vygotskian theorising which underpins this. But what are the implications of the contingent control approach for conceptual understanding? From the Vygotskian perspective, the data presented above also have a number of promising features when it comes to conceptual growth. As noted already, the provision of contingent control boosted both the number of valid tests during the computer-based activity and the number of appropriate conclusions. While valid testing lies fairly and squarely within the experimental domain, the drawing of appropriate conclusions has a strong conceptual dimension in addition. Thus, in drawing appropriate conclusions while working with the computer, the pupils were performing at a higher conceptual level than they were at pre-test. Moreover, they were managing this jointly, for the computer-based activity was collaborative. This is what is important from the Vygotskian angle, for one of the main Vygotskian mechanisms for effecting growth is the internalisation by individuals of jointly achieved progress (see, for example, Vygotsky 1978). The implication is, then, that the provision of contingent control in the context of hypothesis testing created conditions where conceptual as well as experimental understanding should have been boosted.

The question of whether boosting is achievable in practice was considered in five further studies conducted at Strathclyde University, for these studies (reported in Howe *et al.* 1990; Howe *et al.* 1995; Howe *et al.* 1992; Tolmie *et al.* 1993) were all direct attempts to explore the relation between conceptual growth and collaborative activity. The studies started with individual pre-tests to over 100 8- to 12-year-old pupils to ascertain initial conceptions regarding the topics to be covered (object flotation, motion down an incline, or heat transfer). Subsequently, the pupils were assigned to groups of four to work on tasks which were presented to them via workbooks. These tasks invited the pupils: (1) to formulate individual predictions about relevant events – for example, whether provided objects would float or sink in a tank of water; (2) to share individual predictions and negotiate a joint position; (3) to test the joint prediction empirically; and (4) to agree an interpretation of what transpired. Group dialogue was videotaped, and videotapes were coded for, amongst other things, the adequacy of conclusions drawn when interpreting outcomes and the extent to which these conclusions were in fact 'agreed'. All five studies involved individual post-tests to group participants about four weeks after the group task, with one study also including immediate post-tests and another post-tests after eleven weeks as well as four. Progress was ascertained from pre- to post-test change.

By and large, the group tasks proved beneficial, with statistically significant progress from pre-test to post-test. The greatest growth was observed in pupils whose initial conceptions contrasted with those of their fellow group members. Pupils from groups where initial conceptions were similar showed more limited change. Nevertheless, growth was general, suggesting a positive impact of collaborative activity on pupil conceptualisation. Yet, despite this, there was no support in the results for Vygotskian mechanisms. Far from being dependent upon jointly achieved progress, pre- to post-test change was unrelated to conclusions drawn during the group sessions (these often being worse than pre-test ideas) or to the extent to which these conclusions were joint as opposed to individually achieved. Indeed, further analysis suggested that when progress occurred, it resulted from the post-group (and therefore private) resolution of debates which occurred within the groups. For one thing, pre- to post-test change was correlated with the exchange of ideas; for another, there was strong evidence for delayed effects. In the study (Howe *et al.* 1992) which used immediate and four-week post-tests, there was no gain over pre-test performance at immediate post-test; it was only at four weeks that growth was observed. In the study (Tolmie *et al.* 1993) which used four- and eleven-week post-tests, there was progress from pre-test to four-week post-test but much greater progress from four-week post-test to eleven-week.

Perhaps, though, encouragement can be drawn from the fact that collaboration proved productive, even if Vygotskian mechanisms were not involved. After all, in the studies which were described in the previous section, the contingent control software was used by *groups*. It is possible that the dialogue held around the software involved the debate which the subsequent studies have shown to be helpful. If this is the case, it is equally possible that contingent control can support experimentation, while its *deployment* in collaborative contexts can provide the missing ingredient when it comes to conceptual growth. The possibility is certainly worth considering, but there are several reasons for caution. In the first place, there was evidence in the earlier studies that the prompting from the supported software had an intrusive effect upon the group interaction. It broke the dialogue up, producing puzzled requests for alternative ideas and increased numbers of inappropriate suggestions. It did not, in short, stimulate debate. In addition, though, there is the point made by Piaget (for example, Piaget 1932) that the interpolation of an expert 'voice' into group interaction may be incompatible with genuine debate. When experts speak, they are not heard as expressing alternative views to be considered along with one's own; they are heard as expressing received views which should replace all others. Since the prompts and all that surround them constitute an expert voice, contingent control might be expected from the Piagetian perspective to oppose conceptual growth. Thus, in general, tension might be anticipated between contingent control and conceptually supportive interaction, and this unfortunately seems to have been the case.

Debate, consensus and contingent control

At this point, the situation as regards hypothesis testing, experimental skill and conceptual growth appears rather bleak. However, it should be remembered that within the Strathclyde research into contingent control, the pupil interaction took place *around* the experimental activity. There was as a result no opportunity to discuss ideas except in the context of planning and testing. It may be preferable to separate the opportunities for debate from the provision of prompting, while ensuring that both remain part of the same coordinated activity. The most promising approach would appear to be a learning situation where pupils first discuss their beliefs, and are then guided in methods by which they establish if these beliefs are correct. In such a situation, the pupils would (via their beliefs) be setting the agenda, and the expert voice might therefore come across as supportive rather than intrusive. Thus, there is a chance that the prompting would mesh with the debate by appearing to serve it rather than act in opposition.

Nevertheless, even if the approach sounds promising, a number of uncertainties remain. The first relates to how pupils should debate their beliefs. In the five studies that were outlined in the previous section, the main discussion of beliefs took place when interpreting outcomes, within a task which had an (individual and joint) predict–test–interpret format. However, if this format has to precede the teaching of experimentation, the implication is a sequence involving predictions, observations, interpretations, hypotheses drawn from interpretations, supported experimentation and further interpretations. From certain angles, this might appear unnecessarily cumbersome, so might it not be possible to short-circuit somehow? Perhaps pupils could be asked to discuss beliefs directly, via (for example) the appraisal of statements regarding 'the things which do or do not matter' within the topic area. Having done this, they could proceed without further ado to the guided testing of their ideas; that is, hypotheses, supported experimentation and interpretation. In addition, though, there is the fact, noted already, that despite being asked to agree interpretations, consensus is not always achieved within groups of pupils. However, without consensus, it might be difficult to create situations where all pupils feel that their beliefs are being tested. Perhaps it would be better to force a consensus, by (for example) getting pupils to write down agreed positions. The point is that even if consensus is not necessary for conceptual gain alone, it may be helpful when conceptual understanding is being coordinated over time with experimentation.

Such considerations guided the design of two recent and previously unpublished studies, one conducted by both authors in collaboration with Andy Tolmie and the other by the first author in collaboration with Andy Tolmie and Val Duchak. The key intervention in both studies involved pupil debate plus written consensus over beliefs followed by experimentation guided by contingent control. However, to assess the intervention's effectiveness, three comparison interventions were also used: (1) debate without consensus followed by contingent control; (2) debate plus consensus followed by nonguided experimentation; and (3) experimentation guided by contingent control without debate. The first study took *flotation* as its topic, and was designed to investigate the simpler form of debate, consensus plus contingent control – that is, an immediate launch into the appraisal of statements rather than a more gradual approximation through predicting, testing and interpreting. Seventy two pupils working in groups of three were given nine statements to consider, for instance: *There's a special paint you can buy which helps things float in water*, *Having an engine is a great help to floating in water*, and *It's better to be big than small when it comes to floating in water*. The pupils were instructed to discuss the statements, and *agree* ratings for each one in turn (terrible, okay, good, brilliant) depending on how accurate they were thought to be. Debate without consensus involved making ratings individually and then deciding together whether each pupil's ratings in turn were better or worse than a hypothetical further pupil's. No comparisons were made between the pupils themselves. No debate involved individual ratings alone.

Thus, all forms of intervention in the first study centred on ratings, and ratings were the focus of the investigative sessions – in which the groups participated a few days later. In these, the pupils who were receiving contingent control went through a group-based exercise equivalent to the supported software described earlier in the chapter. The exercise was directed at establishing the ratings' accuracy. The pupils who were not receiving contingent control went through a group-based exercise with a similar theme but equivalent this time to the unsupported software. The only difference from the earlier work was that on this occasion the exercise was led by a researcher rather than a computer, and this researcher provided the prompts. Pre- and post-tests were administered to assess the effectiveness of debate, consensus plus contingent control against the three comparisons. The results were disappointing: debate, consensus and contingent control was never the most effective intervention, and was sometimes significantly less effective than one or more of the comparisons. Inspection of videotapes recorded while the groups were interacting made it clear what had gone wrong. Discussion of statements was altogether too abstract for the pupils to cope with. Thus, their 'debates' were extremely brief, and served only to demotivate. The upshot was that when the pupils came to the experimentation they were already disengaged. This contrasted markedly with the five studies described in the previous section where the discussions had been prolonged and animated. Since these studies began as noted already with predict-test-interpret cycles rather than direct discussion of statements, the pointers were clear. Despite its seemingly cumbersome nature, there was a suggestion that predict–test–interpret–hypothesise–test-under-guidance–interpret might be the way to proceed.

Accordingly, the predict–test–interpret–hypothesise–test-under-guidance–interpret format was explored in the second of the new studies, this study taking *shadows* as its topic area. Using the equipment described earlier, pupils were asked to make individual predictions of the consequences for shadow size of various set-ups; for instance, a small, grey triangle with the lamp at maximum brightness but both the triangle and the lamp positioned at the middle distance from the screen. Then, working in groups of three, they were asked to share their predictions and come to an agreement. Having done this, the pupils were instructed to switch on the lamp, observe the actual shadow size, and discuss why things turned out the way that they did. For the *debate without consensus* intervention this was all that the pupils did, but for the *debate with consensus* they were asked to agree and write down the things that are important for shadow size and the things which do not matter. They were invited to imagine that they were preparing a list to help other pupils. Whatever the pupils had written down became the focus for the experimentation a few days later, with guidance being provided or not depending on the type of intervention. Because nothing was written down for debate without consensus, the pupils were fed back ideas which they had mentioned during their debate. In this study, half of the 200 or so pupils who participated were led through both the debate stage and the experimentation by a researcher; the other half were led by a computer. Pre- and post-tests were again administered to ascertain learning, and this time the results were extremely promising: the combination of debate, consensus and contingent control outstripped everything else. Importantly, it did not matter whether the intervention was person- or computer-led: the superiority of debate, consensus and contingent control remained unsurpassed.

Conclusions and practical applications

The recent research seems then to have unearthed a workable method. However, it is not the most obvious method nor the most straightforward. It is important therefore that teachers wishing to emulate the method are absolutely clear about what is involved. Accordingly, Table 13.1 lays out the key steps in the sequence, in generic form, for application to any topic and using examples from Strathclyde research for illustration. The implication of the Strathclyde research is that, although the sequence should be followed by pupils working in groups, it matters little whether the groups are guided by a teacher or by a computer. Selection here can be informed by personal inclination and/or practical constraints. In other words, computer-presentation can proceed with minimal intervention from teachers but it might not be to everyone's taste. Teacher-presentation will almost certainly prove demanding. It will probably involve organising matters so that one group can receive more or less individual attention, particularly when experiments are being designed and conducted. This may mean taking a subset of the class at any given time, while the remainder work on different activities (scientific or otherwise) which require less supervision.

If teachers introduce exercises which follow Table 13.1, they will be taking their pupils through a hypothesis-testing activity which stands a good chance of promoting both experimental skill and conceptual growth. As such, they should be respecting current educational policy, for as noted already the co-ordination of experimentation and conceptual growth is advocated by both the *National Curriculum* and the Scottish *5–14 Programme*. More than this though, teachers will be giving their pupils experience of what it means to be a scientist, and this too would be consistent with current policy. Indeed, in deploying exercises which began with debate, teachers would actually be creating a richer sense of scientific practice than the policy documents appear to envisage. Science as practised professionally is an inherently social activity, and debate would add this dimension. Beyond this, though, science is an activity in which research teams have lengthy discussions regarding the plausibility of ideas *before* their investigatory work begins, and hence the separation of debate from investigation would also ring

Table 13.1 Key steps in the promotion of debate, consensus and contingent control

---

Step 1 Ask pupils to make individual predictions of outcome, by writing these predictions down (e.g., Shown a small grey triangle at the middle distance with a bright lamp also at the middle distance, ask pupils to predict the shadow size from three options by ticking on cards).

Step 2 Place pupils in groups and ask them to share predictions and come to a single agreed prediction.

Step 3 Ask pupils to ascertain whether their agreed prediction is correct by setting up the equipment and observing the outcome (e.g., tell them to put a small grey triangle in the holder, place the holder at the middle distance, turn the dial on the lamp to bright, place the lamp at the middle distance and switch the lamp on).

Step 4 Ask pupils to discuss in their groups why things turned out the way they did, and then to imagine that they were helping someone else in their class learn about the topic. Ask them to write down what is important for the outcome and what doesn't matter.

Step 5 (This can take place after an interval of several days.) Take pupils in the same groups as for Steps 2 to 4. Show them the ideas that they wrote down under Step 4, and ask them to choose one to test out.

Step 6 Ask pupils to discuss in their groups how the equipment should be set up to test the idea. Prompt erroneous decisions following contingent control principles (e.g., Offer pupils three choices for each of triangle size, lamp brightness, lamp position, triangle position and triangle colour. Prompt failure to manipulate the key variable and/or failure to control the other variables.)

Step 7 Once decisions have been made, encourage pupils to set up the equipment, predict what will happen and observe the outcome.

Step 8 Ask pupils to decide in their groups whether they need to conduct more tests to determine if their idea is correct (and cycle back to Step 6 if more tests are deemed to be necessary].

Step 9 Once the pupils decide that all necessary tests have been conducted, ask them to draw a conclusion (e.g., show pupils a card containing the statement 'Lamp brightness is important/doesn't matter for shadow size' if lamp brightness was the tested variable. Ask them to circle a phrase to indicate the conclusion they wish to draw).

Further ideas from the list generated at Step 4 can be tested if desired.

---

true. In fact, when one thinks about it, pre-investigatory discussion amongst scientists often refers to evidence of a casual and anecdotal kind, and this of course is precisely what the sequence in Table 13.1 implies. Once this is recognised, it may then be possible to take a different perspective on what earlier was acknowledged to seem cumbersome and non-obvious: despite (and moreover because of) its numerous steps, our suggested approach turns out to resonate closely with authentic science activity.

Acknowledgements

The research described in this chapter was supported by ESRC grants C00232426, R000233481 and R000236714 and Leverhulme Trust grant S903274. Grateful acknowledgement is made of the assistance provided by: (1) the ESRC and the Leverhulme Trust; (2) the staff and pupils of the schools involved in the research; and (3) Val Duchak, Karen Greer, Mhairi Mackenzie, Catherine Rattray, Cathy Rodgers, Stuart Ross, Nick Sofroniou, Claire Stevens and Andy Tolmie. For a *full report* of research and/or details of the software, please contact the Secretary, Centre for Research into Interactive Learning, Department of Psychology, University of Strathclyde, 40 George Street, Glasgow G1 1QE.

References

Crook, C. (1994) *Computers and the Collaborative Experience of Learning,* London: Routledge.

Department for Education (1995) *Science in the National Curriculum*, London: HMSO.

Howe, C.J., Rodgers, C. and Tolmie, A. (1990) 'Physics in the primary school: peer interaction and the understanding of floating and sinking', *European Journal of Psychology of Education* 4: 459–75.

Howe, C.J. and Tolmie, A. (1998) 'Computer support for learning in collaborative contexts: prompted hypothesis testing in physics', *Computers and Education* 30: 223–35.

Howe, C.J., Tolmie, A., Greer, K. and Mackenzie, M. (1995) 'Peer collaboration and conceptual growth in physics: task influences on children's understanding of heating and cooling', *Cognition and Instruction* 13: 483–503.

Howe, C.J., Tolmie, A. and Rodgers, C. (1992) 'The acquisition of conceptual knowledge in science by primary school children: group interaction and the understanding of motion down an incline', *British Journal of Developmental Psychology* 10: 113–30.

Jackson, A., Fletcher, B.C. and Messer, D.J. (1986) 'A survey of microcomputer use and provision in primary schools', *Journal of Computer Assisted Learning* 2: 45–55.

McAteer, E. and Demissie, A. (1991) 'Writing competence across the curriculum', report to Scottish Office Education Department.

Piaget, J. (1932) *The Moral Judgment of the Child*, London: Routledge.

Rogoff, B (1990) *Apprenticeship in Thinking: Cognitive Development in Social Context*, Oxford: Oxford University Press.

Scottish Office Education Department (1993) *Environmental Studies 5–14*, London: HMSO.

Tolmie, A.K. and Howe, C.J. (1994) 'Computer-directed group activity and the development of children's hypothesis testing skills', in H.C. Foot, C.J. Howe, A. Anderson, A.K.Tolmie and D. Warden (eds) *Group and Interactive Learning*, Southampton: Computational Mechanics Publications.

Tolmie, A., Howe, C.J., Mackenzie, M. and Greer, K. (1993) 'Task design as an influence on dialogue and learning: primary school group work with object flotation', *Social Development* 2: 183–201.

Vygotsky, L.S. (1978) *Mind in Society: the Development of Higher Psychological Processes*, Cambridge, MA: Harvard University Press.

Wellington, J.J. (1988) 'The place of process in physics education', *Physics Education* 23: 150–5.

Wood, D. (1989) 'Social interaction as tutoring', in M.H. Bornstein and J.S. Bruner (eds) *Interaction in Human Development*, Hillsdale, NJ: Lawrence Erlbaum.

14

IT IN PRACTICAL WORK

Assessing and increasing the value-added

Roy Barton

Introduction

Practical work has been a part of science education for over 100 years and throughout this time its role and function has been the subject of debate and disagreement amongst science educators (see chapter by Jenkins). Whatever views are expressed about the purpose of practical work, its scope in school has always been limited by logistical factors such as equipment and time – for example, by the amount of data which can be collected during a science lesson, often lasting between 50 and 70 minutes, and by the measuring instruments available in the school laboratory. These logistical factors have also influenced the roles adopted by the teacher. The need for teachers to support pupils as they collect and process data tends to dominate lesson time relative to other activities such as helping pupils to discuss and analyse their data. This chapter aims to explore the impact which computer-assisted practical work can have in changing these logistical constraints and the roles adopted by the teacher in a school laboratory. We must guard against being so familiar with existing constraints that we are slow to appreciate new and perhaps radical opportunities.

Following the theme of equipment a little further, those who have been involved in science education for long enough will have witnessed a slow but steady development of equipment, with the most rapid changes taking place via the Nuffield Projects in the late 1960s. For example, I can remember measurements of velocity and acceleration using Fletcher's Trolley (Abbott 1963); later came devices such as ticker-timers; and currently light gates and motion sensors connected to computers are available. When considering these, and other equivalent changes, are we seeing a smooth and continuous set of developments? I will argue that we are not, and that the move to computer-assisted practical work represents a discontinuity in this line of development which has the potential to change radically not only the starting points for school-based science practical work but also to change its nature fundamentally.

The scope of practical work in schools is so wide that, for the purposes of this chapter, it will be necessary to limit the range of the discussion. Broadly, practical activities can be grouped into illustrative and investigative activities (see chapter by Woolnough). Illustrative practical work is used to demonstrate a facet of science, and pupils are usually guided by a series of step-by-step instructions, whereas investigative practical work stems from pupils' statements and predictions in response to what they have seen, experienced, or discussed with the teacher. Whilst there is much current interest in the use of investigations and it seems likely that computers will be able to offer considerable advantages for pupils' investigative work, I will concentrate on illustrative practical work. I will do so since many of the criticisms made of practical work focus on difficulties related to teaching 'theory' through practical work.

Difficulties with conventional practical work

Before exploring a possible role for computer-assisted practical work and its potential for 'value added', it is useful to identify some of the problems which have been associated with the conventional approach. It has been my experience that those who are most vociferous in their criticism of computer-aided practical work often seem to imply that conventional practical methods are unproblematic and largely effective. In this context it will be useful to outline just three of the most commonly stated areas in which problems have been identified with traditional practical work.

Time overhead

A common criticism levelled at practical work is related to the amount of time which needs to be devoted to it.

> There is good reason for believing that much of the time presently spent in busywork laboratory exercises in the sciences could be more advantageously employed in formulating more precise definitions, differentiating explicitly between related concepts, generalising from hypothetical situations, and so forth.
> (Ausubel *et al.* 1968: 344)

Is this criticism justified? Many would see practical work as offering an essential opportunity to link first-hand experience in the form of practical work with concepts and ideas. Unfortunately, too often the time and effort expended in collecting and processing the data tend to squeeze out activities related to analysis and interpretation. How often does data collection and processing dominate the lesson time? How often do we resort to, 'draw the graph for homework'? In this case the link between the first hand experience and our attempts to relate them to the appropriate concepts may be very tenuous indeed.

Information clutter

Despite our hope that nature will 'reveal itself' to pupils via practical work, often a degree of 'inside knowledge' is required before it is possible to interpret what has been observed. Pupils have the problem of identifying what is relevant and what is peripheral. This has been described as 'information clutter' by Hodson (1993). It takes a number of forms: clutter associated with equipment; problems in identifying what is relevant to observe; and what Hodson calls, 'mathematical noise' – that is, computational and numerical difficulties which obscure the purpose of the activity. These distracting effects associated with practical work can obscure the purpose of the activity for many pupils.

Linking practical experience with abstract concepts

This lies at the heart of the purpose of much of the illustrative practical work conducted. For example, data collected during an experiment on a freezing liquid is used to draw a cooling curve. We do this as a means of helping pupils to understand and to form a link with the abstract idea of latent heat. Helping pupils to make this link is an important but difficult process, and one which forms a core activity for science teachers. Forming a bridge between personal experience and abstract ideas has been identified as problematic by a number of writers:

> Imaginative understanding was not a sequel to successful experiments. On the contrary, it was an essential prerequisite.
>
> (Solomon 1980: Preface)

> Students need to spend more time interacting with ideas and less time interacting with apparatus.
>
> (Gunstone 1991: 74)

> Practical work can be used to create the illusion of active and purposeful learning.
>
> (Osborne 1993: 118)

Are these intrinsic difficulties associated with practical work in general, or are they associated with some of the constraints imposed on conventional practical work in schools? Often our attempts to form this link to abstract ideas begins with the presentation of information in a graphical form. There is considerable research evidence (Archenhold *et al.* 1991; Austin *et al.* 1991; Bell *et al.* 1987; Swatton and Taylor 1994), together with teachers' everyday experiences, to suggest that producing and interpreting information in a graphical form is problematic for many pupils. These problems impose a barrier which make it difficult for pupils to move on to interpret and analyse the data they have collected.

Given these and other problems, an outsider might ask why we continue to place so much emphasis on hands-on practical activities. Despite these difficulties pupils do enjoy practical work and through it develop important skills related to scientific work. Perhaps more importantly, there is often no substitute for experiencing science at first hand to assist in developing an understanding of scientific phenomena. Practical work has the potential to challenge pupils' ideas and to draw them into learning about science. Can we retain the best features and tackle some of the problems identified?

Computer-assisted practical work

Computer-assisted practical work relates to the use of sensors, interfaces and software to monitor and display data collected during practical science activities. In Britain this is often referred to as 'data logging' and in America sometimes as 'MBL' (microcomputer-based laboratory). At first sight this would seem to be simply an alternative and rather expensive option, in comparison to the tried and tested conventional practical approach. However, I would like to show that when used appropriately, it has the potential not only to tackle some of the problems highlighted earlier but also to provide new teaching and learning opportunities.

Computers and time

Practical work takes up a considerable amount of lesson time. Since teachers often cite the difficulty of fulfilling the requirements of the science curriculum within the time limits available, this would suggest that any innovation which held out the promise of significant time saving could be very beneficial. The case is quite simple: if pupils are presented with data in a graphical form on the computer screen as the experiment is in progress, then this will save a significant amount of time which was previously spent in collecting and processing data for manually drawn graphs.

In addition to a common-sense analysis which would suggest this to be the case, there are also some objective data. For example, I have conducted a comparative study in which I compared pupils using computer-generated graphs to others who plotted the data manually. The context of the study was a secondary science practical activity involving electrical characteristic graphs. For a description of the methodology and the data collected, see

Barton (1997). The data revealed clear, if not unsurprising results. Pupils spent between two and four times longer producing graphs manually than those using the computer. The disparity between the computer and the manual approach was most significant for the younger pupils in the study (Year 8). Working with pairs of pupils extracted from normal science lessons, I found that pupils using the computers spent the largest proportion of their time involved in question and answer sessions with the teacher, whilst those using manual methods spent most of their time processing data. These activities included the time taken to introduce the system to those pupils using the computers. These findings are supported by others:

> Comparing the time profiles of IT and non-IT groups there was a trend whereby IT groups spent more time in discussing their data, and they tended to move on to discussion and extension questions sooner in lessons.
>
> (Rogers and Wild 1996: 133)

Focus effect

Earlier in the chapter the problem of 'information clutter' during practical work was highlighted. A feature of computer-aided practical work, reported by a number of studies, is the focusing effect the computer screen seems to have. Nakhleh and Krajcik (1993), comparing pupils' performance on acid-base titrations whilst using different levels of technology (from microcomputer to chemical indicators), suggested that a key factor was the way new technology can have the effect of narrowing the focus of the pupil's attention to the evolving graph on the screen. They also suggested that any unexpected behaviour of the graph on the computer screen seemed to stimulate pupils to search for explanations and to generate predictions. During my research, pupils from all year groups were seen to observe the screen closely as the data were collected. This effect was particularly noticeable when the data plotted on the screen were different from what the pupils had expected. For example, the transcript below was obtained when a pair of Year 9 pupils (a boy and a girl) investigated a device new to them (a diode) which was concealed from them in a 'black box'.

As the diode started to conduct:

Pupil 1: Oh my gosh.
Pupil 2: An upside down bulb.
Teacher: Do you want to fill in some of those points?
Pupil 1: I didn't think it was going to go like that.
Pupil 2: It can't be a resistor, they go straight.
Pupil 1: It can't be a bulb because it hasn't got that part in, [*Points to the screen.*]

241

Teacher: So how would you describe it? Think about what it's doing. You know a bit more about current now.

Pupil 2:   There's not much current going into it then suddenly it goes up – there's loads of current.

In this case there was not only a clear reaction to the unexpected data on the screen but also spontaneous links with previous knowledge. These data were collected with a teacher working with just one pair of pupils. However, Newton (1997) has spent time observing pupil–pupil interactions when pupils were using data-logging equipment in a whole class setting, and he strikes a note of caution in relation to the focus effect of the computer screen. He reports that, left to themselves, pupils tend to do little more than passively watch the graphs as they appear on the screen. This suggests that the tasks set and the role of the teacher are crucial if the potential benefits of the 'focus effect' are to be exploited.

Computers and the role of the teacher

Despite the different emphases placed on how science should be taught, all authors seem to agree on the importance of communication in learning science. It is widely acknowledged that the spoken and written word has a vital role in establishing scientific understanding. From a psychologist's perspective, whilst Piaget saw involvement with physical reality as the most important element in learning, Vygotsky stresses the importance of language in cognitive development: 'children solve practical tasks with the help of their speech, as well as their eyes and hands' (Vygotsky 1978: 26).

Edwards and Mercer feel that both action and discourse have a role to play and when discussing Vygotsky's work suggest that 'children undergo quite profound changes in their understanding by engaging in joint activity and conversation with other people' (1993: 19). Recently, ideas on the Constructivist view of learning have been combined with ideas on the role of discourse. Driver *et al.* (1994) argue that the construction of scientific knowledge involves both individual and social processes. This would suggest that discussion plays an important part in learning science. Indeed, whenever studies have looked closely at what pupils do whilst using computer-assisted practical work they all identify the importance of the particular tasks set by the teacher and the interactions between pupils and teachers (Nachmias and Linn 1987; Mercer 1994; Rogers and Wild 1996; Barton 1997). Using computer-assisted practical work will not automatically provide a learning benefit but it does facilitate changes in the style and structure of practical work which can. There are two areas to consider: what tasks should we set for pupils who are using computers; and what role should the teacher take during this activity?

Task setting

In situations where graphs are produced in real time – namely, at the same time the data are being collected – it is not sufficient to replace pupils' activity in recording data with their simply being asked to view the emerging graph passively on the screen. The novelty value is soon lost and so a set of activities is needed to capitalise on the opportunities presented. This could involve pupils being given prompt questions to encourage them to consider the data as they emerge. In my research (Barton 1996) I found that pupils were much better able to describe and analyse graphs when they were observing graphs overlaid on one axis; a common situation when using a computer to collect the data. For example, Figure 14.1 shows graphs for a bulb and a resistor together on the same axes, making it much easier for pupils to make comparisons between the behaviour of the two devices.

The idea of using sketch graphs as a means of encouraging pupils to make predictions of the data they are going to collect is not a new idea and could be considered to be an example of the Predict–Observe–Explain (POE) method suggested by Gunstone (1991). However, it becomes a powerful tool when used with computer-assisted practical work. Plotting in this case is achieved quickly and the facility to overlay a number of graphs can lead to further predictions being made, encouraging pupils to take ownership of the problem. For example, in my research, a pair of average ability Year 10 pupils followed up their prediction on the shape of the resistance against voltage graph with an investigation comparing the resistance of a bulb when increasing and decreasing the voltage across it at different rates. Plotting graphs using derived quantities such as resistance is simply not an option when using manual methods.

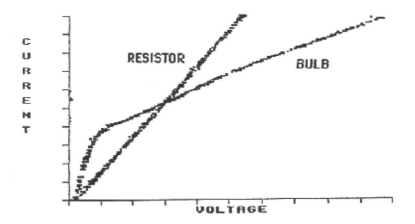

Figure 14.1 Graph of current against voltage for a bulb and a resistor

Teacher interaction and the 'vocabulary of graphing'

It is becoming apparent that if the potential benefits of computer-assisted practical work are to be realised in practice, then this will involve a pedagogical shift by science teachers. We need to identify ways in which teachers can make effective use of the lesson time once they are freed from assisting in the collection and processing (and even presentation) of data.

Whilst working closely with pupils, as part of my research, it became clear that their understanding of the features of the graphs and their ability to relate them to the experiment itself are initially in a very fluid state. The transcripts show the ways in which the teacher – using nothing much more than a few prompt questions, asking pupils to think more about what they have said – can significantly affect their interpretations of the data. The conclusion is that simply the act of talking to pupils about graphs improves their ability to describe them and encourages them to reflect on their meaning (see chapter by Sutton). It was also apparent that pupils do not find it easy to provide verbal descriptions of graphs. Words such as 'steep' and 'slope' were often provided by the teacher when pupils could not improve on 'goes up more'. Part of this problem seemed to be a lack of experience in the verbal descriptions of graphical information. Swatton and Taylor (1994) commented on this, and noted that pupils find it easier to use geometric or numeric descriptions rather than referring to physical variables. They suggested that more needs to be done in terms of explicitly teaching the skills of giving verbal descriptions. Rogers (1995) when discussing the possibilities offered by data logging, has provided what might be called a *vocabulary of graphing*, which could be used as part of this process. It would seem that the computer-based method provides the opportunity for pupils to become more effective in describing graphical data.

I have already discussed the fact that the use of computers increases the time available for discussion to take place. However, what is also new is the way in which the data on the screen can act as a catalyst for this discussion. Newton (1997) talks about the computer as 'another group member', and I have seen the ways in which pupils refer to and point to the screen graph as an integral part of their explanations. In addition, pupils can 'call on the computer' to collect new data quickly and to act as an arbiter when disputes arise. It is during these exchanges, which need not be extensive, that the teacher is able to probe the level of understanding which pupils have.

In my comparative study (Barton 1996), the difference in performance and coverage between the computer and the conventional approach was particularly noticeable with the younger (Year 8) and least able pupils. Indeed, with the support of the computer (and the teacher), these pupils seemed capable of achieving much more than one would expect of pupils of this age and ability. This is consistent with the findings reported by Jackson *et al.* (1993), who used computer-generated graphs with less able pupils and noted the ways in which these pupils responded positively to the higher expectations placed on them. In this context it is important to note that with a computer-aided approach the pupils' first graphical experience is qualitative; that is, the traces on the computer screen. This contrasts with the conventional approach where pupils have to work quantitatively – that is, collect and plot data values – before they can start a qualitative analysis.

But what will we lose if we use computers?

Alongside the potential benefits of computer-assisted practical work we need to consider what disadvantages are associated with their use if we are to assess the possible value added truly. Scaife and Wellington (1993: 23) have made the distinction between what they refer to as *authentic* (that is, desirable and purposeful) and *inauthentic* (unnecessary and irrelevant) labour. The question is, are the labour-saving features of computer-assisted practical work taking away important educational experience for learners and relegating them to mere bystanders? The suggestion is that they will lose the hands-on feel for events and that it will all become too slick, with everything done by 'black boxes'. This is a serious point which deserves close scrutiny.

When using computers, experiments are still conducted on the laboratory bench and the equipment still needs to be assembled and arranged. Therefore, I feel that concerns about lack of hands-on experience with equipment are largely unfounded. The main difference with the computer-based approach seems to relate to the mode of measurement. In one case sensors collect and transfer data to a computer, whereas in the conventional approach, pupils need to read scales and record the data manually on paper. There are two issues here: possible advantages related to pupils' reading scales and benefits associated with manually recording data.

The question about a better 'feel' for the data when reading scales largely depends on the type of measurement. Perhaps it could be argued that a liquid-in-glass thermometer gives a different feel for the data than digits on a computer screen, although the use of such devices in schools is becoming increasingly anachronistic. For other measurements, such as reading the scale on an electrical meter, there is the practical disadvantage that many pupils are unable to read the values correctly. Clearly, a balance needs to be struck and the main purpose of the activity needs to be identified. Is the purpose of the activity to improve pupils' skills in reading a specific scale, or is it more important to get good-quality data quickly so pupils can move on to evaluate them? In some cases I feel the more traditional methods of measurement are invested with benefits with no supporting evidence.

The issue of manual recording is more clear-cut in my mind. I have observed the ways in which manual data recording can become an end in itself (Barton 1996). Pupils seem to 'switch off' during this time, taking on specific roles of reading or recording data with no apparent thought for the meaning or significance of the values they are measuring. Those who talk in terms of pupils becoming more detached from the experiment seem to overlook this point. It should be noted that, whilst the sensors are collecting the data in the computer-assisted approach, the experiment is still taking place in front of the pupils on the laboratory bench. For example, when a gas syringe is being used with a position sensor to monitor the rate of a reaction, the pupils are still able to observe the evolution of gas as they have always done. Indeed, it could be argued that by freeing pupils from routine data gathering they are in an even better position to observe these events during the experiment, with the additional benefit of being able to relate them to the graphical representation on the computer screen.

Are pupils in a better position to interpret data if they have had to produce a manual plot of the data? This question seems to imply that the act of plotting data manually helps pupils to understand the relationship between the variables. My research suggests that this is simply not the case and at best there is no difference between pupils' ability to interpret graphical information whether they have it presented on a computer screen or have plotted it for themselves. However, there are a number of problems associated with the manual approach which extend beyond the time penalty already discussed. It may be that since pupils see the data as a series of individual numbers, they are less likely to see them as part of a continuous relationship between the two variables. The fact that pupils are seen to concentrate very hard on manual graph plotting seems to emphasise the significance of the individual points, particularly for the least able. As I observed pupils struggling to locate points on a sheet of graph paper there seemed to be little sense of a relationship emerging between the two variables. This contrasts sharply with the way pupils, when using the computer, would talk in terms of the overall shape of the graph, suggesting a much better feel for the relationship between the two variables. 'It curved more than I expected' was a telling remark from a pupil whilst watching the data emerge.

With the manual approach, once individual points have been plotted it is sometimes possible for a range of alternative lines to be legitimately drawn through the points. This choice may well be influenced by prior experiences; for example, the expectation that the data will form a straight line. There-fore it could be argued that manual plotting places an additional burden on pupils, since they are required to try to set aside their pre-conceived ideas to plot the best fit line before they move on to interpret the meaning of the graph they have plotted. Pupils using the computer are equally likely to expect straight line relationships but they have the benefit of seeing the graph produced on the computer screen before moving on to try to interpret the shape of the graph. To summarise, my research suggests that there are no advantages associated with manual graph plotting in the context of exploring the relationship between two variables.

Before leaving this discussion I don't want to suggest that there are no problems related to the use of computer-assisted practical work. Resource limitations and logistical difficulties are not insignificant. Even if a science department had sufficient computers available for practical work, their maintenance and management pose problems for even the best-organised science department. However, in my view, many of the problems relate to lack of familiarity on the part of staff and pupils. Clearly, when new hardware and software are first introduced there are considerable teething problems, but it is remarkable how quickly pupils in particular become familiar with new software. The 'jungle telegraph' in the classroom is a powerful dissemination tool if only teachers would give it enough time to operate. It is my contention that despite these logistical difficulties the main problems to be overcome in the effective introduction of computer-aided practical work are the teaching and not the technical issues. If teachers are persuaded on sound educational grounds then they are extremely skilled at finding ways and means. In my view the slow progress in this area is mainly due to the fact that for too long technical issues have been seen as more important than 'hearts and minds'.

New opportunities

Much of the discussion in this chapter has so far centred on comparisons between conventional and computer-aided methods. This can only take us part of the way towards evaluating the potential value added of the computer-based approach. I now wish to explore the features of computer-based methods which cannot be compared directly with a conventional approach. These features relate to the software tools which enable the data collected to be investigated, manipulated and analysed. In effect, the production of a graph becomes the new starting point for practical work. So what can be done with this new starting point and these new tools?

Software tools facilitate the exploration of graphs in a number of ways. At its simplest, cursors can be used to read data values, present pupils with time intervals and evaluate gradients, ratios and the area under the graph. Given appropriate prompts, pupils can use these tools to explore the significance of their data in much greater detail. Other tools, such as the ability to zoom in and out, enable a dynamic exploration of the effect on the shape of the graph of changing the plotting scale – an area well-known to cause problems for pupils (Archenhold *et al.* 1991). The facility for the software to draw the best straight line or to fit points to a curve can be used to good advantage to help pupils to appreciate what is meant by 'lines of best fit'. By changing individual data values pupils can explore, again in a dynamic way, the ways such changes affect the trace produced by the computer.

These tools also provide the opportunity for pupils to explore the significance of both straight lines and curves. Pupils can look for patterns between variables as they move the cursor in simple multiples on the x-axis (for example, values at 10, 20, 30 sec., etc.). However, other tools provide alternative and complementary ways to analyse the data, such as comparing the ratio of the two variables at different points on the graph or reading the gradient at different places. All these are theoretically possible with conventional methods but the software tools facilitate the exploration, removing some of the 'mathematical noise' discussed earlier. Investigating rates of change are important in a number of contexts, and Rogers (1997) explores how the software tools can enable pupils to explore a range of alternative methods of analysing the data, either by considering average rates or instantaneous rates. The point is that pupils are in a position to think about alternative ways of analysing their data and to consider which approach is likely to yield the most relevant and significant results in a particular case.

These software tools provide the option for a new kind of practical science activity where pupils start by collecting data but spend most of their time considering the significance of the data by exploring it. To illustrate this idea, let us look at one example which would be appropriate for Year 9 pupils. This investigation explores the question 'Can we use the brightness of a bulb as a means of measuring the current flowing through it?' Many pupils will have been introduced to current measurement by comparing bulb brightness in this way. By monitoring the current flow through a bulb whilst measuring the brightness, pupils can explore the relationship between the two quantities. It is sensible to try to engage pupils in the problem by asking them to make a prediction via a sketch graph, before collecting the data. The question can be framed so that pupils are asked to draw the shape of the graph, assuming that using the brightness of a bulb was a good way to measure the current. This will encourage them to look more critically at the data they collect.

Collecting the data gives the result shown in Figure 14.2.

Pupils can use the software tools to explore the two graphs and to try to answer the original question. It is useful to display the data in bar charts (as shown in the graph) in addition to the line graphs, since, as the cursor is moved across the graph, the relative size of the two bars gives a clear visual indication of the ways in which they vary relative to each other. This relationship can be explored further by considering a plot of light against current. Again pupils are more likely to become involved if they are asked to predict the shape of this graph. At this stage it is easy to set up the software to plot light against current, which gives the graph shown in Figure 14.3.

By giving this example (there are many others), it is important to stress that it will take time for pupils and teachers to become sufficiently familiar

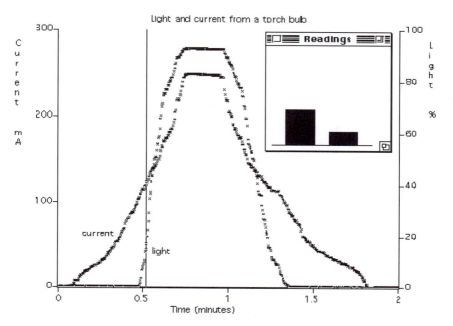

Figure 14.2 Graph showing how the light from a torch bulb varies as the current through it is slowly increased and then decreased. Plotting both of these quantities against time gives a simple picture of how they change relative to each other

with the software tools to explore all the facilities they offer. Whenever we begin to use any new software, such as a word processor, we initially do the simple things, but as time goes by we begin to explore some of the other features available. We do this with a mixture of, 'I wonder if it can . . . .', and seeing other people demonstrate features we were not aware of. What is needed is for teachers gradually to build up a repertoire of techniques and to feed them into lessons at an appropriate rate as pupils become more experienced and confident.

Looking forward

I began this chapter by aiming to explore the potential value added associated with computer-aided practical work. Its introduction has coincided with dramatic changes in science education in Britain, centred on the introduction of a National Curriculum in 1988 and major revisions in 1991 and 1995, which have tended to deflect attention away from considering its potential. All my experiences related to using computer-aided practical work have reinforced my original conviction about its enormous and as yet largely untapped potential. What has become clear is that, in order to

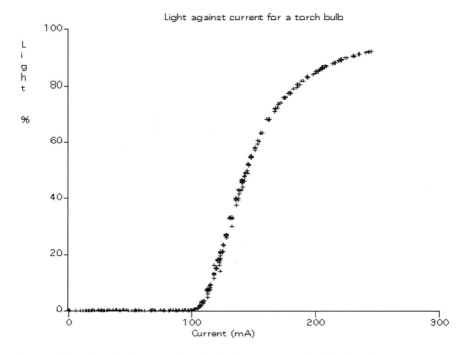

Figure 14.3 Graph showing the light from a torch bulb plotted against the current flowing through it. This shows that light only begins to be emitted once the current exceeds 100mA and that subsequently the light output is not proportional to the size of the current

exploit this potential in schools, teachers will need to refine and to modify their approach to the way they support pupils' practical work. This will inevitably be a gradual process, but one which I feel will eventually bring 'value added' and lead to improvements in the quality of science education.

References

Abbott, A.F. (1963) *Ordinary Level Physics*, London: Heinemann.

Archenhold, F. Austin, R., Bell, J., Black, P. *et al*. (1991) *Assessment Matters No.5: Profiles and Progression in Science Exploration*, London: SEAC.

Austin, R., Holding, B., Bell, J. and Daniels, S. (1991) *Assessment Matters No.7: Patterns and Relationships in School Science*, London: SEAC.

Ausubel, D.P., Novak, J.D. and Hanesian, H. (1968) *Educational Psychology: A Cognitive View*, New York: Holt, Rinehart and Winston.

Barton, R. (1996) 'Computers and practical work in science education', unpublished PhD thesis, University of East Anglia.

—— (1997) 'Computer-aided graphing: a comparative study', *Journal of Information Technology for Teacher Education* 6(1): 59–72.

Bell, A., Brekke, G. and Swan, M. (1987) 'Diagnostic teaching: graphical interpretation', *Mathematics Teacher* 119: 56–9.

Driver, R., Asoko, H., Leach, J., Mortimer, E. and Scott, P. (1994) 'Constructing
scientific knowledge in the classroom', *Educational Researcher* 23(7): 5–12.

Edwards, D. and Mercer, N. (1993) *Common Knowledge: the Development of Understanding in the Classroom*, London: Routledge.

Gunstone, R.F. (1991) 'Reconstructing theory from practical experience', in B.
Woolnough (ed.) *Practical Science: the Role and Reality of Practical Work in School
Science*, Milton Keynes and Philadelphia: Open University Press.

Hodson, D. (1993) 'Re-thinking old ways: towards a more critical approach to
practical work in school science', *Studies in Science Education* 22(93): 85–142.

Jackson, D.F., Edwards, B.J. and Berger, C.F. (1993) 'Teaching the design and
interpretation of graphs through computer-aided graphical data analysis', *Journal of Research in Science Teaching* 30: 483–501.

Mercer, N. (1994) 'The quality of talk in children's joint activity at the computer', *Journal of Computer Assisted Learning* 10: 24–32.

Nachmias, R. and Linn, M. (1987) 'Evaluations of science laboratory data: the role
of computer presented information', *Journal of Research in Science Teaching* 24(5):
491–506.

Nakhleh, M. B. and Krajcik, J. S. (1993) 'A protocol analysis of the influence of
technology on students' actions, verbal commentary, and thought processes
during the performance of acid-base titrations', *Journal of Research in Science
Teaching* 30(9): 1149–68.

Newton, L.R. (1997) 'Graph talk: some observations and reflections on students'
data-logging', *School Science Review* 79(287): 61–8.

Osborne, J. (1993) 'Alternatives to practical work', *School Science Review* 75(271):
117–23.

Rogers, L.T. (1995) 'The computer as an aid for exploring graphs', *School Science
Review* 76(276): 31–9.

—— (1997) 'New data-logging tools – new investigations', *School Science Review*
79(287): 49–54.

Rogers, L.T. and Wild, P. (1996) 'Data-logging: effects on practical science',
Journal of Computer Assisted Learning 12: 130–45.

Scaife, J. and Wellington, J. (1993) *Information Technology in Science and Technology
Education*, Milton Keynes: Open University Press.

Solomon, J. (1980) *Teaching Children in the Laboratory*, London: Croom Helm.

Swatton, P. and Taylor, R.M. (1994) 'Pupil performance in graphical tasks and its
relationship to the ability to handle variables', *British Educational Research
Journal* 20(2): 227–43.

Vygotsky, L.S. (1978) *Mind in Society: the Development of Higher Psychological
Processes*, London: Harvard University Press.

15

MULTIMEDIA SIMULATION
A threat to or enhancement of practical work in
science education?

Linda Baggott (with Jon Nichol)

Simulation is neither an alternative to, nor an imitation of,
lab-based practical work: it is a form of knowledge representation in its own right. This chapter discusses the nature,
advantages and disadvantages, uses, and future application of
simulation programmes in science education. It presents a
recently conducted evaluation of a novel simulation currently
under development. The chapter concludes with a discussion
of the evolving pedagogy of the new information and
communications technologies in general and simulation in
particular.

The nature of simulation and
the teacher's 'second record'

'Virtual reality' is the most extreme example of how multimedia can induce
in participants a sense of reality that is in fact unrelated to the circumstances
in which they find themselves. Here the mapping and representation of the
'model' is so realistic that the illusion becomes mistaken for the reality. As
such, the ability of the mind to enter into a fantasy world created through
the written, visual or spoken word is a well-recorded facet of the human
state. Explanations of what occurs at the interface between the minds of
those accepting the illusion and the illusionist have been central to academic discourse for well over 2,000 years, moving from the world of the
Platonic theory of forms to Gombrich's exegesis on representation in *Art and
Illusion*. Concepts of illusion and reality are central to the whole question of
simulation, where the simulation is a substitute for the reality that it is
supposed to mirror. More, it requires an act of will on behalf of the
participant to accept that the simulation is a substitute for 'the real thing'.
The nature and role of simulation in education directly relates to the issue of
illusion, representation and reality. Are we merely seeing a conjuring trick

performed with a set of reflecting mirrors? Or is there a deeper and justifiable educational purpose to simulation that relates the illusion to the reality that it is supposed to represent?

The issue was explicitly raised in Lewis Carroll's post-Darwinian masterpiece, *Through the Looking Glass*. The question of whether simulated practical work is a threat to or an enhancement of traditional school practical work is directly related to the question of whether 'school science' is the same as scientists' science, however defined. If we accept that there is synchronicity between the two, progression involves both substantive (know 'that' knowledge) and syntactic (know 'how' knowledge) understanding of skills and processes. Accepting that sensory exposure to multimedia optimally engages a student's awareness, multimedia has the potential to ensure a pupil's conceptual understanding. This is in contrast to most laboratory work, which is often unfocused, 'ill-conceived, confused and unproductive' (Osborne 1993).

A simple concept in relation to multimedia simulations is that of what can be called the teacher's 'second record' (Hexter 1971). The second record is all that knowledge, experience and understanding that the teacher brings to bear upon the 'first record' – that is, the body of scientific knowledge presented to their pupils. Shulman (1987) classified the knowledge bases that teachers need to promote pupil understanding via scientific simulations:

1   *Content knowledge*: the depth and organisation of knowledge in the mind of the teacher. Shulman divides this into substantive knowledge (organisation of basic scientific concepts and principles) and syntactic knowledge (ways in which facts of science are established) – this is the 'first record';

2   *General pedagogical knowledge*: the broad principles and strategies of classroom management and organisation which transcend the subject matter of science;

3   *Curriculum knowledge*: content and workings of the National Curriculum in Science (in the UK);

4   *Pedagogical-content knowledge*: the most useful ways of making a particular science topic accessible to pupils;

5   *Knowledge of pupils and their characteristics*: individual and group relationships and how these affect learning in science;

6   *Knowledge of specific educational contexts*: the local school, regional and national situations in which the teaching and learning in science take place;

7   *Knowledge of generic educational contexts*: purposes and values; historical and philosophical roots of teaching and learning of science.

The 'second record' covers categories 2–7 above, activated in what Shulman has called a cycle of pedagogical reasoning.

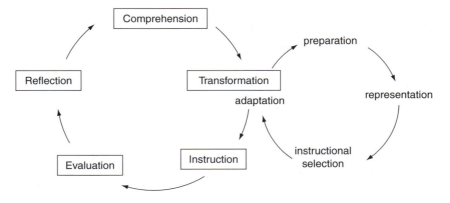

Figure 15.1 Shulman's Cycle of Pedagogical Reasoning
Explanatory note: The cycle begins and ends with an act of comprehension on behalf of the teacher. Given an understanding of the ideas to be taught, and the curricular purposes to be achieved, she then transforms these into a form which is pedagogically potent. This involves her in another cycle of action: preparation (critical scrutiny and choice of teaching materials, based on intimate knowledge of them) ⇒ representation (consideration of how the key ideas can best be represented to the pupils) ⇒ instructional selection (choice of class management and teaching strategies) adaptation ⇒ (methods of differentiation).

A typical practical session in science actively involves the teacher's 'second record' in the necessary planning and preparation. The teacher thus provides the pupil with a surrogate 'second record' to make the practical experiment work. The extent to which this detracts from or enhances a pupil's learning opportunity is part of the professional decision making of the teacher. The simulation is an extension of the teacher's expertise, as is a textbook or other resource. For any new topic the teacher draws on their 'second record' to decide where on the illustrative / investigative continuum to concentrate. Like the practical work which it replicates, an exploratory simulation is interactive. It forces the student to make decisions and respond to consequences that result in a changed set of experimental parameters. The degree to which computer simulations and laboratory practicals fulfil the same aims and objectives highlights the question 'What *is* authentic practical work?'

As with other episodes of teaching, the process of using simulation in science education starts with the act of transformation (Shulman 1987; Grossman *et al*. 1989), that is, the series of decisions which underlie the choice of pedagogical strategy to use in transferring a teacher's knowledge and understanding of a topic to the pupils. Here preparation involves the choice of materials of instruction: in this case the decision whether to use a simulation in preference to a live practical. Representation follows this, and here the manner in which the key ideas are represented in the simulation will influence the teacher's decision about use. The next choice is one of instructional selection of the most appropriate teaching approach: how the simulation will be employed during the lesson, including the roles of pupil and teacher. Finally, the possibilities afforded by the simulation for differentiation will influence a teacher's decision about how, and indeed whether, to use it.

Drawing upon the teacher's second record, for a pupil to devise and design an investigation takes a cognitive and intellectual effort similar in kind to that of a research scientist. The difference lies in the depth and sophistication of background knowledge and understanding which informs and guides the subsequent series of decisions and actions. This background knowledge base is composed of a wide range of substantive knowledge and syntactic concepts. Operationally, these take the form of skills and processes. The pupils are pushing back their own frontiers of knowledge by engaging in what appear to them to be original school-based science investigations. The structure and form of the simulation, 'the model' it presents, free the pupil to exercise higher-level skills such as hypothesising, analysis, deduction, inference (divergent thinking) and concluding. The concept of invisibility has long exercised those working in the area of computer simulation; namely, the provision of a man–machine interface that convinces that student of being engaged with a reality. So it is entirely legitimate to use a computer program to generate data or to simulate a practical situation or to exercise discrete skills as part of curricular provision for science.

Simulation is therefore neither an alternative to nor an imitation of lab-based practical work: it is a form of knowledge representation in its own right.

Simulation programs – the pros and cons

A relatively small number of effective simulations are available. Their use is warranted however, because simulations have a number of distinct advantages. An effective simulation puts the learner in an *active* role in an environment which has a set of rules, either static or changeable. The nature of that *activity* is the major contributing factor to the effectiveness of simulations. But little research has been done to investigate their effect on learning. The quality of existing research does not allow firm conclusions to be drawn. As with many aspects of computer-based learning, for simulation a pedagogy grounded in research does not yet exist.

Active learning

The construction of knowledge requires learners to be *active* decision makers, choosing between a number of options instead of the passive recipients of another's interpretation. The grandees of learning theory,

Piaget, Dewey and Bruner, all advocated involvement of the learner in the learning process. The defining characteristic of a simulation is the requirement of the player to make decisions in order to accomplish a goal. A simulation allows pupils to take control of the organisation and content of their own learning. In this regard, the play aspect of simulation is an important motivator (Blissett and Atkins 1993). Play requires an act of imagination that stimulates the pupil's mind through engaging in a rule-based activity that brings expectation of differential rewards. The imaginative faculty requires the pupil to speculate, to project permutations, to anticipate outcomes and mentally to create different situations and scenarios. The rewards (or disappointments!) result from the outcome of a choice or choices made from a range of options. This heightened gaming stimulus from projecting expectations involves developing pupils' understanding beyond the options provided by conventional teaching (Vygotsky 1978; Wood and Attfield 1996: 68).

This 'edutainment' element may account for the pupil-appeal reported in a recent simulation evaluation (Watson and Baggott 1997). Well-designed simulations are therefore not a break from learning but a most effective learning strategy: they challenge a learner's fantasy and curiosity within the context of rule-bound 'play'. However, we should not lose sight of the fact that reality is much, much more than simulation. Substantial differences exist between the real world and the simulated world. To appreciate the difference fully, the pupil needs to experience both.

Unlike many multimedia learning packages, a good simulation departs from the book metaphor, and in doing so can provide for the teaching of skills and processes as well as content knowledge and understanding. Further aspects of the ways in which simulations provide exemplars for active learning lie in their potential for continuous assessment and evaluation. 'In flight' self and teacher checks of understanding are easily built into such programmes.

Cost

Another considerable advantage of simulation programs is that they are almost always cheaper than the real thing. They can also be considerably safer (for example, virtual reality surgery training developments, and the Cytovision program [Stringer et al 1994] for training cytologists), and more ethical simulations, such as that of the frog nerve–muscle preparations. Simulations can be as realistic as the live situation, although a good simulation need not exactly emulate the real thing, as long as the learning process is valid and the outcome comparable. This raises the issue of the validity of the process of working from a simulation. If the simulation provides ready access to an accurate representation of a real situation and makes it more accessible, then its value as a learning tool increases proportionately.

Skill transfer

Some evidence from the American military suggests that simulation can provide more effective transfer of skill than other methods of instruction which involve comparable time and effort from the trainees. For example, pilots learning in flight simulators can transfer to aeroplanes more quickly than those who have received their instruction on flying in lecture theatres. Here the critical factor is the closer cognitive and affective engagement of the tutee with the simulated reality. A realistic environment is experienced. This gives the learner an appreciation of reality that transfers to real-life situations. Where a situation might induce apprehension, by engaging the learner with reality in a 'play' context, simulations can bridge the gap between illusion and reality. The rat dissection simulation is an example of a less anxiety-provoking learning situation for some pupils as compared to the live (or rather, dead!) alternative. Simulations can be more revealing than other teaching and learning approaches. For example, lecture-style exposition with little engagement of the individual provides the opportunity to switch off, whereas in a simulation a student's understanding is revealed.

Critical thinking and discussion

In the teaching of critical thinking simulation allows the possibility of asking 'What if?' questions. A pupil can then pursue them to their conclusion because of immediate feedback and teasing out the implications of the questions. Research evidence suggests that computer-based activities are commonly effective for motivating interaction and stimulating discussion. In this respect, simulations can develop collaboration and cooperation and can foster learning through peer interaction, both cooperative and dissonant. Through discussion, the simulated practical exercise in science involves negotiation, estimation and examination of alternative ideas, demonstration of different interpretations of evidence. This enhances the development of pupils' social (Mercer 1994) and scientific skills. It forms an aspect of a pupil's learning environment, providing secure opportunities for competition and leadership practice. The teacher should understand that competition may overshadow collaboration and cooperation, and carefully control this factor.

Time and control

All wet-bench practicals, but particularly biological investigations, can be time consuming and uncertain in outcome. An effective simulation on the other hand will maximise the use of learning time. The length of time pupils spend on a simulation is far more controllable and predictable.

Simulations can change the time-base of events to fit into the learning time available. Thus very slow processes such as plant growth or rock formation can be speeded up, and very quick events such as propagation of nerve impulses or sound waves can be slowed down. All of these can also be repeated as often as necessary for the learner, which would be impossible in a live practical class. The simulated situation is also controlled and therefore predictable and repeatable. Evidence from the higher education sector has clearly shown that a good quality of student learning experience can be gained in a single afternoon practical session from the use of a simulation of neurophysiological experiments which would take an experienced researcher days to perform. The ability to get clear results quickly contrasts markedly with a not atypically discouraging experience – quite common in biological investigation at all levels – of confusing results and the time taken to get to grips with the equipment (National Committee of Inquiry into Higher Education (1996) Evidence from the Computers in Teaching Initiative). A note of caution here, however: simulations may not achieve the learning objectives claimed in the advertising/support material, and careful preparation including thorough familiarisation with the package, is essential.

The information and communications technology revolution

Simulation is a vital part of the revolution which we are currently experiencing in information and communications technology (ICT) with its potential for distance learning. That IT motivates and stimulates students (NCET 1994) is based on a growing body of educational research, including many evaluation studies of curriculum developments in various subjects. The extent to which this affective role also leads to cognitive gains is open to debate. Simulation programs became increasingly popular from earliest days in the 1970s (for example, Nervax, and the SiP Software developed by ILEA). The psychological basis for these simulations in Skinnerian programmed learning materials was reflected in the limited nature of such software. The attempts to provide software that reflected a different psychological model, that of Piaget, through Papert's development of LOGO as a tool for learning (Papert *et al.*, 1979) have failed to have lasting influence. As hardware became increasingly powerful, cheaper and therefore more accessible through the 1980s and 1990s, the sophistication and range of simulations increased. However, a high proportion of instructional software still remains in the Skinnerian skill-and-drill or linear tutorial model.

The reason for this possibly lies in the fact that it is easier to teach declarative information – content – than to teach syntactic skills and processes. 'What?' is simpler than 'how?' or 'why?' Skill-and-drill software, in supporting the 'what?' is therefore widely used. On the whole it is easy to develop and it certainly emulates a didactic teaching strategy more comfortably. The necessary pedagogical shift (see Barton's chapter in this book) involves change in overall teaching functions such as planning, setting of course objectives, class management including teacher–pupil interaction, practical work and assessment as well as detailed pedagogical-content knowledge central to the effective teaching of any science topic. Coupled with this is the requirement for an easy confidence and comfort with the use of ICT applications.

However, the use of computer simulations also requires a 'match' between them and the curricular goals that the National Curriculum in Science, as reflected by its OFSTED enforcer, demands. The limited availability of 'good' simulations of this kind is a major barrier to their adoption. Appropriate use of multimedia techniques can enrich and extend current practices in science education, but only if the simulations that they enhance map on to the teacher's requirements and expectations. This is where the emphasis in educational multimedia and telematics research now lies (Collins *et al.* 1997; Someckh and Davis 1997).

A new generation of educational simulation

The use of computer simulation is an important aspect of the use of IT in science education, and one which is attracting increasing attention. The reasons for this are relatively simple: it is a cost-effective way of bridging the gap between expensive and managerially difficult practical experimentation and the classroom. The simulation presented in this chapter, the Interactive Microscope Laboratory (IML), currently under development, represents the attempt to unite academic and pedagogical subject expertise by bringing together a team of research scientists, educationists, teachers, student-teachers, pupils, computer programmers and multimedia experts (Baggott, 1996; Baggott and Watson 1997; Watson and Baggott 1997).

The basis for the IML is to promote high-quality observation in biology education. Observation is a basic and primary skill of the scientific process and the springboard for many other higher-order skills, and as such it is of fundamental importance in a student's learning of the processes of biology. Moreover, appreciation of the very nature of the living world in its almost infinite variety and beauty is essentially a visual experience. This is particularly true at the microscopic level, and it is from such study that a deeper understanding of the structure and functioning of living things arises. But paradoxically, as the cellular and even molecular structures and functions of organisms are probed and revealed by ever more sophisticated (and costly) equipment and refined scientific expertise, and the quality of the images is improved, so these first-hand encounters are further removed from the school biology lab.

Biology as a study comprises about a quarter of the National Curriculum in Science, which is itself a core subject: pupils between 14 and 16 spend up to 20 per cent of the school curriculum time engaged in it. This means that all pupils in mainstream education in the United Kingdom have to study biology, and that, by the end of the compulsory period of education, will have done so for a considerable proportion of the available time. At one level, biology is a user-friendly and therefore popular science: pupils are themselves organisms living in an environment, and so it is of the most direct relevance to them. However, the basic unit of life, the cell, is very small, and has an intricate structure and highly complex function, its mechanisms being based on an intricate underlying chemistry. It is at these microscopic and submicroscopic levels that a detailed understanding of the processes of life arises; indeed, this is reflected in the requirement of the National Curriculum, that 'pupils' learn about the ways in which plants and animals function as organisms should be related to cell structure and the underlying chemical reactions'.

The typical school bench-top microscope, seen in comparison to other types of scientific apparatus in school labs, is a relatively sophisticated and expensive item. Usually, only one pupil can look at a specimen at once, and all biology teachers are aware of the problems of interpretation arising from this constraint. Few schools can boast a class set of really good microscopes for KS4 pupils, and usually results lack the necessary definition, and are therefore disappointing to pupils of the 1990s who have a high expectation of visual stimuli. Witnessing biological events at the cellular level is not realistically within the scope of the school biology lesson, and the time taken to acquire the skill to use even an unsophisticated microscope to its full potential is disproportionate to the time available. Although relatively few pupils will continue with the study of biology post-16, it is a very, if not the most popular of the sciences with this age group. A small proportion of these 16–19 year olds will continue with biology into HE courses, and even fewer will become professional biologists or biomedics. Gaining an appreciation of the cellular world through good, accessible images is thus more important than an acquisition of skills in microscopy.

The Interactive Microscope Laboratory (IML)

The IML is an innovative system for learning about the sub-optical world. It uses a CD-ROM that simulates the functionality of a microscope, and enables students to investigate biological materials in their own time and place. This interactive CD-ROM offers pupils of all abilities a unique opportunity to use the new multimedia technologies to simulate the latest techniques of microscopy which are not normally available even to undergraduates in colleges and universities. The IML can augment their practical experience with school microscopes and provide them with opportunities for practice and review. They can therefore have an equivalent experience of investigation and discovery of the sub-optical living world to that of a graduate student at a fraction of the cost and technical mastery, thus further empowering them with the skills of biological investigation.

Educational multimedia is a burgeoning field, but there is little or no information from research about how effective such materials as CD-ROMs are in teaching and learning. Many of the available products act essentially as books on a computer screen, and although they are accessible and visually attractive, do not involve pupils in skills-based learning. To date, computer simulations for science education are based on activities, processes, concepts or theories that are too dangerous, difficult, expensive or abstract to be demonstrated experimentally in the laboratory (see Scaife and Wellington, 1993). Currently available examples include: *Gravity Pack* (Cambridge Micro Software), *Predator–Prey Relationships* (AVP), *Bridge Building* (Longman), *Moving Molecules* (CUP) and *Survival of the Fittest* (SPA). The nature of the interactivity in these is limited to the ability of pupils to alter variables, observing the effects. Some also offer the chance to explore and hypothesise. In contrast, the central idea of the IML is to provide a way of getting at the facts and concepts of cell biology through rehearsing a range of science skills, thus giving pupils greater learning opportunities than they might experience with either text-based materials or conventional laboratory apparatus.

Interactive technologies such as computer-mediated learning (Modell 1990), videodisc (Hall 1989; Huang and Aloi 1991; Stringer *et al.* 1993; Baggott and Wright 1996a), PhotoCD (Baggott 1995; Baggott and Wright 1995; Baggott and Wright 1996b), have already made an important contribution to science education. See also Hartley (1994) and Collins *et al.* (1997) for reviews of the use of interactive multimedia. The IML simulation represents the next step in using new multimedia technology. In considering the general question of developing simulations to support practical work in science we asked the questions 'Is there any added value of simulation – are any important skills being replaced?' and 'What impact does a simulation have on the practising of skills of the scientific process?' We developed a list of these based on the demands of the National Curriculum in Science, and considered in turn whether a simulation could be designed to provide an opportunity to exercise the skills. In the IML prototype, we simulated the popular but tricky school practical involving measuring the changes in heart rate of a water flea *(Daphnia)*, over a range of environmental temperature. Table 15.1 shows how the science skills were covered in this investigation.

In summary, the Interactive Microscope Laboratory (IML) is a simulation of a functional microscope on CD-ROM for use in biological education for school pupils and students in further and higher education (for a description of the technical details of this, see Baggott and Watson 1997). The IML offers the following functions linked to an image database:

Table 15.1 Coverage of science skills in a simulated practical investigation

Generate hypotheses	Form a hypothesis to test the idea that the metabolic rate of a water flea (derived from heart rate) changes with environmental temperature change.
Test hypotheses	In this investigation you will test the hypothesis that increasing the temperature of the water around the water flea will increase its heart rate.
Plan experiments/investigations	Design an investigation in which the external temperature is varied within the range 1°C–30°C. Why is this range limit suggested?
Ask questions	Editable teacher's notebook
Fair tests – control variables	What conditions will you keep constant? How will you record the results?
Predict	Do you expect an increase or a decrease in the heart rate of the water flea as the temperature rises?
Use equipment	Set the temperature of the water to 10°C.
Make estimates	How many beats per minute do you estimate the water flea's heart will make at 10°C?
Observe	Look at the water flea, and use the diagram to locate the beating heart. Use the camera to take a micrograph of the water flea specimen, and label the heart and any other organs you can identify on the micrograph.
Measure	1 Use the counter to count the number of heart beats over a time of 15 seconds, then multiply this number by 4 to get the number of heart beats in 1 minute. 2 Increase the temperature to 15°C, and repeat the heart-rate count, entering your results in the table.
Repeat measurement/observation	3. Repeat the process, increasing the temperature by five degrees each time until you have recorded the heart rate at 30°C.
Record evidence	Record the number of heart beats in each case in the table on your jotter.
Present data clearly	Print out the table from your jotter, and plot your results as a graph.
Use graphs	From your graph, say how many heart beats would be expected at 17°C and 28°C.
Identify patterns, trends	What does the graph tell you about the effect on the heart rate of the water flea when you increase the temperature of the water?
Draw conclusions	What can you say about the way water fleas control their metabolic rate over a range of temperatures?
Explain conclusions	Why does the heart rate of water fleas vary with changes in temperature?
Evaluate	Can you think of any ways in which the accuracy of this investigation could be improved?

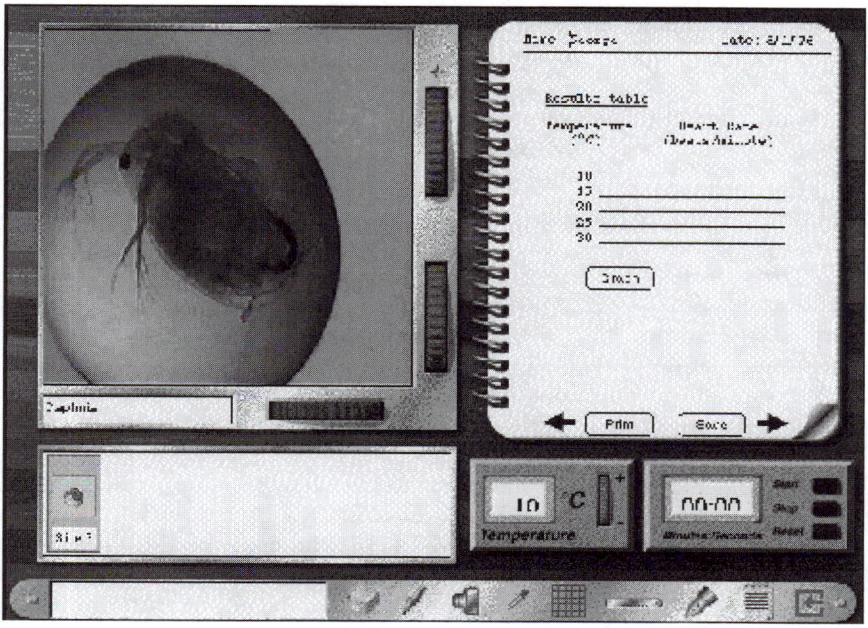

Figure 15.2 IML student activity: forming and testing a hypothesis about the effect on metabolic rate of *Daphnia* of varying the environmental temperature. The IML uses the metaphor of a laboratory workbench, here set up for an investigation into the heart rate of a water flea. In addition to the microscopic field-of-view, a slide box, a notebook and a tool bar, there is a thermometer, which also 'alters' the temperature of the water around the flea, and a stop clock for timing the heart rate. *Daphnia*, the water flea, is a small crustacean that lives in slow moving fresh water. Like all invertebrates, it cannot maintain a constant body temperature, and when the temperature of its surroundings changes, so will that of its body. This has an effect on its metabolic rate, which will alter in response to changes in the environmental temperature. You can assume that the heart rate of *Daphnia* is a measure of its metabolic rate.

- changing magnification
- panning
- focusing
- staining
- counting (haemocytometer)
- measuring (micrometer)
- timing.

The IML is based on a workbench metaphor (see Figure 15.2), and apart from the simulations of the microscope and other laboratory equipment such as thermometer and stop clock, it includes worksheets, support material and a jotter facility on which the user may type notes to save to disk or print out at the end of a session. Uniquely, the Interactive Microscope Laboratory offers the opportunity to work in a 'virtual laboratory' without the need for any paper resources.

Evaluating the use of simulation

Evaluation of new multimedia technology features infrequently in recent publications. Cox (1993) in reporting on the ImpacT project, observed that very little evidence has been gathered from pupils themselves about the extent and nature of their IT use in the classroom.

We carried out an evaluation of a prototype of the IML in which the responses of pupils in English secondary school science departments to the simulation were observed and evaluated. This study sought to lay a foundation for understanding how such products are likely to affect teaching and learning in secondary schools. Data were collected by interviews, questionnaires and observation of pupils aged 14–17 who used the IML. All pupils filled in a response sheet about their use of computers and microscopes at home and in school. Some questions probed how the pupils felt about using a CD-ROM compared to setting up a real microscope in a laboratory. In 75 per cent of the schools, pupils were able to use the IML and to work through some exercises before making responses. In 25 per cent, it was not possible for the pupils to use the IML, and they merely saw it being demonstrated.

In this evaluation, the comments of pupils recorded during the time they worked on the IML were generally enthusiastic. This echoes the point made above that multimedia applications can be designed to be highly motivating and entertaining. There was a novelty value about the IML which captured pupils' attention.

Three-quarters of the pupils sampled had access to a computer at home, and about half of these pupils used the computer every day or on most days. Regular use of computers at school was less frequent. Eight per cent of pupils claimed that they never used computers in school. This statistic, if it is an accurate reflection of the wider situation, is somewhat alarming, given that there is a specific requirement in the UK National Curriculum to provide pupils with training in IT. The ImpacT project reported by Cox (1993) found that pupils in some secondary classes did not use IT at all in spite of having the same level of resources available as other classes which made regular use of computers. A possible explanation for the total lack of computer contact reported by some pupils may be linked to the marked reluctance noticed in this study of some teachers to engage with and use the computer simulation on the CD-ROM. Cox (1993) and Collins *et al.* (1997) have noted a restriction on IT use in the classroom imposed by limited flexibility and possibly also a lack of enthusiasm of the teacher. There is a staff development issue here: some teachers may need support in developing expertise and confidence in their use of IT. Those who lack confidence about using computers will be much less likely to incorporate IT into their lessons, thus depriving their pupils of contact with computers and also the chance of practising transferable IT skills.

The use of microscopes was much rarer at home than at school, though 16 per cent of pupils claimed to have access to an instrument at home. Even in schools, microscopes were used infrequently, as might be expected for instruments that have a specific use in the science curriculum.

By far the most common use of computers by pupils at school was for word processing. Playing games was cited as the next most common use. Some pupils had to be reassured that this was an 'acceptable' use to record. It seems likely that this represents a substantial underestimate of the true figure. The only other relatively common use reported was for information retrieval or research using electronic encyclopaedias such as *Encarta*. There was also some use of the Internet and e-mail. Whether access was gained to the Internet via a terminal at home or at school, and whether it was used to gather information, was not apparent from the data collected in this study.

The survey showed that pupils are using IT over a wide range of activities. It was perhaps surprising that so little use seems to be made of computers in revision and review of work, given the ease with which information stored on a computer can be accessed. There was a minority of pupils who approached the technology cautiously: when questioned about computer use, one pupil wrote 'Only when I have to'! This raises the issue of support needed by pupils who are less confident about using IT. The predominant impression gained during this study was that a majority of pupils use a range of applications enthusiastically and creatively but there are some who are positively resistant to using the technology.

When pupils were asked whether they felt that using the IML was 'real science', or 'cheating', an interesting pattern emerged in the data. Of the group of pupils who used the IML, nearly twice as many thought that it offered real science, compared to those who regarded it as cheating. However, among the pupils who only saw the IML being demonstrated, the pattern is reversed: relatively few regarded the IML as real science and over half the group thought that it was cheating. The question caused some difficulty for pupils, perhaps because there was no 'correct' answer, and many were either undecided or did not fill in a response. The variation in attitudes between those pupils able to use the simulation and those who only watched a demonstration may have been due to the fact that groups who used the IML were actively engaged in collecting experimental data in the water-flea investigation described above. Each group filled in a short worksheet as if it was a laboratory investigation and answered questions about the observations that they made. In contrast, the pupils who were not able to use the IML just saw a series of images on a monitor and did not have the same 'hands-on' experience of data collection. As the demonstrations took place in laboratories, it cannot have been the surroundings that were influencing the opinions of pupils. There was something fundamentally different about a truly interactive experience with the simulation that encouraged pupils to view it as a contribution to their science education.

In a linked enquiry, pupils were asked to rate the IML as better than, the same as, or not as good as doing experiments in a lab with equipment. Results are shown in Figure 15.3. Reflecting the views discussed above, the responses of the pupils who actually used the simulation ('users') were predominantly in favour of the IML as a method of collecting experimental data. Those who merely saw a demonstration ('observers') were notably less enthusiastic about the simulation. Again, there was a group of pupils who felt unsure or who declined to fill in this section of the response sheet. The difference in reactions between the users and the observers of the simulation was quite marked.

These results give a very clear indication of the importance of getting 'hands-on' experience with an interactive computer simulation. The pupils who did not use the IML took a mostly passive role in the session and did not experience the interactive aspects of the simulation at first hand. They were understandably muted in their response: merely watching somebody else having fun is no contribution to experiential learning.

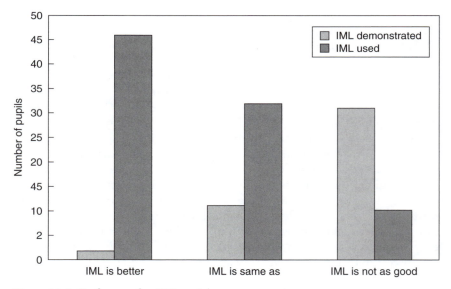

Figure 15.3 Preference for IML or laboratory experiment

Pupils who used the IML worked together in small groups at a computer and collected data. After completing the experiment, most pupils said that they would prefer to use the simulation rather than a real microscope. Less mess and fiddling about, thus saving time, and a concern for the welfare of water fleas featured among reasons given for preferring the IML. On the other hand, there was a sizeable minority who liked doing practicals with live material and felt that doing the experiment would give them greater ownership of results. Some realised that they would be unable to acquire the skills of microscopy without doing work in the lab. Pupils are generally eager to use computers, but a 'virtual laboratory' on screen should not be regarded as a substitute for 'wet' practical work. In connection with this, Blissett and Atkins, 1993, suggest that the intellectual, academic roles of the teacher in the classroom (or lab) will remain as important as ever, even with integration of computer-based technologies into lessons.

Class management using simulation

Obviously, the most crucial decision the teacher has to make is whether to use the simulation at all. What makes it more worthwhile to use a simulation for teaching as opposed to a traditional or different strategy? As with many ready-made teaching materials, it is often all too easy to provide a simulation and let the pupils get on to it without a clear objective. This can considerably detract from its effectiveness. By their nature it is all too easy just to run or allow unstructured exploration of simulations. To avoid this the teacher should provide a structured activity. Having decided to use a simulation, what is the teacher's role in preparation, supervision and debriefing?

Here we return to the idea of the 'second record', and to the cycle of pedagogical reasoning, (see page 254). As with any other teaching resource, simulations need adaptation to local needs and conditions; to curriculum demands, to abilities of pupils, class size, physical constraints of the room/ accommodation; the topic (safety, impossibility of some experiments); available IT equipment; teacher's knowledge, confidence and class management skills (skills and standards of teaching; time of day and so on). All these aspects of a science teacher's pedagogical-content knowledge apply equally to IT resources, and particularly to simulations because of their close mimicry of a practical situation.

The role of the teacher during pupils' work on simulations can range from referee to coach, to helper, guide or IT trouble shooter. The teacher must be available for 'teachable moments', those brief periods when the windows of a learner's mind are wide open and receptive. Any instructional procedure requires some form of post-activity discussion, but this is parti- cularly important in simulations. Those issues, concepts and procedures covered in the simulation must be aired in order to set the real context, as well as to consolidate these. Misconceptions within the topic of the simulation can also be identified and rectified.

Evaluating the simulation is a vitally important aspect of its use. Whether the simulation accomplished the desired cognitive/affective objectives should always be explored. In this regard, the question of what changes should be made next time can be illuminated as much by such means as gathering student opinion as by a pre-/post-testing regime.

These aspects of the second record are of immediate pertinence to the deployment of simulations by the science teacher. The speed and depth in operation of the second record will vary as much with the experience of the individual as with the choice of simulations in front of them.

The necessary pedagogical shift

This phrase, purloined from Barton's chapter in this book, refers to the 'new think' required by teachers and their trainers/mentors to make effective use of the new information and communications technologies. In the context of science simulations this really starts from the notion of prepared materials for teaching: how raw is raw? To what extent does teacher or technician preparation detract from or enhance a pupil's learning opportunity? This brings us back to the title of this chapter, and to a parallel between the live and the simulated practical. The liberating effect (discussed in a section of Barton's chapter on 'authentic' and 'inauthentic' labour) of freeing pupils from the time-consuming business (for example) of drawing graphs has to be balanced against the possible de-skilling of the pupil in graph drawing. There is clear evidence that pupils spend longer on, and get more quickly to, the higher-order science skills such as questioning and interpreting if they are emancipated from the 'drudgery' of lower-order, mechanised tasks by a computer. Can this then be extended to practical skills like counting the heart beats of a water flea under a microscope?

It seems entirely appropriate that maximising the level of a pupil's intellectual engagement in this way, particularly when coupled with the practice of needed IT skills, should take precedence in the lesson planning of today's science teachers.

Acknowledgement

Thanks are due to my colleague Kate Watson, for her painstaking and thoughtful research in the IML evaluation project.

References

Baggott, L.M. (1995) 'Management of electronic images for teaching and learning in biology', invited paper at the Association for Training Technology International Conference.

—— (1996) 'An interactive microscope for biology education', Association for Learning Technology Conference Programme, Abstract No. 249, p. 54. Glasgow.

Baggott, L.M. and Watson, K.E. (1997) Interactive Microscope Laboratory Project: an interactive virtual microscope for teaching and learning', *Microscopy and Analysis* 61: 27–9.

Baggott, L.M. and Wright, B. (1995), 'Interactive learning in biology with PhotoCD and associated software', *Association for Learning Technology Journal* 3: 62–8.

—— (1996a) 'The use of interactive video in teaching about cell division', *Journal of Biological Education* 30: 57–66.

—— (1996b) 'PhotoCD and biology education', *American Biology Teacher* 58: 390–5.

Blissett G. and Atkins M. (1993) 'Are they thinking? Are they learning? A study of the use of interactive video', *Computers and Education* 21: 31–9.

Collins, J., Hammond, H. and Wellington, J. (1997) *Teaching and Learning with Multimedia*, London: Routledge.

Cox, M. (1993) 'Technology enriched school project – the impact of IT on children's learning', *Computers and Education* 21: 41–9.

Gombrich, E.H. (1959) *Art and Illusion: A Study in the Psychology of Pictorial Representation*, London: Phaidon Press.

Grossman, P.L., Wilson, S.M. and Shulman, L.E. (1989) 'Teachers of substance: subject matter knowledge for teaching', in M.C. Reynolds (ed.) *Knowledge Base for the Beginning Teacher*, New York: Pergamon.

Hall W. (1989) 'Using Hypercard and interactive video in education: an application in cell biology', *Education and Training Technology International* 26: 207–14.

Hartley JR. (1994) 'Multimedia views of science education', *Studies in Science Education* 23: 75–87.

Hexter, J.H. (1971) *The History Primer*, New York: Basic Books.

Huang, S.D. and Aloi, J. (1991) 'The impact of using interactive video in teaching general biology', *American Biology Teacher* 53: 281–4.

Mercer, N. (1994) 'The quality of talk in children's joint activity at a computer', *Journal of Computer Assisted Learning* 10(1): 24–52.

Modell J. (1990) 'The computer as a teaching tool – how far have we come? Where are we going?' *Computers in Life Science Education* 7.

National Committee of Inquiry into Higher Education (1996) Evidence from the Computers in Teaching Initiative, http: //www.york.ac.uk/inst/ctipsych/Dearing/Dearing.html.

Osborne, J. (1993) 'Alternatives to practical work', *School Science Review* 74(271): 117–23.

Papert, S., Watt, D., DiSessa, A. and Weir, S. (1979) *An Assessment and Documentation of a Children's Computer Laboratory*, Final report of the Brookline LOGO Project, Brookline, MA.

Scaife, J. and Wellington, J. (1993) *IT in Science and Technology Education*, Buckingham: Open University Press.

Shulman, L.S. (1987) 'Knowledge and Teaching: foundations of the new reforms', *Harvard Educational Review*, 57: 1–22.

Someckh, B. and Davis, N.E. (1997) *Using IT Effectively in Teaching and Learning: Studies in Pre-service and In-service Teacher Education*, London: Routledge.

Stringer *et al.* (1995) *Cytovision*, software developed by Applied Imaging, Sunderland SR5 3HD.

Vygotsky, L. (1978) *Mind in Society*, London: Phaidon.

Watson, K.E. and Baggott, L.M. (1997) 'An evaluation of pupils' responses to a prototype microscope simulation on a CD-ROM – the Interactive Microscope Laboratory', CAL97 International Conference, *Superhighways, Super CAL, Super Learning?* Conference Proceedings Abstract no.1, pp. 327–35.

Wellington, J. (1994) *Secondary Science – Contemporary Issues and Practical Approaches*, London: Routledge.

Wood, E. and Attfield, C. (1996) *Play, Learning and the Early Childhood Curriculum*, London: Paul Chapman,

Interactive Microscope Laboratory

More information about the IML project can be found at: http: //www.ex. ac.uk/telematics/IML/

16

VIRTUAL SCIENCE

A practical alternative?

John Wardle

The Internet is emerging as a viable and powerful educational technology. Though often used as a source of information, the inherent networking functionality of the Internet lends itself to extending the range and scope of practical science in schools. Experiments can be illustrated, reported and commented on, data can be combined, shared and made available as secondary sources to all.

This chapter will consider the implications of the Internet for practical work in school science and explore the possibilities and alternatives offered using this emerging educational medium.

Introduction

Though the Internet was originally designed as a defence tool, its use (Wardle, in Thompson 1997) was pioneered by scientists who were quick to realise its potential. Indeed the World Wide Web (Web or WWW), the most useful incarnation of the Internet, was developed by a physicist, Tim Berners-Lee, working at the CERN laboratories. He realised the potential of the Internet and developed this more accessible system driven by a graphical user interface and the powerful hypertext[1] method of linking documents.

The Internet is multi-functional. It is a vast source of information, a global communication network and a powerful publishing medium. Electronic information can be transferred on a one-to-one basis or made available to all. This information transfer includes small electronic mail messages, numeric or scientific data files and software packages. Above all, these functions are accessible to all users.

This accessibility through the hypertext medium of the World Wide Web is now attracting a wide educational audience. Even with the advantages of newly emerging technology, much of this use places the learner in a passive role, not uncommon in many multimedia and IT situations. The challenge to the educator is to harness the power and flexibility of the Internet and develop it in order to enhance teaching and learning in schools. This could be no better used than to support the science curriculum and, in particular, to extend the practical opportunities for pupils in schools.

There are many different reasons for carrying out practical work in science, some clearly valid and justifiable, some not quite as convincing in terms of developing pupils' understanding of science. What is clear, is that educators must consider this intrinsic value and have specific objectives in mind before adopting any teaching strategy. Research carried out by the University of Durham's Exploration of Science project (Foulds *et al.* 1992) identified clear examples of primary schools carrying out practical activities involving traditional experimentation and data collection. These data were displayed by the children, but few examples were found where the process was extended or continued to encourage children to question, reason and draw conclusions from the data collected. Ros Driver (1983) reflected on this common approach to practical work: 'practical lessons end abruptly when the prescribed task is complete and little, if any, time is given to the interpretation of the results obtained, although this is just as important as the activity itself'.

Though the method of collecting data provides perspective and context for the learner, it is the ability to interpret and reason, often referred to as higher-order skills in science, that develops understanding of the concepts and procedures involved. Making sense of the data collected is crucial to effective learning. Pupils need to be engaged in this process through meaningful activities, presented in realistic contexts. They have to be given the opportunity to explore, test and reason, using data from both primary and secondary sources. It is making concrete sense and judgement from empirical evidence or observation that leads to conceptual understanding of the science involved. In order to achieve this the learner needs to have access to *quality* data. The definition of quality may be interpreted in different ways and may vary according to situation. Some common criteria can be identified: pupil ownership, valid sample size, limited extraneous results, for example. Providing data, or supporting the provision of data, electronically can improve pupils' access to *good* data. Datalogging, simulation and the Internet are possible sources of data for this learner interaction. IT has a crucial and integral role in supporting schools' science practical work both now and in the future. The use of IT does not, however, imply redundant activity for the teacher. Many observers quote the changing pattern of pedagogic activity for the teacher when using IT in the classroom; skills, processes and attitudes need to be taught and nurtured for pupils to work in this way. The remainder of this chapter will focus on the use of the World Wide Web in science education, and in particular on its role in enhancing and extending practical work.

The Web

The World Wide Web is a sub-set of the Internet (Krol 1994). If we imagine the ubiquitous analogy of the Internet as a highway, then the Web can be considered as the cars we use to travel as opposed to buses or bicycles. They all do a similar task but some faster (more capacity), more effectively (better designed for the task) and in more comfort (user friendly) than the others. Like many scientific and technological terms, the 'Internet' and 'Web' are used interchangeably in common language, we should not be too concerned at this. The important aspect is to define the function of the system we are using and evaluate its potential from that standpoint.

Learning in science should be *interactive*, it should involve the learner in making decisions at all levels, it is inherently experimental or *investigative*, and it relies on *information* or knowledge. Mapping these criteria on to the functions of the Web reveals the potential of the technology and system.

Different modes of use of the Internet

The Internet can be used to support practical work in science in a range of ways, each exploiting a particular aspect of the system. The majority of the science-based material on the Web can be categorised as a source of information. The type of information required to support practical work will vary, depending on whether it stems from teacher or pupil demand. For example, a teacher may be looking for teaching materials directly applicable to the classroom, whereas pupils may be looking for factual information to support investigation topic research. In both examples, retrieval of information implies a limited one-way process between the user and the Web.

Teaching materials: instructional *and* illustrative

For many teachers the initial starting point is to look for resources or materials which can be used directly in teaching or as an inspiration for activity. Finding material relevant to the UK science curriculum suited to a particular Key Stage is not an easy task on a vast, open-ended system such as the Web. Search engines can be used to find specified topics which are located anywhere on the Web, raising the issue of the acquisition of necessary information handling skills by the user. These powerful software tools (for example InfoSeek, Yahoo, Excite, Lycos) are commercially driven databases able to search on words or phrases and even include Boolean operators (AND, OR). However, the search mechanisms and sheer volume of the Web can make their use time-consuming and frustrating. Most teachers prefer, sensibly, to use sites recommended by colleagues, the media or their Internet Service Provider (ISP).

Directly relevant· to practical work are instructional materials or

Setting up

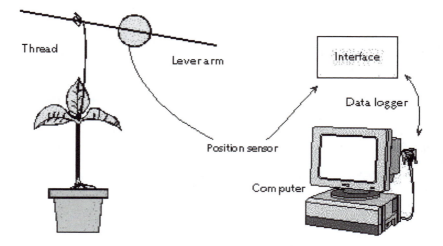

Figure 16.1 Resources such as worksheets can be made available over the Web

worksheets for experiments. These are likely to be *closed* resources by their nature and often fit the recipe category of practical science. However, positive reaction and feedback have been received from teachers accessing worksheets for experiments stored on the author's Schools Online Science Web site.

At this level the Web is being used for no more than a repository and source of teaching material, a predominantly *instructional* or *illustrative* mode of use. Books, journals and magazines could offer similar facilities. The enhancement or added value built into the system is the *electronic* retrieval of the material; files are downloaded from the Web site and saved locally on the user's computer or network. The teacher now has the option of printing out the material and using it in original form or modifying the material to meet the specific needs of the learners. Experience suggests that teachers feel more comfortable in using material they have *contributed* to in some way. Allowing adaptation of material removes many of the barriers preventing teachers from implementing new ideas (the 'my kids couldn't use that' syndrome). *Ownership* of material is also a great motivator of people. Developers of material which is made available in this way have to be prepared to accept the copyright issues raised by this practice. A commonly held view at the moment, legally incorrect, is that by placing material on the Web you are waiving any rights to protection. I suspect that increased commercial interest on the Web will change this situation. The need for a teaching resource bank is without question; who provides it is the more contentious point. Ideally, this would be a primed and supported resource, but with a collective responsibility from all users – you take out and put in!

Support for pupils' investigations

Pupils can also be encouraged to use teaching materials directly from the Web. Schools taking part in the Schools Online Project have used the bank of investigation ideas as a stimulus for Sc1 investigations. Researching ideas and collecting content information to support their investigations is a worthwhile and authentic use of the Internet for pupils. It mimics the use research scientists might make of the Web. The Pupil Researcher Initiative (Harrison and Mannion, 1996) was set up to strengthen the links between the research community and schools. One of the investigation briefs produced as part of the project is the 'Cosmic Web Site'.

Pupils have to design a Web site (some are on-line to see), from information presented and investigations completed. This perhaps takes the reporting aspect of investigative work to its extreme at the current time, though clearly increasing use will be made of the medium by both scientists and pupils in schools.

The *ScI-Journal* is a Web-based pupil journal produced specifically for

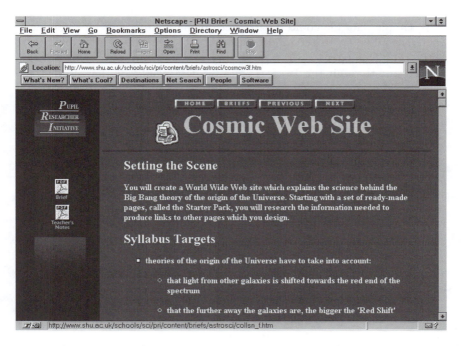

Figure 16.2 Pupils can be encouraged to investigate and publish on the Web

reports of investigations and experiments. Pupils' reports include statements of aims, hypotheses to be tested, details of experiments and results, and conclusions from investigations. Communicating ideas and demonstrating understanding is a valuable part of investigative work and is intensified by the global medium of the Internet. No longer is feedback on pupil reports restricted to the teacher's comment. Fullick (1995) writes of 'motivation of writing for a potentially large international audience', citing comments to Hampshire pupils involved in the project from Australian pupils reading the journal. The effect on self-esteem and confidence is a factor not to be overlooked when assessing the potential of the Internet in science. The shift from consumer to producer (Nadelson 1997) also focuses pupils to produce high quality-work – they are aware of the potentially large and critical audience who may access their work.

Providing secondary data

The idea of supporting investigations with the Internet can be further extended by developing the instructional approach and provision of resources. The type of material available on the Web for downloading is wide-ranging, from software to data files. Virtually any type of file can be made available, immediately increasing the interactivity and value of Web pages.

A sample data file could be attached to the instructional or informative material, allowing direct interrogation of experimental results relating to the topic. This opens up the possibility of data-handling activities being carried out through the Web. Typically, data would be downloaded and saved locally, as previously described, but then appropriate software (such as datalogging, spreadsheet) can be used by the pupil for analysis and inter-pretation. Clemmitt (1996) refers to the advantages of using uncontrived and statistically valid data sets from the Internet for teaching Earth sciences. The availability of data in this and other traditionally difficult practical areas – astronomy, for example – makes the topic area more accessible and relevant for the learner.

A number of examples of this approach have been trialed on the SOL Science Web site. Teachers and pupils have reacted positively to using the data both comparatively and as a method of teaching and developing data-handling skills with realistic data sets.

In the example shown, the context is described and a series of questions presented. The questions involve interpretation of the data presented and range from 'after we opened the freezer door, how long does the air in the freezer take to get back to normal?' to 'what does the gradient of the lines tell you about freezing food for storage?' Finally, pupils are encouraged to do an experiment themselves: 'try this for yourself. You can choose the food, but do see how your results compare when you use fatty food.' The Web is

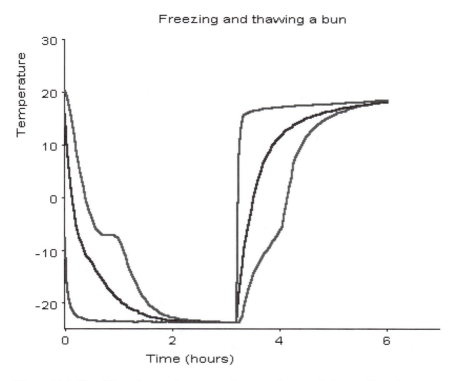

Figure 16.3 Providing data and structured approaches can help pupils to interpret data

being used as the distribution medium for this type of activity; though some of the interpretation could be done from the graph alone, this is greatly enhanced by the use of software analysis tools (Rogers 1995), typically found in data-handling software.

Sharing and comparing data

The provision and availability of data on the Web reveals the true potential of the Web as a medium to support practical science. The insulatory nature of the classroom and limited scope for data collection restricts many practical activities to semi-trivial exercises. Breaking down these barriers can infinitely increase the bench space available. We have begun to explore some of these possibilities on the SOL Science site. A simple, but relevant, example designed by teachers in the project uses the Web to collate data from a variation investigation. This is a typical introductory piece of work carried out in schools throughout the country yet with no reference made to national trends, other groups or classes. By agreeing a common approach,

277

through a brief on the Web, pupils collect their data and tabulate them in a downloaded spreadsheet template. The spreadsheet is returned by e-mail and made available to other schools. This allows comparisons across geographical and demographically varying areas to be made and, when added to the cumulative set of results, immediately increases the number of pupils to a statistically meaningful sample. This raises the task from a routine classroom activity to a relevant and realistic investigation, which also involves a collaborative responsibility on behalf of the pupils and schools.

The Global Learning and Observations to Benefit the Environment (GLOBE) project, initiated in the United States, uses pupils to collect environmental data in a similar way. This international initiative has more than sixty subscribing countries endorsed by their government. Once the country has been recognised as a member, schools can opt into the centrally organised and controlled project. Pupils are encouraged to collect daily observations of weather and environmental data. The data collected are published on the Web and are a valuable resource for both the research community and schools around the world. Interesting comparisons of global climatic conditions can be made using the data collected. An interesting illustration of this was found when looking at the most recent data collected. This revealed a temperature difference of 40°C between a Japanese and Australian school from the previous days recording. This immediacy and availability of data are unique to the Internet. A criticism of the project is that little guidance is given to the analysis and interpretation of this vast data bank which is crucial if pupils are to develop their understanding of both concepts and process.

As more data become available, interpretation becomes a more accessible procedure for pupils. Unfortunately, many sites making data available are produced by academics reporting their findings. Profitable pupil interaction will only result from sites designed to meet educational objectives. The teacher-designed Green Issues Web site exemplifies an educational approach to suggesting and testing hypotheses around meaningful contexts of environmental topics, such as travel and energy consumption. Data are collected in a collaborative way by users of the site, though no quality checks are made, by completing on-line forms. Pupils are then encouraged to suggest and test a hypothesis relating to the data collected. The author of the site has also presented the data in a graphical and visual format for pupils to interrogate, making it accessible to the learner.

The pupil as a researcher

Extending this approach to other content areas, such as energy surveys and radiation measurement, elevates the position of the pupil to a researcher who can genuinely contribute to data gathering, an activity which is valued by the research community. Observations of near astronomical bodies are often neglected by researchers, but schools using the Bradford Robotic Telescope are encouraged to collect sets of images which are used to inform academic research as well as to stimulate and enlighten pupils. The telescope is controlled through the Internet, and requests can be submitted on-line for images to be taken, which are subsequently downloaded to the user's computer. This process exploits the interactivity of Web-based technology and demonstrates the possibilities for future development.

Similar glimpses into real life have been pioneered by the MagNet project in Australia. This project relays datalogging experiments on to the Web in real time. Linking this to real time video, which is currently available, will allow pupils to conduct remote experiments or participate in experiments in other schools, laboratories or universities.

On-line simulations

The development of operating systems and browsers running programming languages, such as Java, will further extend on-line practical opportunities. Animations and simulations are already evident on Web sites. For example, the Virtual Optical Table can be used to investigate a range of optical elements.

Rays are traced on the optical table and the effect of changing focal length, position, wavelength and so on can be investigated. These simulations are downloaded using small programs called applets, and can be run in

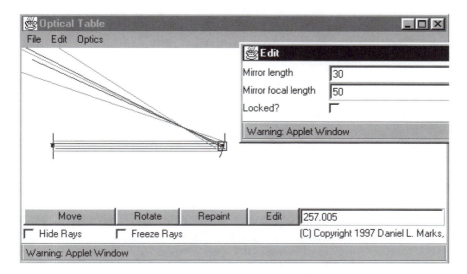

Figure 16.4 The scope for interactive involvement is developing through Web-based simulations

real time on- or off-line. Although this type of software simulation is not particularly innovative or original (versions were written for the BBC computer), by producing it on the Web the accessibility and user base are increased. When combined with the functionality of reporting and sharing of experiences, the potential of this model is further raised, offering wide-ranging opportunities for investigation.

Structuring on-line and off-line activities

Much of the interaction discussed uses the Internet as a medium for other operational tasks to be performed. Most of the analysis is done off-line using appropriate data-handling packages such as spreadsheets and datalogging software. Taking data from the Web is a relatively simple and mechanical procedure requiring some limited IT competence. Development of science understanding comes from the interaction with the data. In much of the author's work this *secondary* IT use is crucial to procedural development, but in itself has been part of the *hidden curriculum* or agenda for both teachers and pupils.

Evidence from classroom observations and reports from teachers suggests that effective models of Web use by pupils will be tightly structured (an antithesis to the anarchism of the Web) and time limited. Pupils are likely to go on-line to collect resources or information, pursue some off-line activity and return at a later stage to submit data or reports or to communicate with others. This is by no means a universal model, but does appear to be a manageable operational practice.

In summary

This chapter has described some of the ways in which the Web can be and is being used to support practical science activity. The Web will play a central role in communication, education and home learning for the next decade. How it is to be used and exploited in schools is still emerging. Teachers are faced with the issues of management, provision and location of resources and development of skill and competence familiar to all technological innovations. These require support, training and critical evaluation if they are to be used effectively in the learning environment. Priority should also be given to developing high-quality resources matched to the needs of pupils and the science curriculum.

There are genuine opportunities for *supporting and enhancing* practical science activity in schools through the Internet. This activity may not directly involve pupils carrying out experiments on the Web, though we have seen that this is possible, but is more likely to engage pupils and teachers in collecting resources, sharing data, collaborating with others and reporting on their work. It has to be used in an active, contributive and collaborative way. Pupils will not just receive but will take part in learning through this medium. This clearly meets many of the objectives we would wish to address as science educators moving into the twenty-first century.

Notes

1 Hypertext – a powerful feature allowing cross-referencing and linking of pages and sections of information. Links are usually denoted by an alternative colour. Mouse clicking on the link automatically moves to a new section of text or page which may be used to explain the word, as in a glossary, or provide information related to the word.

References

Clemmitt, S. (1996) 'Accessible Internet Data', *The Science Teacher* 3(3): 48–50.

Driver, R. (1983) *The Pupil as Scientist*, Milton Keynes: Open University Press.

Foulds, K., Gott, R. and Feasey, R. (1992) *Investigative Work in Science*, Durham: University of Durham.

Fullick, P. (1995) 'Teaching science using ScI-Journal', *Education in Science* 165: 27.

Harrison, W. and Mannion, K. (1996) 'Experimental and investigative science', *Education in Science* 167: 18, 19.

Krol, E. (1994) *The Whole Internet Users Guide and Catalog*, Sebastopol: O'Reilley and Associates.

Nadelson, L. (1997 'Online assignments', *The Science Teacher* 64(3): 23–25.

Rogers, L.T. (1995) 'The computer as an aid for exploring graphs', *School Science Review* 76: 276.

Thompson, D.L. (1997) *Science Education in the Twenty-first Century*, Aldershot: Arena.

Web references

GLOBE	http://globe.fsl.noaa.gov/welcome.html
Pupil Researcher Initiative	http://www.shu.ac.uk/schools/sci/pri/index.html
Schools Online Science	http://www.shu.ac.uk/schools/sci/sol/contents.htm
Green Issues	http://www.rmplc.co.uk/eduweb/sites/egriffin223/index.html
Bradford Robotic Telescope	http://www.eia.brad.ac.uk/eia.html
MagNet	http://mag-ic.edfac.unimelb.edu.au/
Virtual Optical Table	http://dionysus.phs.uiuc.edu/Osa/edu/table.html

EPILOGUE

A collection of chapters such as those above, from authors with established track records in science education, hardly needs a pretentious epilogue from me. In many ways the end of this book should be deliberately left hanging because, quite simply, we have posed questions more often than we have given answers. It is hoped that this book will add something to the debate on the future of practical work and, more specifically, its place in a statutory national curriculum. Part of the common ground between authors here is that there should be curriculum change, not least to reflect technological change. In this section I plan to be provocative and suggest, partly as a result of the process of studying and getting to grips with the chapters in this book, certain recommendations for a future science curriculum. What should it, and what should it *not*, include, given a statutory curriculum and the considerable constraints (of resources, of time and of space) imposed by the nature of schooling? Below are my personal views, stated roughly and as briefly as possible. They have not been fully worked out. However, any comment on them is most welcome – but please address it to me as the points below are not a joint statement.

The science curriculum should include practical work, and indeed many of the current approaches and practices in practical science are educationally valuable and well worth preserving. However, a balanced science curriculum should *not* be dominated by a *single* set framework or format for practical work – and it certainly should not pretend that the practical work in a teaching laboratory mirrors the nature of 'real' science. This book has argued for a balanced practical curriculum, involving a variety of different activities rather than a set, standard approach. This balance would include several elements, which are outlined below.

As several chapters have shown, when scientists tackle real scientific investigations they not only use their 'hands-on' apparatus and equipment but also use their 'minds on' handling and interpreting data. Therefore, at least one element of the practical curriculum should involve looking at someone else's data, preferably someone pupils don't know. It could be a figure from the past, it could be from another learner – for example, via the Internet – or it could be a piece of contemporary science. It could involve the kind of historical case study discussed in chapters above.

A balanced practical curriculum should include the critical use of simulations – the case for simulations in developing understanding and giving a feel for abstract ideas (which 'hands-on' cannot achieve) has been well-made by authors in this book and need not be repeated. The simulation could be computer based – for instance, on disc or CD-ROM, from the Internet, or handled using paper-based materials. Students at a later phase could learn how to look closely and critically at how the simulation was constructed, which model or models it is based on, and what its limitations are.

Practical activity should sometimes involve the use of IT and the use of data-logging even if not carried out as a whole-class practical. It should be used to show the benefits (and possible drawbacks) of using computers in practical science. It should emphasise the interpretation of the data rather than their collection and processing.

At least one element of work (probably as project work) should look at a contemporary, controversial issue which is science-based. For example, this could be the BSE debate, the issue of cloning and genetic engineering, global warming, pollution, or the use and supply of energy. Practical activities would include: looking at data, who collected them and how; the interpretation of data and the concept of evidence; media coverage of the issue, the 'evidence' and the experimental work; and the perspectives and prejudices of the people involved (the scientists included).

There has been a growth of standard, set practicals – masquerading as 'Investigations' – which pupils have done before and will do again largely because they fit into a template which has been laid down by a centralised curriculum. Quite understandably, these have been passed from one teacher to another, exchanged within and across regions, and picked up at in-service events or support groups, simply because: (1) they can be done within the appreciable constraints of a school laboratory and the time constraints of a school timetable; (2) they fit the format or 'strait-jacket' of a statutory curriculum; (3) they can be assessed using a single template and tailored so that pupils can (or cannot) reach certain levels at the right age or key stage. In contrast, pupils should carry out at least one *genuine* scientific investigation – that is, a research project, over an extended period of time, which does not follow a set format or template. If this could be based in the community or local environment, involve fieldwork, or even link with local employment that would be an added bonus. It could certainly involve extended observations over a period of time – for example, fieldwork, environmental monitoring, or astronomical work such as observing the sky over a period of time. Whatever its focus, it should require pupils to use secondary sources. One project leading the way here is the Pupil Researcher Initiative. The PRI is aimed at broadening pupils' experiences of investigations and their concept of evidence by exposing them to a range of activities: meeting real scientists and engineers; linking with PhD research students; visiting interesting sites and industries; sharing and communicating with other learners, and many other initiatives going beyond the constraints of school labs and a statutory curriculum. The key aim is to develop a broad concept of 'scientific capability' involving skills, attitudes and understanding.

In doing investigations and other practical work, the importance of pupils' implicit knowledge and skills needs to be acknowledged, recognised and developed in some way. To develop pupils' competence in these skills they need to be practised but not always written about. Students may have the ability to 'do science' even though they are unable to articulate it – that is, write it down. The current model of investigational work places huge demands on pupils' language abilities by asking them to write down (at considerable length in many cases I have seen) their planning, observations, conclusions, explanations and evaluations. Some investigations are almost done to death by an elaborate framework and the writing demands of assessed coursework. The assessment of practical work then becomes a measure of the pupils' ability to write clearly, articulately and elaborately rather than a measure of their scientific ability.

Finally, and most generally, teachers and pupils need to be clear about different types of practical work and why they are doing them. The purpose of any practical activity needs to be stated to pupils – how can they be expected to see the point of a practical exercise if they are not given some indication from the teacher who asks them to do it? Pupils also need to be shown and told that not everything in science is connecting with doing. Time needs to be allocated to discussing ideas, to interpreting data, and to making the link between things observed and ideas. Science is a practical subject but it is also a theoretical subject.

One message which all the authors here seem to agree on is that there is a need for curriculum change and development. However, changes and improvements will come about only if due account is taken of teachers' viewpoints and practical concerns. As past experience has shown, there is a vital need for careful professional development. Science teachers have become bruised and bitter about the impositions made on them in the area of 'experimental' science. The days of investigations by order, and of dropping IT onto school doorsteps, must be seen as past mistakes not to be repeated.

Comments and feedback on this book and any of the points or suggestions made in it are welcome. Please send them to Jerry Wellington, either by post to the University of Sheffield or by e-mail to: j.wellington@sheffield.ac.uk

FURTHER READING

The chapters above draw upon a wide range of references to published studies or critical analyses of the role of practical work in science education. A literature search was also carried out using 'Dialog', an on-line search tool; databases such as ERIC, British Education Index and Social SciSearch were explored using combinations of keywords such as 'practical work', 'school science', 'transferable skills', 'authenticity' and so on. This search led to the short, annotated list of articles below, which is my own selection of some of them. They all relate to practical work in the last twenty-five years, and may be valuable for those who wish to read further in this area.

Clackson, Stephen G. and Wright, David K. (1992) 'An appraisal of practical work in science education', *School Science Review* 74(266).
    Argues that, although practical work may have helped in teaching measuring techniques and manual dexterity, it has been of little benefit in helping students to understand the concepts of science.

Cuthbert, L.G. (1981) 'Microprocessors in schools?' *Physics Education* 16(3): 136–40, 151.
    One of the early studies of reasons for including 'microprocessors' in school curricula. Indicates that practical work with microprocessors is not easy and discusses problems associated with using and constructing the control and processing abilities of micro computers.

Denny, Michael and Chennell, Frank (1986) 'Exploring pupils' views and feelings about their school science practicals: use of letter-writing and drawing exercises', *Educational Studies* 12(1): 73–86.
    Examined views, attitudes, and feelings of 112 English secondary school pupils concerning practical work in their school science classes, by asking students to complete a letter-writing or a drawing exercise about their practical work. Results show that students associated practicals with learning scientific theory within a confirmatory rather than an investigatory mode, as a teaching device to reduce boredom, as a means of developing

self-esteem, and as a source of enjoyment. The relative merits of the two attitude-measuring tools were compared: the letter-writing exercise was considered to be more useful than the drawing exercise, although the latter revealed more about pupils.

Dynan, M. and Kempa, R.F. (1977) 'Teacher-based assessment of practical work in sixth-form physics', *Physics Education* 12(6): 364–9.
  Reports the findings of a study involving teacher assessment of practical work in secondary level physics courses taught in Northern Ireland, where assessment is made by a single standardised examination.

Fairbrother, R.W. (1986) 'Perspectives on the assessment of practical work', *Physics Education* 21(4).
  Discusses a range of approaches to the assessment of practical work.

Gayford, Chris (1988) 'Aims, purposes and emphasis in practical biology at Advanced Level – a study of teachers' attitudes', *School Science Review* 69(249): 799–802.
  Describes a study which examined teachers' attitudes about the value of practical work, attitude changes from previous studies, how teachers' aims relate to their teaching emphasis, and the differences between teachers who teach for practical exams and those who use teacher assessment of practical work. Presents methods and results.

Gunning, D.J. and Johnstone, A.H. (1976) 'Practical work in the Scottish O-Grade', *Education in Chemistry* 13(1): 12–14, 16.
  Describes the evaluation of an alternative chemistry syllabus that emphasises the role of practical work. The evaluation includes an assessment of the amount of practical work being done, the teacher's objectives, the pupils' achievement, and whether the pupils' achievement could be measured by a paper and pencil test.

Hellingman, C. (1982) 'A trial list of objectives of experimental work in science education', *European Journal of Science Education* 4(1): 29–43.
  Describes the rationale, need for and purpose of three lists of objectives (included in appendices) for skills and abilities related to experimental practical work in biology, chemistry and physics.

Hodson, Derek (1985) 'Philosophy of science, science and science education', *Studies in Science Education* 12: 25–57.
  A review article organised under several headings: aims of science education; the image of science; why a philosophy of science?; the nature of scientific knowledge and the role of theory; scientific method; practice of science by the community of scientists; and the role of practical work.

Hodson, Derek (1992) 'Assessment of practical work: some considerations in philosophy of science', *Science and Education* 1(2): 115–44.

Argues that a skills-based approach for the assessment of laboratory work is philosophically unsound, educationally worthless and pedagogically dangerous. Proposes an alternative, holistic approach to assessment, based on a more valid model of scientific practice.

Johnstone, A.H. (1991) 'Why is science difficult to learn? Things are seldom what they seem', *Journal of Computer Assisted Learning* 7(2): 75–83.

Suggests that the difficulties of learning science are related to the nature of science itself and to the methods by which science is customarily taught without regard to what is known about children's learning. The discussion addresses the nature of science concepts, the need for multilevel thought, the utility of practical work via experiments, and the 'language barrier'. An information-processing model is proposed to guide thinking and research in this area.

Johnstone, A.H. and Wood, C.A. (1977) 'Practical work in its own right', *Education in Chemistry* 14(1): 11–12.

Describes process-based practical work used in Scottish high school examinations and evaluates this work against a standard of course objectives for practical work in general.

Lock, Roger and Davies, Vaughan (1987) 'Assessing practical work in biology using the OCEA Scheme', *Journal of Biological Education* 21(4): 275–80.

Describes the Oxford Certificate of Educational Achievement (OCEA) and the principles on which it is based. Discusses ways in which biology teachers can develop their confidence and proficiency in making assessments of process-based work. Stresses the advantages that a scheme such as OCEA can bring to a biology department.

Lock, Roger (1989) 'Assessment of practical skills Part 1: the relationships between component skills', *Research in Science and Technological Education* 7(2): 221–33.

Reports a study of the relationships between the component skills involved in practical work assessment. Skills assessed included observing, manipulating, planning, interpreting, reporting and self-reliance. The literature relating to inter-skill relationships is reviewed.

Mathews, J.C. and Leece, J.R. (1975) 'Nuffield Advanced Chemistry: the free response questions and assessment of practical work', *School Science Review* 57: 199, 362–7.

Describes the results of utilising examinations which allow freedom of choice and response, and lists the outcomes of assessing practical work internally by teachers.

McWethy, D.D. (1984) 'Practical work evaluation: how and why', *Canadian Vocational Journal* 20(2): 25–28.
Describes the development of a detailed, structured evaluation method to assess students' practical work performance systematically. Reports that a survey of 5 secondary vocational teachers and 125 students showed that both groups favoured the detailed evaluation approach.

Napier, J. (1988) 'Woodland decomposition', *School Science Review* 69(248): 469–76.
Outlines the role of the main organisms involved in woodland decomposition and discusses some of the variables affecting the rate of nutrient cycling. Suggests practical work that may be of value to secondary school students either as standard practice or long-term projects.

Newton, Douglas P. (1979) 'Practical work in the sixth form', *Physics Education* 14(2): 74–77.
Divides the stated aims of practical work, listed in some of the A-level syllabuses of the GCE examining boards, into four groups and discusses each: didactic aims, the development of skills, the scientific method, and affective aims.

Nott, Mick and Wellington, Jerry (1995) 'Critical incidents in the science classroom and the nature of science', *School Science Review* 76(276): 41–6.
Describes a range of critical incidents which have been used with experienced and trainee teachers in order to promote discussion and reflection on the nature of science. Discusses teachers' views on critical evaluation of practical work, reliability and replicability of experiments, accepted scientific explanations, scientific evidence, religious beliefs and moral dilemmas.

Pugh, Malcolm and Lock, Roger (1989) 'Pupil talk in biology practical work – a preliminary study', *Research in Science and Technological Education* 7(1): 15–26.
The development of a framework for analysing pupil talk is described and the reliability of scoring transcribed conversions using the framework discussed. Definitions and examples of the terms used in the framework are appended.

Sands, M.K. and Forrest, G.M. (1981) 'A scheme for teacher assessment of practical work in Advanced Level biology and its moderation', *Journal of Biological Education* 15(2): 146–50.

Describes a procedure for assessment of student performance in laboratory work (practical work) in Advanced Level biology in England. Some historical background is included.

Tawney, D.A. (1975) 'Books on experiments and projects at A Level', *Physics Education* 10(2): 76–8.

Outlines the aims of practical work carried out by students doing investigations and projects. Provides a list of sources found useful as experimental guides, ideas for projects, and background information for A Level Nuffield physics.

Turner, P. (1974) 'A resource based learning system for practical work in science', *Physics Education* 9(4): 228–230.

The need is discussed for non-print materials to help students get an indication of how to set up an experiment and how to proceed with the work. The use of closed circuit television as an instructional aid is described, and other audio-visual aids are briefly reviewed.

Verkerk, G. (1984) 'Practical work in Dutch school physics examinations', *Physics Education* 19(5): 229–32.

Investigates the abilities and objectives which can be measured on practical tests. Results suggest that these tests be composed of separate parts which measure the ability to perform an experiment and the ability to interpret and analyse an experiment. A brief description of the Dutch school system is included.

Watson, J.R Prieto, T. and Dillon, J. (1995). The effect of practical work on students' understanding of combustion', *Journal of Research in Science Teaching* 32(5): 487–502.

Interviews were carried out, and questionnaires given to a total of 299 students aged 14 and 15 years in England and Spain on their understanding of combustion and on the teaching and learning styles used. The study concluded that the extensive use of practical work in English schools had only a marginal effect on their understanding of combustion. (Includes the questionnaire used.)

Watts, Mike and Ebbutt, Dave (1988) 'Sixth-formers' views of their science education, 11–16', *International Journal of Science Education* 10(2): 211–19.

Investigated were 17-year-old British students' comments on their previous science education. Satisfying science education entails (1) relevance, coherence and continuity; (2) concern for student needs; (3) and practical work such as inquiry activity.

Wilson, James M. (1977) 'Practical work in physics in Scottish schools', *School Science Review* 58(205): 783–90.

Reports on a survey of 191 Scottish secondary physics teachers to determine teachers' (1) aims of practical work, (2) types of practical work undertaken, (3) methods of organising work, (4) reasons for science demonstrations, (5) pre-experiment instructional techniques, and (6) methods of recording work.

Woolnough, Brian E. (1976) 'Practical work in sixth-form physics', *Physics Education* 11(6): 392–7.

Presents the results of a survey of English physics teachers concerning the proportion of classroom time they spend in practical work, the objectives of practical work and their use of student projects.

Woolnough, Brian and Toh, K.A. (1990) 'Alternative approaches to assessment of practical work in science', *School Science Review* 71(256).

Argues against an 'atomistic', criterion-referenced approach to the assessment of practical work; advocates a 'holistic' approach to scientific investigation which can be assessed through teachers' professional judgements.

Wyatt, H.V. (1984) 'Writing, tables, and graphs: experience with group discussions in microbiology practical work', *Journal of Biological Education* 18(3): 239–45.

Suggests that microbiology activities/experiments are suitable for teaching skills in designing experiments, manipulating tables/graphs, and the rewriting of work. Shows how students design an experiment using a table and how another experiment provides material for a group discussion on writing and rewriting.

INDEX